American Indians in British Art, 1700–1840

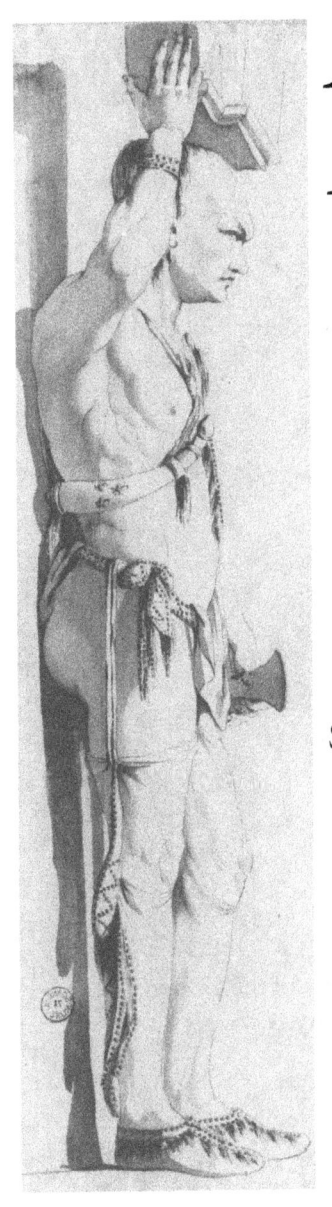

American Indians in British Art, 1700–1840

STEPHANIE PRATT

UNIVERSITY OF OKLAHOMA PRESS : NORMAN

For my parents

This book is published with the generous assistance of the Paul Mellon Centre for Studies in British Art.

Library of Congress Cataloging-in-Publication Data

Pratt, Stephanie, 1958–
 American Indians in British art, 1700–1840 / Stephanie Pratt.
  p. cm.
 Includes bibliographical references and index.
 ISBN 978–0–8061–4200–5 (paper)
  1. Indians in art. 2. Art, British—18th century. 3. Art, British—19th century.
 I. Title

 N8217.I5P73   2005
 704.9'499700497'00941—dc22

                                                    2005041713

The paper in this book meets the guidelines for permanence and durability of the Committee on Production Guidelines for Book Longevity of the Council on Library Resources. ∞

Contents

Illustrations

Black-and-White Figures

American Indians in British Art, 1700–1840

Introduction

ASK ANYONE THE world over to identify a figure in buckskins with a feather bonnet and the answer "Indian" will be given, no matter how little further information about that culture could be supplied. As an iconic type, the American Indian is an instantly recognizable individual in the gallery of the world's peoples. That this figure is a cliché, derived from selective understandings of Plains culture in the nineteenth century, is not in doubt, but it serves to demonstrate the power of images in creating identities. For many of us, the only real Indian is one who is shown living in a tepee on the Plains and dressed in appropriate nineteenth-century garb.

The scholarly treatment of issues surrounding the European depiction of other so-called racial or exotic types, such as the "Black" or the "Oriental," has met with considerable attention in recent years, probing the discourses of knowledge and power that have produced these categorical identifications.[1] Surprisingly, however, although they are relatively well documented, relatively little attention has been paid to the analysis of images of American Indians as similarly constitutive of categorical types, even in the United States itself. There is simply no equivalent study of visual images made of American Indians to compare with the Menil Foundation's publication of *The Image of the Black in Western Art*.[2] This is especially true of the eighteenth century, which lies sandwiched between the earliest European images of America produced in the sixteenth century and the development of an Indian iconography in the United States during the nineteenth century based largely on Plains Indian culture. First-contact images have been the subject of some extremely important analyses, as have some of the images associated with the frontier in the nineteenth century. However, the seventeenth and eighteenth centuries have tended to be overlooked, lacking either the excitement of European discovery and curiosity in the New World or the mystique of the westward-moving frontier as the United States of America came into being.[3] The middle centuries, when the eastern seaboard was a colonial outpost of Britain, lack the glamour of the two founding moments, which lie on either side of them. Similarly, the art produced then might seem to advance but little on what the sixteenth-century record shows and to be incapable of providing the kind of documentary realism often attributed to Frederic Remington and George Catlin.[4] This historiographical gap in the analysis of European and American visual representation of American Indians is unfortunate, as it leaves many underlying issues and premises underexplored. No synoptical study of European artistic representations of American Indians has been undertaken since Hugh Honour's two important and seminal publications, *The New Golden Land: European Images of America from the Discoveries to the Present Time* (1975) and *The European Vision of America* (1975–76).

In terms of the history of art, however, the relative exclusion of eighteenth- and early-nineteenth-century imagery is puzzling. It is notable that several important publications on Orientalism and on the representation of blacks in art concentrate on precisely this era, taking in as they do the growth of colonialism and the attendant European discourses devoted to the documentation of other cultures.[5] One might ask why it is that interpretations of black and Orientalist images have not inspired other scholars to produce a sustained analysis of the images made of those "first" American peoples whose own cultures and presence

4

were being effaced on the map of a new United States during this era. Certainly, the explanation cannot lie in a dearth of materials. Europeans continued throughout the eighteenth and early nineteenth centuries to document, examine, discuss, write about, and image American Indians in a wide variety of contexts.

It is perhaps worth speculating that our relatively meager interest in eighteenth-century images of American Indians may have something to do with institutional positions in contemporary society. It is right and proper that art history examines how the imaging of other races has produced particular effects, and by the same token, it is important that art history do this in respect of contemporary understandings. The position of African Americans and of peoples of African descent worldwide is rightly seen as an important topic to which scholarship can make a contribution. Similarly, since the 1940s, world politics has put a premium on attempting to overcome the prejudices that might hinder comprehension of the peoples of the Middle East. If art historical scholarship can help illuminate past and present perceptions of different cultures, so much the better. Yet the relative dearth of art historical studies devoted to the image of American Indians suggests that the contemporary situation of American Indians in the United States is not perceived to occupy as important a place in modern consciousness. A consensus seems to exist that analysis of their imaging, and the lessons we might draw from it, is not as urgent a task as the analysis of other groups subjected to the colonial gaze.[6]

This book, then, attempts to fill in this gap in scholarship, to reveal the ways in which American Indians were imaged by British artists in a relatively neglected era and how these images fit into a larger pattern of perceptions, concepts, understandings, and misunderstandings. I have chosen to take a synoptic overview of the material, as this best suits my purpose, which is to demonstrate the breadth of imagery as it appears in differing contexts. In placing these various contexts for representation side by side, I hope that the reader will begin to see the connections to be made between images made for different contexts, such that as a whole they contribute collectively toward the elaboration of several all-embracing American Indian types and typologies. This overarching and synoptical viewpoint is thus the mechanism that allows us to see the patterns and proclivities of visual representations of American Indians as they were constructed during the eighteenth and early nineteenth centuries. What I have lost in detailed examination, I hope to have gained in the presentation of recurrent themes within the imagery as a whole. Broadly speaking, these themes might be described as expressive of a tension between older, allegorical positionings of America and its inhabitants, on the one hand, and realizations of the historically contingent impact of actual American Indian groups, on the other. At a time when art practice itself eschewed the particular in favor of more idealized understandings of the world, the realities of American Indian warfare, diplomacy, and delegations to London found artistic accommodation somewhere between a symbolic and a naturalistic kind of representation.

One key concept regularly associated with the image of American Indians is that of primitivism. "Hard" and "soft" primitivisms were identified by Arthur O. Lovejoy and George Boas in 1935 as the two characteristic variants on the theme, respectively identifying a spartan and rigorous life ignorant of luxury and a life blessed with natural bounties in a benign climate. Both of these ways of living could be deployed as alternatives to contemporary European culture. Hard primitivism suggested an elemental, reductive culture that called into question the moral laxity of modern Europe; soft primitivism offered a vision of an almost Edenic state, free of the inhibitions, frustrations, and artificial pleasures of European life. Hard primitivism influenced most European accounts of America. The American Indian was perceived as the quintessential noble savage from at least the time of Montaigne, whose *Essais* (1580) celebrated the stoical attitudes of the Brazilian Indians. European understanding of Woodlands Indians in North America, especially the Hurons and Iroquois, tended to follow this pattern. American Indians, seen in this primitivist light, lived a life that offered a severe lesson to a sybaritic and morally uncertain European. As we shall see, there were a number of attempts to find parallels in American Indian life with the remotest beginnings of European civilization, itself an era that offered a lesson to contemporary life. American Indian rhetoric, morality, martial valor, and even bodily form could all be compared and contrasted with the best and worst that Europe had achieved.

The idea of the American Indian noble savage as a dominant eighteenth-century concept is well known. My contention, however, is that eighteenth-century Britain had other means of apprehending the peoples of America, not least because the colonial wars that dominated the era required an effective policy to work with them as allies. This is still a story that needs telling. It suggests a more nuanced understanding of American Indians in British society, albeit an understanding that rapidly waned with the loss of Britain's American colonies. From a methodological point of view, it proposes that the construction of race in European visual culture was not inevitably or solely a process of imposing a set of European values on another culture without resistance. In the case of America, the reality of the "middle ground," that liminal space between American Indian and European territories where a hybridized culture developed, where mutually acceptable trade flourished, and where Indians and non-Indians temporarily achieved a certain amount of coexistence, offers an understanding of colonial affairs that moves away from that older historical model's assertion of the European extirpation of Indian culture. British responses to American Indians in the eighteenth century can be shown to exhibit some of the complexity already revealed for the "middle ground." We can profitably dispense with the idea that every image of an American Indian is inevitably an image of a noble savage and work within a wider field of possibilities. Eighteenth-century images of American Indians, no matter that they were saturated with often complacent understandings of "savagery," noble or ignoble, were also capable of representing Indians as participants in contemporary history. Alongside images of "generic" Indians occupying the predetermined space outlined by the noble savage concept, we can also find specific encounters with named individuals whose diplomatic and military skills were recognized and celebrated in Britain.

This book is concerned mainly with British visual representation of American Indians in the period from about 1700 to the first half of the nineteenth century. Given that the book's focus is primarily on images made during this period, the concentration on British imagery is not surprising. It is precisely in this era that British colonial interest and domination of North America climaxed and then began to wane. Britain's colonial ventures were to take place largely on North

America's Atlantic seaboard, and it is on the colonial contacts with tribal groups living in or nearby these settlements that much of the discussion will center. Although comparative analyses of the British Empire and its subject peoples in separate colonial regions can bring to light interesting patterns, there is nevertheless some merit in examining British and American Indian relations in a geographically and temporally delimited zone, which has occasioned some very insightful recent historical analysis.[7] During the eighteenth century particularly, attitudes toward American Indians were adapting and changing to new circumstances. Important studies have emerged that propose innovative models for analysis of this period of Indian-white contact.[8] Historians of empire, Anglo-American historians, and members of the British Association of American Studies have all recently devoted more attention to the investigation of relationships between Britain and the American Indian peoples who fell under the sway of the empire during the eighteenth and early nineteenth centuries.[9] All of these factors have gone into deciding that a book about eighteenth- and early-nineteenth-century British images of American Indians is a worthwhile project.[10]

In chronological terms, this study is also deliberately limited. Where appropriate, I have included brief reminders of earlier patterns of representation, if only to demonstrate the staying power of tropes established as early as the sixteenth century. However, the bulk of this book is concerned with the years of struggle for North America as Britain fought with and against American Indian groups in its conflicts first with France and then with the rebellious colonies. From skirmishes in the 1690s through the Seven Years' War, the American Revolutionary War, and the War of 1812, the period may be said to end with the Treaty of Ghent in 1814, which settled the Canadian border and ended British hostility to the United States. I have, however, given a brief indication of British interest in American Indians after 1814, as the idea of the collapse of Indian culture emerged. George Catlin's activities in London in the early 1840s thus stand as the termination of my narrative, rekindling an interest that had been dwindling for thirty years.

The book is therefore divided into five chapters, each of them moving progressively forward in time. Chapter 1 examines a symbolic and standardized allegorical figure standing for America, analyzing the changing uses of this figure and the metamorphoses it undergoes. Chapter 2 is concerned with the ways in which American Indians had become important figures of diplomacy and negotiation for the British during the wars for empire from the early to mid-eighteenth century. Chapter 3 concentrates almost completely on the history paintings of Benjamin West, the American expatriate painter living in London. It considers whether West's pictures that contained American Indian figures resorted in the end to standardized or stock types of representation of Indians. This may have happened in spite of West's direct experience with Indian peoples during his early life in Pennsylvania and his ownership of American Indian objects, which he used in his studio to clothe his figures. Chapter 4 examines the changing circumstances of the relationships between American Indians and Britain during the Revolutionary War period and its aftermath and looks closely at a number of portrait paintings and one work of sculpture to underscore these larger historical shifts. Chapter 5 deals with the period subsequent to the end of Britain's direct involvement with American Indian peoples as allies or diplomatic partners. It takes up a popular theme of the late eighteenth century, the trope of the "dying" Indian, such as was imaged in Joseph Wright of Derby's *Indian Widow* (1785) and which set the stage for a nineteenth-century romanticized and nostalgic view of American Indians.

The range of visual material to be examined thus extends from the highly popular (satirical prints and broadsides) to the less pervasive and more singular, but no less important, "high" art productions (painting and sculpture). That said, this book is not intended to even begin providing comprehensive coverage of British images of American Indians in this period. Rather than adduce a wealth of examples, my intention has been to work with images I consider to be definitive of the wider processes I wish to expose. These processes, I contend, displace the lived experience of American Indian culture and substitute for it a simulacrum that better accorded with European expectations. Such a conclusion, for an art historian, is commonplace, but it is worth emphasizing it here if only to point out that relatively recently published works on the history and exploration of America tend to use artistic imagery as a source of apt illustration without seeking to analyze its contemporary meaning and debt to tradition. A case in point is William P. Cumming et al.'s edited volume, *The Exploration of North America*, 1630–1776 (1974), where no distinction is made between the visual material and the written text in terms of each medium's status as a historical record. Even more problematic is the invitation by some authors that their readers should compare the visual record with written accounts in order to see more lucidly those peoples being described in the texts. Clearly, visual and verbal representations of events and peoples adopt different strategies and operate within distinctive traditions. Each seeks to answer the expectations of its intended audience, but both do this with quite different techniques. To collapse visual imagery into the same category as verbal discourse is to do violence to the specific iconic qualities possessed by images. In a number of recent accounts, this distinction has not been drawn, and the images have been left as mute support or background color to an accurately analyzed verbal text.[11] Nor has art history necessarily done justice to these images. Although a number of them have been analyzed in some depth, they tend to be "high" art instances in the main, whose attraction lies in the fame of their originators—for example, Benjamin West and Joseph Wright of Derby. By separating these canonical images from the broad mass of visual imagery in which they participate, the contextual analysis of the images has been inevitably limited if not frustrated.

If much of this introduction makes claims for new thinking, this is not intended as some discovery of a newfound land of images. Examination of perceptions held about American Indians in the "mind" of particular dominant cultures is a road well traveled, and I am indebted to the many distinguished precedents that exist for this work. Without the accumulated scholarship of generations of historians of art, politics, ethnography, and other relevant disciplines, much of what I have included here would not have been available.[12] I would like to believe, however, that my particular circumstances as an American Indian art historian based in the United Kingdom have given me the distanced perspective that has allowed various patterns to come into focus and the opportunities to pursue this kind of investigation. Like some of the figures discussed in these pages, I am myself between cultures and am drawing on differing heritages. I do not believe that my identity as a Dakota woman offers me a necessarily privileged insight into this material, but it affords me a position, a sense of urgency if you will, that has certainly contributed to my thinking.

1 *The Allegorical Representation of America*

When fierce Pizarro's legions flew
O'er ravaged fields of rich Peru,
Struck with his bleeding people's woes,
Old India's awful Genius rose
He sat on Andes' topmost stone,
And heard a thousand nations groan;
For grief his feathery crown he tore,
To see huge Plata foam with gore;
He broke his arrows, stamped the ground,
To view his cities smoking round.[1]

JOSEPH WARTON'S POEM "The Revenge of America" (1747) personifies the continent of America as an Indian furious at the destruction brought upon his country by Francisco Pizarro's invasion and conquest of Peru.[2] In casting his figure of "Old India" as a feather-crowned emanation of the South American

landscape, Warton was evoking a long-standing and traditional artistic representation of America. From the late sixteenth century to the mid-eighteenth,
America had been depicted allegorically as one of the four continents of the world
alongside Europa, Africa, and Asia.[3]

The use of an allegorical figure to represent American Indian peoples is
fundamental to understanding European perceptions of American Indians
throughout the three centuries following Columbus's voyages. Allegorical
representations became a standard artistic convention in the Renaissance, and
allegorical handbooks that grouped similar allegorical elements under the
appropriate subjects to which they referred were created by designers for artists.[4]

The rhetorical pattern of allegory, where a visual construction stands for (or
replaces) a discursive idea, is used in art as a shorthand method for expressing a
complicated notion within a single visual design. By the late sixteenth century, a
specific iconography had developed for the figure of America, where special
reference was made to the figure as a male "chieftain."[5] In Cesare Ripa's allegorical handbook, the *Iconologia* (first published in 1593), the personification of
America is a male figure, and the objects that ornament and surround him are
intended to typify the essence of America. Of particular note is the South
American derivation of the objects, flora, and fauna that are part of the allegory;
these include an iguana or armadillo, coral, a nautilus shell, Amazonian war clubs,
and feather accoutrement. Also prominent is the inclusion of "gold or gold-dust."
Ripa's work, first illustrated in 1603, was extremely popular and was reprinted as
late as the eighteenth century in a German edition by Johann Georg Hertel
published in 1758–60.[6] It is important to enunciate the iconography of the
allegory as it was first formulated in the Renaissance and then handed on to later
scholars, writers, artists, and designers.

> The personification of America is a dark man, a native chieftain certainly,
> who sits among many objects associated with America. He is elaborately
> tattooed, and wears a feather headdress, many beads, and a decorated
> animal hide. He holds a spear with a jagged head. About the main figure
> are bits of coral, pearls, a basket of gold dust(?), arrows, spotted hides, a

13

large nautilus shell, a human head, war clubs, a bow, and a monstrous animal, perhaps an iguana or an armadillo.[7]

For the majority of viewers in the eighteenth century, their most likely encounter with any imagery of American Indians would have occurred in a symbolic context. Warton's poem relies on the fact that his readers would instantly have recognized the combination of arrows and a feathery crown as the attributes of America. This recognition, in turn, derived not so much from any knowledge of Ripa but from a haphazard encounter with the thousand and one places where the symbolic figure of America might be found: ships' figureheads, inn signs, coats of arms, trade tokens, printed ephemera such as tobacco labels, wallpaper, porcelain, carved or inlaid furniture, tableware, interior decor, masque costumes, and children's books. The Indian figures used in these various products might follow Ripa's original codification of the type, but more typically they offer variants on the theme. The attributes included are often pared down, with the essential elements reduced to the bow and arrow and feather bonnet, and Ripa's male chieftain is frequently replaced by an Indian "princess."

The issue of gender bears further examination. In one sense, given the development of female allegorical personifications for Europe, Asia, and Africa, the need for a woman to symbolize America was no more than a piece of allegorical housekeeping that would unite the four continents at the level of gender. But beyond this conventional explanation lie further areas for discussion.

The hold of the allegory of America on European imagination can be seen in the costumes adopted for Indian characters in the theater. Both John Dryden and Robert Howard's *The Indian Queen* (1664) and Dryden's *Indian Emperour* (1665) invited theatrical designers to clothe the eponymous royal figures in accordance with the allegorical tradition. Given their role, to embody their culture physically and dramatically, the emperor and queen were already positioned in a symbolic world, so recourse to Ripa or one of his derivatives was entirely appropriate.[8] Engravings of actors and actresses in costume for these roles reveal that their appearance as "The Indian Queen" or "Indian Emperor" in costumes made of feather crowns and rich jewels and ornaments was designed to

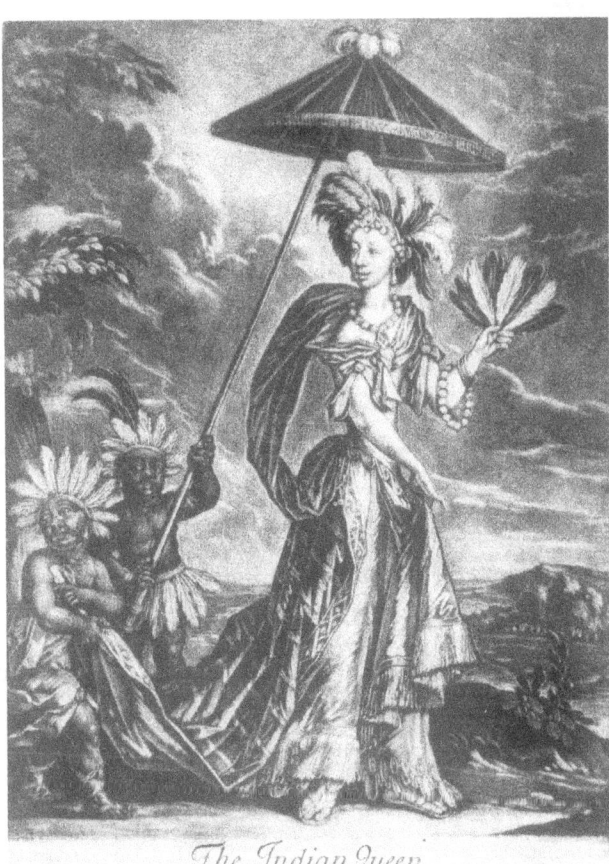

The Indian Queen

Fig. 1.1. Thomas Smith, after William Vincent, mezzotint engraving, ca. 1700, *Anne Bracegirdle as The Indian Queen, Semernia*, from Aphra Behn's *The Widow Ranter*, first performed in 1689. Prints and Drawings, The British Museum, London. Photo © Copyright The British Museum.

function allegorically.[9] It is known that at the turn of the century, the playwright Aphra Behn loaned the King's Theatre a set of feather headdresses and feather garments, which originally had been presented to the author when she was in Surinam, but the use of these items in the performance of a play would have primarily helped codify an allegorical understanding. Certainly, the prints made by William Vincent and Bernard Lens of Anne Bracegirdle in the title role of Behn's own play *The Widow Ranter; or, the History of Bacon in Virginia* (1689) are entirely of a piece with the allegorical figure of America (fig. 1.1).[10]

Necessarily, these representations operate at a highly generalized level, invoking the traditional repertoire of the four continents' Indians rather than any specific reference to particular places or peoples. In Behn's play, the action is set in Virginia and is based on the colonial ventures undertaken by the English to settle the northern continent of America, yet these figures could as well be Inca or Aztec nobility. The conjunction of allegory with history in the theatrical representations of American Indians helped to produce the idea of American Indians as consistent and similar in all their cultures.

This gendering of the figure of America in allegory is itself worthy of comment. In looking at female allegories of America, we need to be mindful of wider considerations of gender and gendered readings of the colonial venture. Helen Carr has discussed the relationship of imagery surrounding colonized peoples alongside a notion of gender, relating the American colonial experience to a gendered and asymmetrical contact. This asymmetry might be expressed as the stark oppositions of man and woman, seducer and seduced, and even rapist and victim.[11] This series of binary oppositions is essentially predicated on the notion of active and inactive gendered roles, where a dominant masculinity (Europe) masters a subordinate femininity (America). The allegorical representation of America might be read as a working out of this set of conflicting positions.[12] Allegory allowed a displacement of the actual contact experience into the realms of symbol and myth. In visual terms, the interaction of figures representative of America and Europe was played out in asymmetrical roles similar to those listed by Carr and certainly grounded in assumptions of gender and gendered behavior. In Jan Stradanus's engraving of *America* from the early seventeenth century, the male explorer Amerigo Vespucci arrives on the shore of distant lands now known as America, after his own first name. The figure of America, a youthful, feather-crowned maiden, is awakened from her slumber in a hammock by the figure of her "discoverer," who literally brings her into being.

The translation into literary terms of the allegorical or representative figure of the Indian reproduces these considerations. The characters in dramatic narratives function as continental emblems (the Indian emperor, the Indian queen) but also as individuals whose interactions with Europeans play out in miniature the interaction between Europe and America. For the Indian princess figure, the gendered nature of this encounter is crucial. In Aphra Behn's tragedy *The Widow Ranter*, her "noble" American Indian character is called Semernia, a royal personage and

16

"Queen of the Indians." Semernia loves the English settler Francis Bacon and loses her life.[13]

Even more notably bound up with the problems of European contact is the love story of Inkle and Yarico. First appearing in Richard Ligon's *History of Barbados* (1657), the narrative details the relationship between a high-born young Indian woman and a white sailor who betrays her love and sells her into slavery. Richard Steele's version of the story, published in 1711, further dramatizes the tale, noting especially that her pregnancy sets a higher price on her sale in the slave market in Barbados. The union of America and Europe is inevitably corrupted by greed, and even love can be commodified into mercantile advantage.

Alongside these allegorical personifications of America as a woman subjected to the colonial encounter there also exists another tradition in which the attributes of strength and aggression seen in Ripa's chieftain are grafted on to the Indian princess. Crispijn de Passe's engraving of America from the early seventeenth century is a case in point (fig. 1.2). De Passe essentially transposes Ripa into another key: here is a dark woman, a Native princess certainly, who sits among many objects associated with America. Although she is not elaborately tattooed, she wears a feather headdress, many beads, and an animal hide. Rather than a spear with a jagged head, it is a human head she holds, and about her are grouped ferocious animals, jewels, and reminders of cannibalism. Scenes of human sacrifice and devil worship animate the background. Here, the conventional expectations of woman as a compliant or subservient figure are overturned, with the Indian princess in full self-possession of her rank and dignity, served by a male warrior. Her ability to take on the mantle of violence and cruelty typically associated with the male adds a particular frisson to this deployment of allegorical America.

Yet, notwithstanding the visual impact of De Passe's engraving, America's role within the representation of the four parts of the world is entirely dependent on her relationship with Europe or Europa, particularly when the figure of America is also an American Indian. The frontispieces of books published in the sixteenth and seventeenth centuries that included the allegories of the continents exemplify the ways in which the representation of Europe in relation to her other three sister continents could work to determine the roles such figures played within the

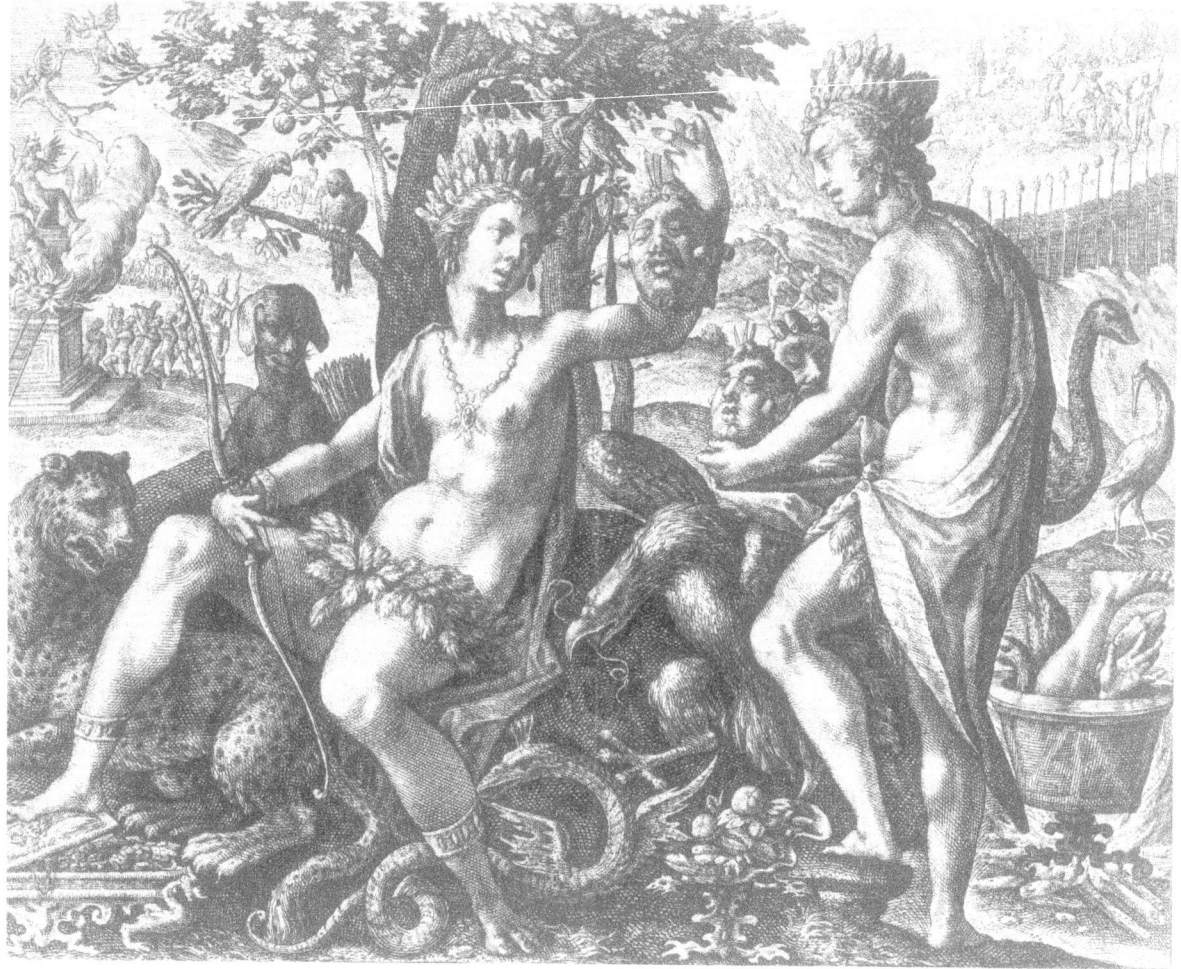

Fig. 1.2. Crispijn de Passe, *America*, engraving, early seventeenth century, Rijksmuseum, Amsterdam. Photo © Copyright Rijksmuseum-Stichting, Amsterdam.

larger symbolic framework of the image. Allegorical figures inhabit an architectural framework, which constructs order out of diversity.[14] Effectively, the placement of an allegorical figure within an overall design containing the other three continents is never one of equality. Even when each continent is given one quarter of the design, the master narrative is European, speaking of the systematic ordering of knowledge and the binding of all world cultures to a European cognitive frame. Frequently, however, the Eurocentric focus of the designs is manifest with the figure of Europa, first among equals, given a more prominent position or possessing qualitatively distinctive attributes. Europa is the fount of civilization, of arts and letters; she is clothed, industrious, and intellectual. America is naked and in a state of nature, and she is known for her economic potential rather than her achievements.

This can be seen when images of the four continents were produced as interior decorations for public buildings, royal palaces, and private homes during the seventeenth and eighteenth centuries. The figures of the continents tend to occupy the extreme edges of the design, as this indicated its cosmological scope. On the level of the formal arrangement, then, these figures were symbolic of the global reach of European powers into all corners of the world. The figure of America seen in combination with the other three continents can be found in a number of ambitious decorative schemes of this period, among them Antonio Verrio and Henry Cooke's painting of 1687–90 in Royal Chelsea Hospital showing King Charles II on horseback and the four continents in supplication to him; the painted panels of 1696 by Robert Robinson that originally decorated a house a 5 Botolph Lane in Aldgate, London; Verrio's painting of the allegories of the continents paying tribute to Britannia, painted for Queen Anne at Hampton Court ca. 1700; the sculpted figure of America of 1737–44 that is part of a design for the four parts of the world paying tribute to Britannia by Peter Scheemakers on the grounds at Stowe in Buckinghamshire; and the overdoor painted panels of 1737–44 by Antonio Zucchi in the dining room at Osterley Park House.

Ceiling decorations carried out by Sir James Thornhill in the years 1718 to 1725 for the Royal Naval College at Greenwich are perhaps the most impressive designs created in England at this time to include the figure of an allegorical American Indian (plate 1). The ceiling painting in the upper hall of the large dining hall contains the visual representatives of each continent, Europe, Asia, Africa, and America. They all display attributes that by this date had become associated with their separate geographical spaces, the most prominent feature of America being her brightly colored red-and-white feather headdress. The decorations on the upper hall ceiling were created with a specific theme in mind. Thornhill's plan was to present the figures of the Hanoverian rulers in such a way as to highlight the technical advances attained under Protestant rule and its patronage. The design has as its main theme a scene with the portrait busts of Queen Anne and King George I being saluted by the Virtues and acclaimed by the world. Each continental figure occupies an area on the edge of the design and is seated above one of the four walls; thus the design reflects the cosmological arrangement of the world into four distinct regions. All the figures' faces have been turned to look slightly upward and outward, as if to direct the viewer toward the center of the ceiling space. Asia and Africa each raise one arm in tribute, and America lifts her unstrung bow as if to indicate allegiance. While all the figures that represent the continents are shown occupying positions equivalent with respect to the rulers' portraits, it is only the figure of Europe that can be glimpsed from the lower dining hall area; she is depicted above the back wall and is seated the "right way up" to those standing on the ground (or seated at the dining tables) and viewing her from below in the larger dining space. A design such as Thornhill's seeks to reiterate the dominant and important position of Europe with respect to the other continents. In like manner, the role of the feminine continental figure for America and the others accentuates their dependence on the central and instigatory participants, the royal personages who graciously accept the tributes and vows of allegiance offered to them.

Thornhill's elaborate allegorical scheme demonstrates the extent to which the four parts of the world as a representational system was still in play in early-eighteenth-century England. At least two further major examples were produced, one in the 1730s, the other in the 1760s. The first of these, by Peter Scheemakers, was commissioned by Lord Cobham for the Palladian Bridge at Stowe (fig. 1.3). Although today this bridge has a superstructure of columns and entablature, when first built one side was paneled to mask the view toward the village of Lamport.[15] Here was installed Scheemakers's large allegorical panel of the four continents. As with Verrio and Thornhill, the figure of America is a seminaked young woman holding a bow. As with many examples of this arrangement of allegorical figures of continents paying tribute to the figure of Britannia or Europe, America appears on the far edge of the design, in this case on the far left, coming to join the others as a somewhat late arrival. Originally, the relief by Scheemakers was flanked by two portrait paintings of Sir Walter Raleigh and Sir William Penn by Francesco Sleter.

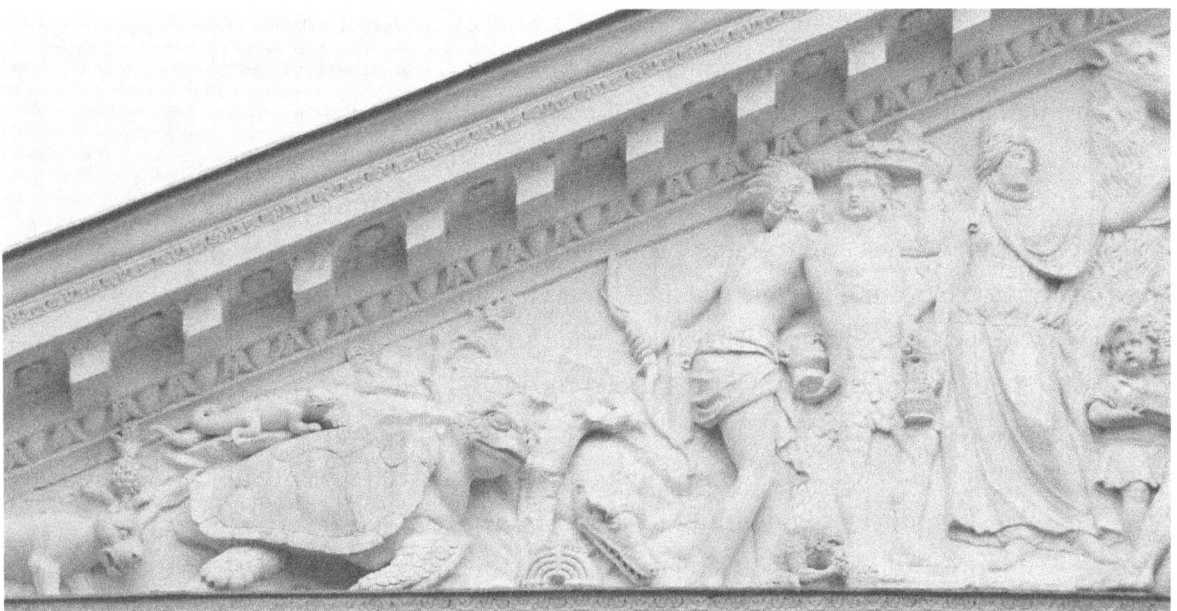

Fig. 1.3. Peter Scheemakers, *America*, part of the design of "Britannia receives tribute from the Four Continents," stone relief sculpture, after 1737, Temple of Concord and Victory, Stowe, Buckinghamshire. Photo by Ian Wood.

In 1762 the relief with the four continents was moved to the Temple of Concord and Victory, also at Stowe, which had just been remodeled in 1761–64 by Richard Grenville Temple, Second Earl Temple and was meant to recall recent British victories in the Seven Years' War and political harmony at home. Inside the temple on the walls are fourteen terra-cotta medallions representing important military victories throughout the empire. It would seem that the allegory of the continents paying tribute to Britannia was a theme entirely in keeping with this celebration of martial victories that had led the nation toward empire.

Inevitably, perhaps, as the eighteenth century wore on, the power of allegory declined. The world conceived symbolically could not contain the pressure of history. In the case of America in particular, the simmering border conflicts broke out into open warfare with France in 1755 and then a struggle with the American colonists in 1775. In these new circumstances, symbolic allegory, with its cosmological interpretation, could have little to contribute. At bottom, the allegorical tradition required a personification of America that was essentially inert, a stable construct whose elements were not required to respond to the modern world. The America that occasioned political and military events of such magnitude throughout the eighteenth century could not be represented thus.

As we shall see in chapter 2, the figure of the American Indian princess gets pressed into service as a satirical device in the prints circulating in the 1760s and 1770s. In one sense, this offered a quick identity check for the reader of the print, categorically locating the satire in an American context. But more than that, by allowing the Indian princess to act and react, to become part of the dramatis personae of the print, the engraver disturbed the inertia and stability of the original allegorical personification. Rather than America being a known place, immutable in its cosmological niche, it was becoming radically unstable, assisting in the process that would produce new identities for the continent.

Moreover, at a time when American Indian diplomacy and military contributions were uppermost in people's minds, the idea of the continent being represented by an essentially passive young woman could only have appeared fanciful. To think of America in the 1760s and 1770s was to think of sachems, kings, and war leaders, rather than an exotic confection of nudity and tropical abundance. This is not to say, of course, that a conventional symbol was unthinkable, but using such a symbol routinely was more problematic than it had ever been.

Just as De Passe's *America* revised the Indian princess figure to introduce a more disturbing female personification, so the figure of the male warrior in Ripa's allegory was also ready for reinterpretation. Famously, the classicization of American Indians was an eighteenth-century creation and became something of a cliché by the end of the period. As is well known, the identification of the American Indian warrior with Apollo was something of a routine maneuver in the eighteenth century. Contemporary interpretations of the Apollo Belvedere commented on the pose of the sculpture, exemplifying a bowman having loosed his arrow, in reference to Apollo's prowess as a hunter. Some interpretations went further, linking this pose with the story of Apollo's striking down of Niobe and her children.[16] In either case, however, as hunter or as wrathful god, from the mid-eighteenth century onward writers were prepared to find Apollo's counterpart in American Indians.[17] Johann Joachim Winckelmann's *Thoughts on the Imitation of Greek Works in*

Painting and Sculpture (1755) refers to Apollo's ideal of perfect form in motion by calling up an image of the "Indian . . . in pursuit [of] the hart."[18] In the same year, John Shebbeare, in his novel *Lydia; or Filial Piety*, made the same connection even more forcefully.[19] One or both of these texts may have prompted Benjamin West's remark in Rome in 1760 when viewing the Apollo Belvedere for the first time: "My God! How like it is to a young Mohawk Warrior!"[20] At first sight, all of these remarks seem radical, taking an ideal of European culture and locating it in a non-European, even barbarous context. But in terms of the perception of American Indians, these comparisons might be said to have achieved a similar result to allegorical representation. In each case, the experience of America is mapped onto a preexisting European scale of values. America and its people thus lose their potential to disturb by virtue of their separation from European values and the challenge that represents.

To sum up, the image of America presented in either of these two modes, the classicizing or the allegorical, was a complacent one. Two examples from the 1790s show how a new understanding of the "truth" of America pushed conventional understandings to a breaking point. In both of them, a set of clichéd devices are undermined and a dissenting vision proposed in their place. The understanding of America derived from either of these images is wholly different from the untroubled symbolism of Thornhill and Scheemakers a couple of generations earlier.

Travels Through the Interior Parts of America in a Series of Letters, by Thomas Anburey (first published in 1789), was published in two volumes in 1791 and included a plate entitled "An Indian Warrior Entering his Wigwam with a Scalp" (fig. 1.4). The figure that comprises the subject is dressed in rather curiously draped leggings and a loincloth and wears his very curly hair wrapped tightly in a knot on the top of his head. The most interesting aspect of this figure, however, is the pose he assumes underneath the framing branches of the pine trees. He is posed and physically articulated on the model of the Apollo Belvedere (fig. 1.5).[21] What is curious is that such a refined pose was incongruously placed within a so-called barbarous context, that the disparate elements of the scalping scene in the background and the classically articulated Indian were somehow reconciled within the minds of those looking on.[22] We, as modern viewers, recoil from the extended

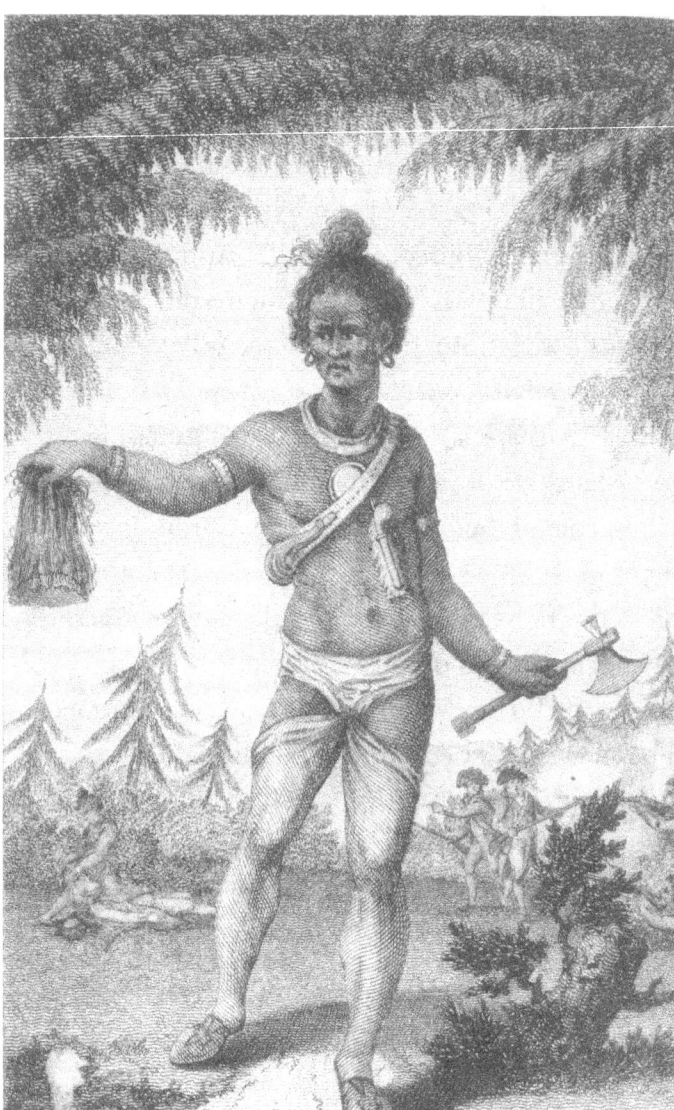

Fig. 1.4. Francis Barlow, *An Indian Warrior Entering his Wigwam With a Scalp*, from Thomas Anburey, *Travels Through the Interior Parts of America*, engraving, 2nd ed., 1791, shelfmark 297.g.16, British Library, London. Photo by permission of the British Library.

hand that holds a scalp, but this may not have been so obviously offensive to those readers in the eighteenth century. It is possible that a connection was discerned between the ethnic qualities of the figure and his classically nude form, insofar as both could be assimilated within the concept of primitiveness. In other words, the Indian's supposed uncivilized behavior (as a social being and as a taker of scalps in wartime) was somehow equivalent to Europe's own "rude" past in ancient Greece

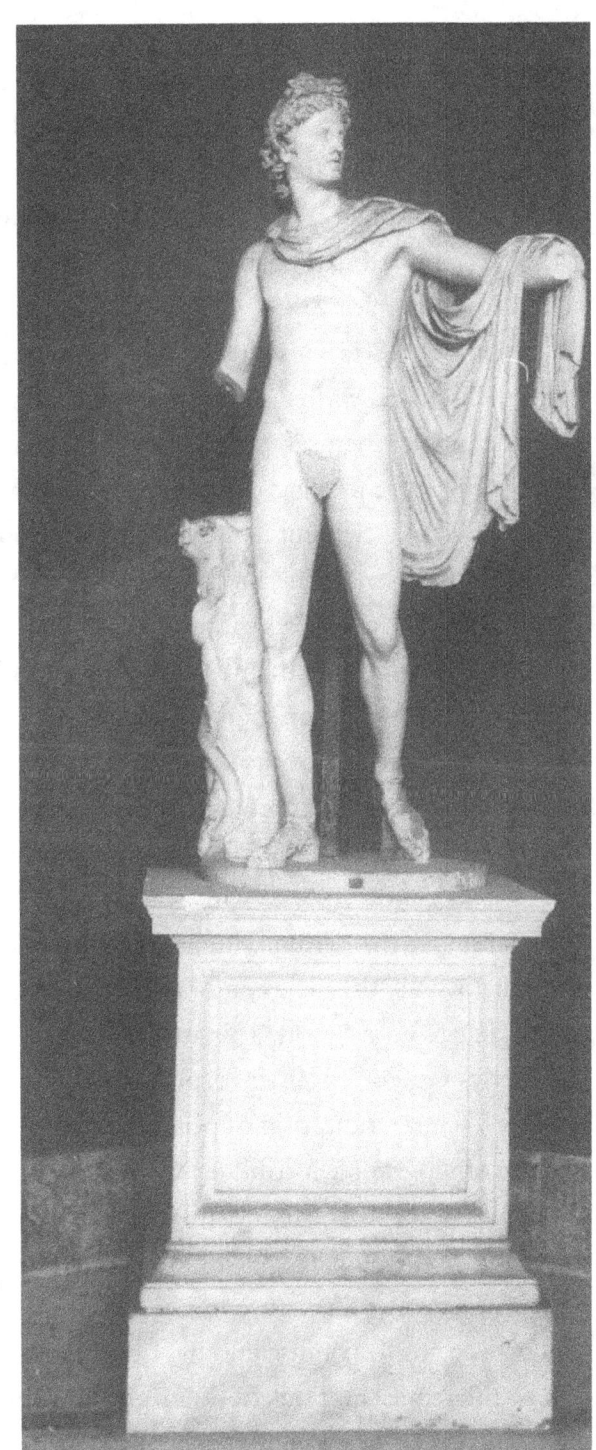

Fig. 1.5. Roman copy, *Apollo Belvedere*,
marble, early Hadrianic period, Vatican
Museums, Rome. Photo by Dr.
Nicholas Penny. From the Conway
Library, Courtauld Institute of Art.
Courtesy of the Conway Library.

and Rome and the many battles fought between neighboring city-states. Be that as it may, the Apollo pose resulted in the first place from the artist's inability to conceive of nude form as anything but classically articulated. He would surely not have had a live model from which to draw the Indian figure. He thus would have had to conceive of an active and physically strong male warrior in the only terms that would approximate such a concept, that of an ancient god, or at least a popularized conception of this.

In some respects, this illustration has an effect akin to the allegorical visions of America discussed earlier, in that the vignette scenes of brutality on the edges of the design make themselves felt as symbolic attributes of the figure of America.[23] In the earlier type of allegory, a severed human head was used to indicate savageness and was one element in a complex system of symbols. In the Crispijn de Passe engraving of America, the Indian princess is receiving a tray of disembodied heads, and the viewer is provided with further evidence of cannibalism by the pot next to her filled with amputated limbs of victims.[24] In Francis Barlow's illustration of the Indian warrior, we see an identically grotesque element acting within the overall scene in the same way as the severed head. It reminds viewers that they are seeing a "savage" capable of committing horrific acts of violence. It also reminds viewers of long-held notions about the symbolic significance of the continent of America. The association of America with scalping thus renews the older association with cannibalism, both bearing witness to the savagery synonymous with America. In the earlier works, the inclusion of a severed head at the foot of the figure of America was a standard convention. This attribute fell out of use as the symbolic iconography of America waned, but it was replaced by the possession of a scalp lock or scalping knife as a similar indication of potential violence or brutality.

The ethnographic attributes, which are superimposed onto the classical framework, seek to locate the figure in an American landscape. Barlow wanted his viewers to recognize the Indian as being of a certain race and climate. The dark skin and curly hair given to this figure might indicate a variety of races.[25] In this way, the engraver begins to confuse and hybridize the image of the Indian warrior, linking him to the representations of other groups of peoples, such as African American slaves and even the aboriginal peoples in Australia. However, the tomahawk and the bloody scalp lock he holds in his left and right hands, respectively, determine most powerfully the country and race of which he is a representative. This grafting on of ethnic traits to a classical form takes the idea of the noble savage to an almost ludicrous extreme, and the production of this hybrid form bears witness to the contrived nature of the solution. The easy identification of Greek sculpture with American Indians breaks down once contemporary references to Indian combat are included. As we shall see in chapter 2, the potential for violence when Indian troops were deployed was recognized at the time. But that very recognition sits ill with the perfection and nobility of the Apollo Belvedere. Barlow surely did not intend to satirize the Indian-Apollo connection, but in deploying it so clumsily he revealed the emptiness of the comparison.

Similarly, it is worthwhile to remind ourselves of the stark conceptualization of the allegory of the continents by William Blake. In an engraving of 1796 entitled "Europe Supported by Africa and America," the artist has provided almost no decorative details for each of the figures (fig. 1.6). Their nude forms signify the continents without the usual cloaking of the body in dress, ornamentation, and accoutrement. Blake's design was used as the finis page to an antislavery narrative by his friend John Gabriel Stedman, entitled *Narrative of a Five Years' Expedition, against the Revolted Negroes of Surinam*.[26] In a weird parody of the three graces, Blake's two "non-European" figures are physically restrained by the figure of Europe. As she coyly averts her eyes from the attention of the spectator, Europe holds Africa's hand in her right hand while she simultaneously wraps her left arm around the neck and shoulders of America. They both give physical support by the placement of their hands around Europe's waist and on her back. The group seems indissolubly linked through pictorial means, such that it is unclear where one figure ends and another begins. Still, America and Africa glare forcibly from the page, as if to call the spectator to witness their inextricable bonds. In fact, a rope-like cable is held between the hands of Europe, encasing all the figures, and this separates the group from those looking on as if to assert the finality of this arrangement. Blake has thus made a mockery of the entire concept of the "four quarters" or parts of the world, in that he clearly reveals the ethnocentrism apparent in the allegory from the beginning. He characterizes the figures in his allegory such that

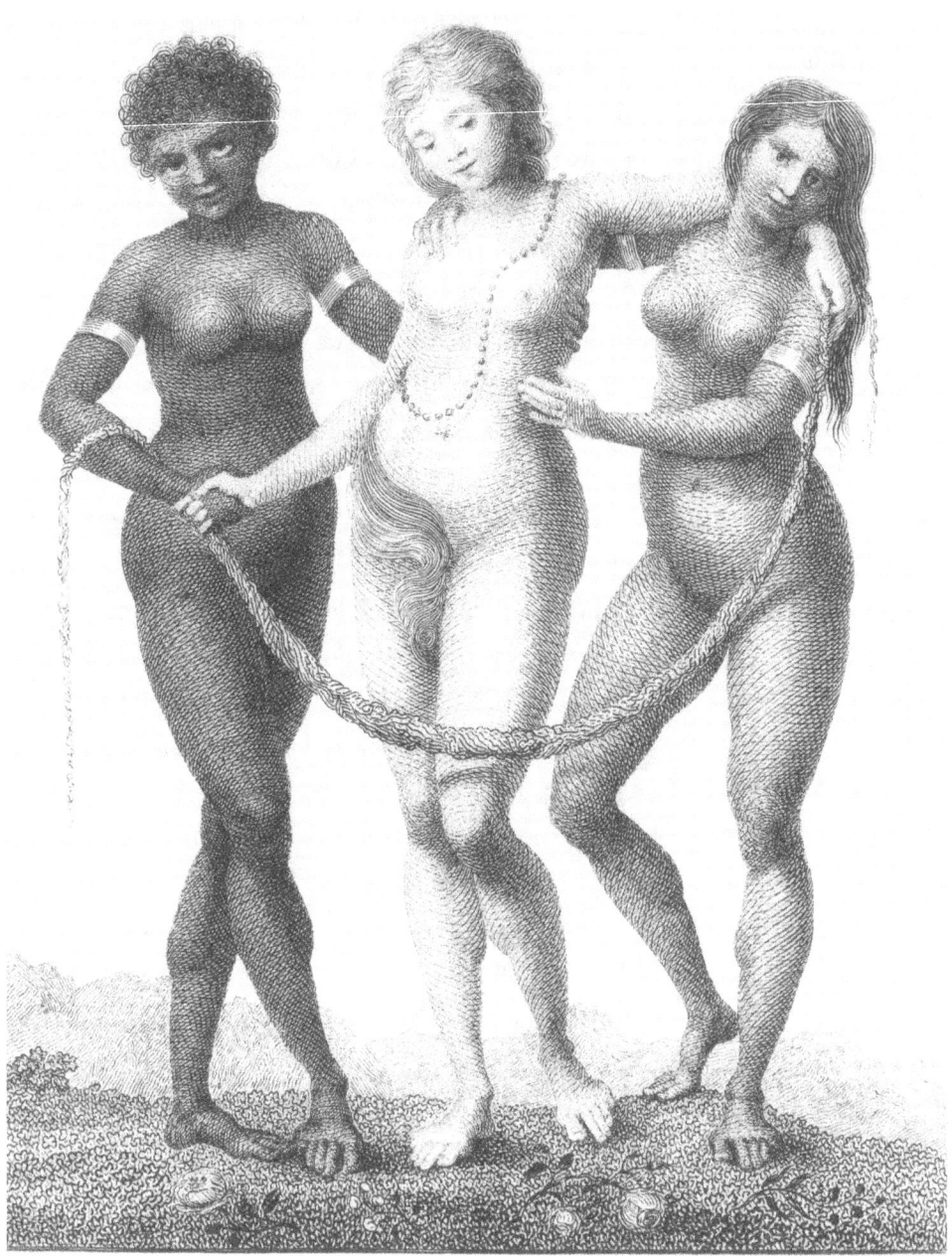

Fig. 1.6. William Blake, *Europe Supported by Africa and America*, from John Gabriel Stedman, *Narrative of a Five Years' Expedition against the Revolted Negroes of Surinam*, copper engraving, 1796, Reference (shelfmark) RHL: 535.1s8, facing 394, Bodleian Library, University of Oxford. Courtesy of the Bodleian Library.

they adopt the strong position of opposites, the dark tones of Africa and America in contradistinction to the whiteness of their captor. Blake's recognition of America's otherness places his work closer to the earlier characterizations of America as Indian queen but subverts them for his own anticolonial purposes. In this satire of the sad state of colonial intervention in distant cultures, this print approaches in emphasis the strategy of the political cartoon, which will be part of the discussion in the following chapter.

2   *Warfare, Diplomacy, and Visual Representation, ca. 1700–1760*

IN THIS CHAPTER, I examine the strategic importance of American Indian groups for British colonial interests in the first half of the eighteenth century until the outbreak of the Revolutionary War and the extent to which that importance was mirrored in graphic representations of Indian diplomatic delegations. With reference to the circumstances of the second decade of the 1700s, Eric Hinderaker has argued that the visit to London of the so-called Four Indian Kings established "a new visual and verbal language of empire."[1] Hinderaker's formulation may be taken as the impetus for much of what follows here, although my focus will deliberately emphasize the visual rather than the verbal language of empire. My primary concern is to trace the emergence of a new Indian persona whose presence signified much more than the generic American Indian associated with Theodore de Bry, whose important set of volumes, *Historia Americae* (1590–1634), became an essential source for images of American Indians, or with the allegorical tradition. Here were tribal emissaries, active within the world of lived experience and subject to the pressures of diplomatic and military development. Yet, as we shall see, their political status was itself contained within the wider frames of reference inherited from the allegorical or generic traditions of representation. The visual language of empire thus attempts to bind living peoples into a structure of representation conformable to British expectations.

The struggle for colonial superiority in America dominates the long eighteenth century. After the Comte de Frontenac was made governor of New France for the second time in 1689, border conflicts stemming from the rival territorial ambitions of England and France were a regular occurrence.[2] These struggles over territory often included indigenous peoples, whose interests were also tied up in the outcome. In 1689 Dover, New Hampshire, was attacked by members of the Pennacook, Ossipee, and Pigwacket tribes, and the following year the town of Schenectady in New York saw large losses of life after a French military force and its Indian allies attacked the city under cover of darkness. During the closing years of the century, in 1697, Haverhill in Massachusetts was raided by a party of Abenaki Indians; many settlers were killed, and some were taken prisoner. After another pause of a few years, 1702 saw the start of Queen Anne's War, during which Deerfield, Massachusetts, suffered a dawn attack in 1704, with about fifty settlers killed and more than a hundred taken as prisoners. In 1711–15 the frontier regions of North Carolina experienced Indian-white conflict during the Tuscarora Wars, and in 1715, farther south on the South Carolina border, the outlying settlements suffered during the Yamassee Wars.[3] This volatile situation not only threatened the expansion of British colonial interests but also raised the distinct possibility that French control of North American territories would seriously harm the existing British settlement of the continent.

The contest for eastern America was essentially a four-way conflict, with Britain, France, American Indian groups, and the European settlers themselves all attempting to secure their own advantage. In these frontier conflicts, the use of American Indian irregulars was commonplace. European powers could make use of their local knowledge for strategic purposes and incite them to aggression by promising territorial or other advantages if victorious over rival tribes, who were themselves enlisted by the enemy for the same reasons. In such circumstances, treaties could be made and broken, federations forged and dissolved, alliances sealed and ignored, as the advantage moved from one party to another. In a bid to secure some stability, it was imperative that as many of the tribes within a European power's sphere of influence be brought under its control. For the French and British governments, settling with the Indians at least had the merit of ensuring a united force to field against the opposition. From the European point of view, the situation was complicated by the fact that the allegiance of any one tribe or community could not be guaranteed in such a fast-changing military and diplomatic situation. British colonial policy in America can thus be regarded as a series of punitive actions or diplomatic activities aimed at pacifying the frontier tribes who threatened British interests.

From the British point of view, the instability of the region in the early eighteenth century was in large measure a result of the same perfidious French tactics developed since the 1680s, stirring up the Indians to assault British interests by proxy. Understandably, then, an anti-French bias can be found in the colonial writings of this period. For instance, in the important and influential account written by Cadwallader Colden, *The History of the Five Nations of Indians, Depending on the Province of New York in America*, first published in 1727 and again in an expanded version in 1747, explicit mention is made of the conflicting interests of the colonial powers.

> The following Account of the Five Nations will show what dangerous Neighbours the Indians have been, What Pains a Neighbouring Colony (who's [*sic*] interest is Opposite to ours) has taken to withdraw their Affections from us, and how dreadful the Consequences may be, if that colony should succeed in their Designs; and therefore how much we ought to be on our Guard.[4]

For Colden, his account is justified by its strategic importance. The Indians have a history, but it is that history's intersection with European history that should matter to his readers. Indeed, Colden is at pains to emphasize the necessity of engagement with tribal groups as opposed to any more disinterested policy.

Besides the consideration of Profit and Gain, he [Governor William Burnet] Considered what Influence this Trade had on the numerous Nations of Indians living on the Vast Continent of North America, and who surround the British Colonies; of what Advantage it might be of, if they were influenced by the English in case of a War with France, and how prejudicial, on the other hand, if they were directed by French counsels.[5]

Colden voices his concern over how far the French have influenced the Indian groups inhabiting all of the frontier regions and whether this will act to their advantage "in case of war." To remedy this, he recommends winning over the Indians, seeing that it is their sympathies and alliances that could well determine outcomes in battle. This desire to win over American Indian groups to the British cause was also in part responsible for the planning and execution of the 1710 visit of the delegation of three Mohawks and one Mahican to London, which I will discuss shortly.

In these circumstances, British diplomats and colonial authorities were quick to recognize the importance of the Iroquois peoples, of whom the Mohawks were but one of five groups formed as a league and known in their own language as the Hodenosaunee (People of the Longhouse). The Five Nations of Iroquois had established themselves as a league some time between 1560 and 1570 and by the early eighteenth century had become a confederacy.[6] The Five Nations of Iroquois was comprised of the Mohawk, Oneida, Onondaga, Cayuga, and Seneca nations, controlling land from Mohawk territories along the Mohawk River in the eastern part of present-day New York to Seneca land in the western part of the state. Of these, the Mohawks were the best known to the British and had by this date suppressed their neighbors, the Mahicans, hence the reference to "Six Nations," over which Tee Yee Neen Ho Ga Row was "Emperor," as found on his printed portrait (fig. 2.1). The Mohawks traded with the Dutch in the seventeenth century in what would become Albany, New York. After the British gained New Amsterdam from the Dutch in 1664, the Mohawks, being the group closest to Albany, continued such trading relationships and the alliances that tended to follow trade. It seems that this ongoing relationship helped to solidify the British and Mohawk alliance, which eventually became part of the Covenant Chain, at least in the American Indians' eyes.[7] The Iroquois as a whole, however, tried to maintain contacts with both competing European powers and to insert themselves into the fur-trading routes that linked places like Albany with the Great Lakes and farther western areas. They became, in effect, the barrier or "cushion" between the budding French empire in Canada and the quickly expanding British equivalent based on the eastern seaboard of America. Their position as mediators would become particularly important for the aspirations of the Pennsylvania and Virginia colonies, especially in the latter's enterprise known as the Ohio Company. Thus, in several respects, the Iroquois had made themselves indispensable by answering to the demands of both sides, British and French, and also by attempting to control a vast area between their homelands in northern New York and those of the refugee Indians, the Algonquin Delawares and Shawnees, beginning to inhabit the coveted Ohio Valley region.[8] As has been explained by a number of historians of the Iroquois, their policies tried to maintain their status as intermediaries and to keep them neutrally available to both the French and the British.[9] At times of stress or conflict, this status could be used to play one side off the other, and thus the Iroquois could maintain their position as powerbrokers within the region. This tactic would eventually split the Great League of Iroquois, but in the beginning of the eighteenth century there was much to play for. After making peace with the French in 1701, the Iroquois effectively came under British jurisdiction under the terms of the Treaty of Utrecht in 1713. Although warfare and diplomacy in this era affected many tribal groups, the Iroquois, and Mohawks in particular, tended to dominate British understanding of Indian affairs.

Between 1700 and 1755, it is possible to chart the inception of a new colonial relationship between American Indian groups and Britain. Population growth along the eastern seaboard of North America increased demands for more land and thus provoked an inevitable clash with the needs of the original inhabitants of the northeastern woodlands. This "land hungry" situation created a volatile atmosphere that had far-reaching effects across the whole of the Old Northwest, extending as far as the eastern Plains. It was evident that new alliances might secure territorial advantage as well as stabilizing this situation. Diplomatic initiatives and formal treaties provided the means to do this, effectively drawing the Indians into a European system of rights and privileges.

According to colonial records, the French first established the idea of bringing some of the most outstanding American Indian leaders to the palace at Versailles. After his captivity with the French, a Boston man, John Nelson, wrote in 1696 to urge the British Board of Trade to create a similar style of diplomacy by bringing over to England "prominent" Indian chiefs.[10] During the following century, several Indian delegations to England are recorded.

The earliest of these embassies to Britain to receive any substantial notice was the visit of the "Four Indian Kings" to the court of Queen Anne in 1710.[11] These four men were often referred to as "kings" but were younger war leaders mainly representing Mohawk concerns and interests. The embassy was organized to secure Mohawk allegiance as a British force readied itself to invade Canada. Waiting only for naval support, the eight hundred men stationed on the New York frontier in 1709 could further strengthen their position with Indian allegiance, especially at a time when many Woodlands Indians were allied with the French. When Queen Anne diverted the fleet to other duties, the need for a British alliance with the Indians became imperative. Taking a group of American Indian delegates to England was thus an essential stratagem within the overall planning for the invasion and the immediate capture of Montreal.

Ffurther wee propose (provided always the ffleet doe not arrive) that some suitable persons be sent home from the severall Governments. Truly to Represent the case to the Queen, and Address Her in that behalfe, that wee may yet be enabled to put in Execution what she has with so much Grace, Commanded us to undertake. Respecting - the Reducing of Canada (which designe without any fault of ours is like to prove unsuccessfull) as likewise that two or three of the Sachims & Principall Captains belonging to Each of the Five Nations be sent over with them, And Laurence the Interpreter, which wee judge the most proper methods for securing the Indians in our Interest, and preventing the Incursions of the Enemy on any part of our Countrey.[12]

As we have seen, French and Indian attacks on British settlements in the late seventeenth century had demonstrated beyond all doubt the need to maintain the loyalty of the Iroquois as allies. Although only Mohawk leaders made the trip, the Mohawks' significance within the Five Nations ensured that the delegation was received with all due seriousness and respect.[13]

The Mohawks' visit is significant on account of its spawning a large and diverse body of visual and literary material that bears some examination. The creative response to the visit is, in some way, a testament to its importance but also to its novelty. For the first time since Elizabethan exploration of the continent, American Indians were being received in London as politically significant individuals. The Indian visual trope, elaborated over two hundred years of allegorical representation, could not accommodate the actuality of Mohawk culture without some strain. Indeed, in just the same way as Queen Anne's ministers needed to establish an appropriate settlement with the Iroquois, so those who sought to represent them needed to establish an appropriate mode of depiction.[14] Four individual portrait paintings of the embassy were commissioned by Queen Anne from John Verelst, a Dutch artist working in England. These were engraved in mezzotint by Jean Simon shortly afterward to capitalize on the public interest in the visit. Each of the Indian men is depicted standing in a landscape background with one hand on the hip and the other hand holding an item relating to his status, either as a clan member or a leadership figure (figs. 2.1, 2.2). The "Emperor of the Six Nations," or Chief Hendrick, carries in his right hand a belt of wampum signifying in colonial terms the peaceful relations that were being secured by treaty and, in American Indian terms, the "brightening of the Covenant Chain" signifying a strengthened commercial relationship as well.[15] Behind him is his totem and clan animal, a wolf, which was also used as his signature on a document establishing friendly relations.[16] In a sense, this mode of depiction attempts to attest to the figure's political importance by fitting him to established visual conventions. All of Verelst's Indian "kings" are placed in standard portrait poses conventionally used for the depiction of the landed elite in this era; as high-ranking figures, they are shown standing in front of their domains, elegantly dressed, armed, and accoutred. But of course this elegant presentation is itself revealing of the particular circumstances of the visit.

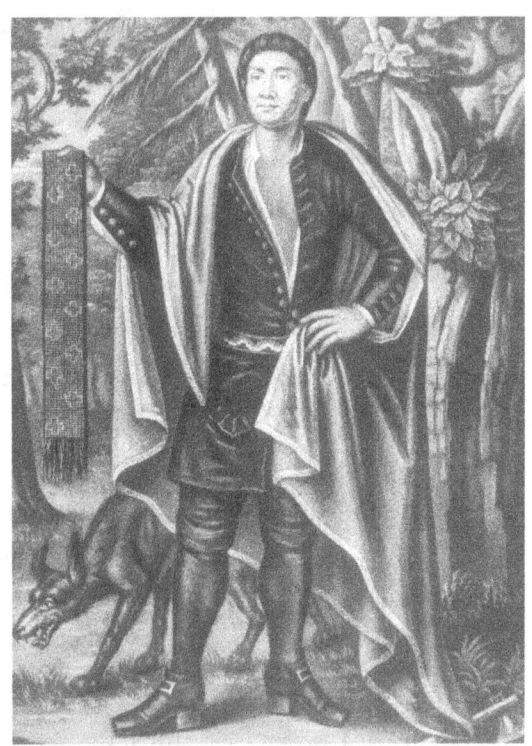

Fig. 2.1. Jean Simon, after John Verelst, *Tee Yee Neen Ho Ga Row, Emperor of the Six Nations*, mezzotint engraving, 1710. Department of Ethnography, The British Museum, London. Photo © Copyright The British Museum.

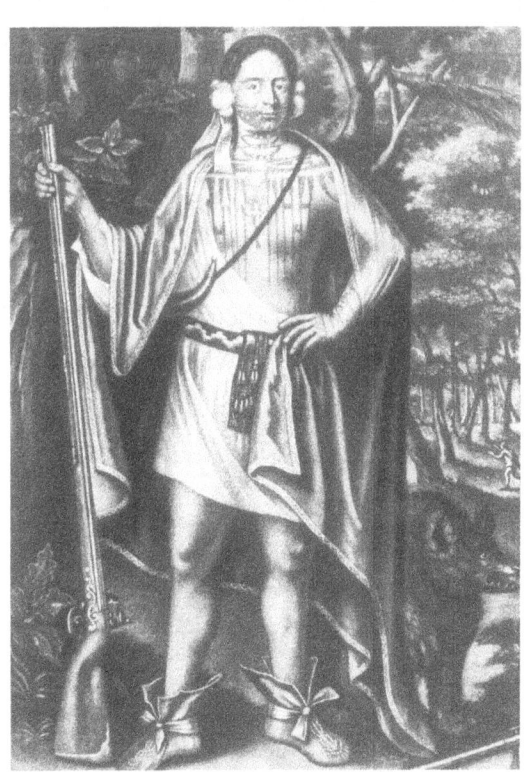

Fig. 2.2. Jean Simon, after John Verelst, *Sa Ga Yeath Qua Pieth Tow, King of the Maquas*, mezzotint engraving, 1710. Department of Ethnography, The British Museum, London. Photo © Copyright The British Museum.

In preparation for their audience with Queen Anne, "dressers of the playhouse" were instructed to fit them out with appropriate garb.[17] "These American Kings were dressed in black under cloth[e]s after The English manner; but, instead of a blanket, they had each a Scarlet-in-grain cloth mantle, edged with gold, thrown over all Their other garments."[18]

Hinderaker has argued effectively that the designation of the 1710 delegation group as "kings" or "Indian kings" was important to the extension of English empire and authority within the American context. This designation posited the existence of Native peoples who were both allies and agents acting in lieu of the crown in the process of building an empire. Taking this idea further, Hinderaker also sees the formation of a "new . . . language of empire" being initiated during this visit in its several representations and that the elements of American Indian and kingliness, chief, leader, or head warrior as well as stately European gentleman were very much a function of this new way of representing empire.[19] Verelst's portraits might be seen, in this light, as witnesses of this phenomenon. The visual presentation of the Mohawk leaders achieves, in graphic terms, a convincing reconfiguration of American Indian culture for a new imperial context. *Tee Yee Neen Ho Ga Row, Emperor of the Six Nations* (fig. 2.1) and *Sa Ga Yeath Qua Pieth Tow, King of the Maquas* (fig. 2.2) can be usefully compared in this respect. First, the "Emperor of the Six Nations" is more closely allied to European standards of deportment than the "King of the Maquas." The latter still wears moccasins and buckskin, his face and body are tattooed, and his hair is decorated. The "Emperor," on the other hand, wears buckled shoes, lace breeches, and an elegant jacket; his hair is plainly dressed. The wampum belt he carries attests to his diplomatic significance, in contradistinction to the musket displayed by the "King of the Maquas." Thus, although both men are posed virtually identically, the "Emperor of the Six Nations" seems to inhabit that pose more easily than his compatriot. In effect, Verelst has proposed a hierarchical reading of the embassy, with paramount power clearly associated with European decorum, while military prowess alone remains subject to its Native context. The "Emperor of the Six Nations" is worthy of his appellation, it seems, by virtue of his ability to participate within the British imperium. Divested of his tribal identity, he enters that liminal world where the empire can do its work. Both he and the "King of the Maquas" offer military potential for Britain, symbolized in each case by the discarded tomahawk at the bottom right, but the consolidation of that potential in a settled alliance is figured as much in the "Emperor's" adoption of European ways as in the wampum belt he proffers. Furthermore, insofar as the "Emperor" is posed in gentlemanly guise, his appearance might be seen as preparing the ground for occupation. He is fitted to a portrait convention in which the subject's surroundings speak of his or her possessions, suggesting thereby entitlement and ownership, which are negotiable commodities in European experience.

Thus the language of portraiture, elaborated to depict British grandees in possession of their lands and titles, simultaneously elevates the embassy to some sort of equivalence with their hosts in the court of Queen Anne, while at the same time rendering the four Indian leaders and their peoples more susceptible to European values. If the Mohawks are now to be understood as British allies, they are so by virtue of their recognition of British superiority and their willingness to enter into trading compacts and military agreements on essentially British terms.

The iconic formula developed by Verelst proved to be lasting, as did other features of the 1710 embassy: the transport of delegations to London, the use of appellations like "king" or "chief," and, when depicted, their visual accommodation to European portrait conventions. The fact that later embassies were presented in similar terms suggests that the language of empire, in Hinderaker's formulation, was capable of working with diverse groups from different regions, binding them all into one discourse.[20]

In 1730 another important Indian delegation, this time Cherokee, accompanied Sir Alexander Cuming to England. The seven "ambassadors" were portrayed individually for the Duke of Montague and collectively in a picture by Markham, engraved by Isaac Basire (fig. 2.3).[21] As in 1710, so in 1730, the British authorities worked with a hierarchical understanding of the embassy, led by a "king" with a clearly distinguished retinue of followers. Their meeting with King George II was recorded by a contemporary witness: "The [Indian] King had a Scarlet Jacket on, but all the rest Were naked, except an Apron about their Middles, and a Horse's Tail hung down behind; their Faces, Shoulders, etc. were painted and spotted

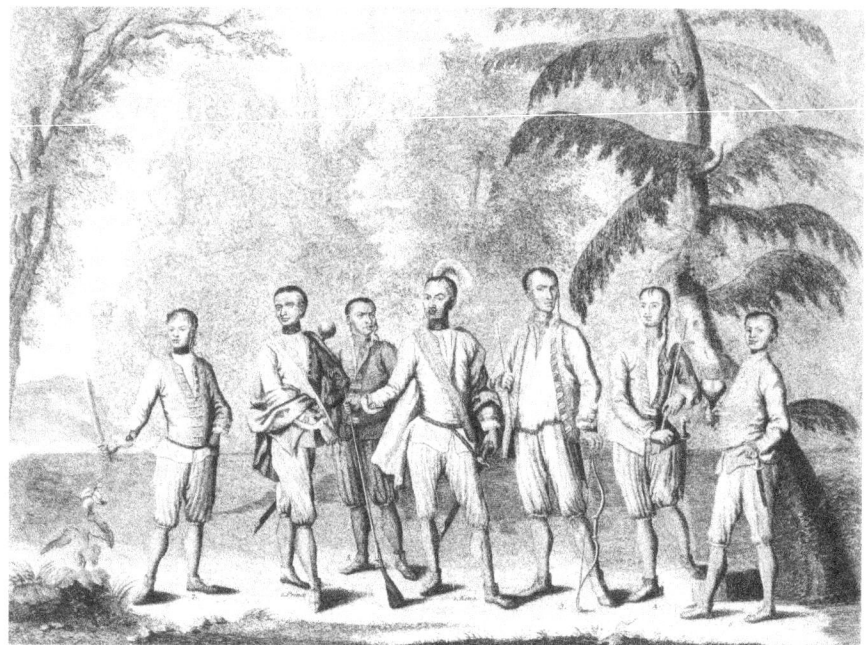

Fig. 2.3. Isaac Basire, after Markham, *Seven Cherokees,* (left to right) *Onaconoa, Catergusta, Caulunna, Oukah Olah, Tathtowe, Clogoittah, Ukwaneequa (Attakullakulla),* engraving, 1730. Department of Ethnography, The British Museum, London. Photo © Copyright The British Museum.

with red, blue, and green, etc. They had Bows in their Hands, and painted Feathers on Their Heads."[22]

Compared to the 1710 embassy, however, the contrast between the "King," Oukah Olah, and his retinue seems to have been much more marked than that between the "Emperor" and the other three Indian "Kings." Partially, this may be explained by the differences between the two embassies, especially as no retinue is recorded for the 1710 visit, whose members might well have appeared less conformable to Western experience than the four sachems they accompanied. Intriguingly, however, this written description of the 1730 group presents a much more alien encounter than the one recorded in visual terms. In the print, the entire delegation wears European clothing, and the inclusion here of European-made breeches and silk or linen shirts to adorn the American Indian men is reminiscent of the style and dress employed earlier during the Mohawk and Mahican visit of 1710. Striking fashionable poses, the "King" and his entourage are ranged in front of a wooded landscape, presumably intended to represent an American woodlands scene. As with Verelst's 1710 portraits, their gentlemanly appearance connotes acquiescence in, if not submission to, Britain's colonial endeavors. Indeed, the process of

40

acculturation detected in Verelst's treatment of the "Emperor of the Six Nations" seems to have progressed to incorporate the entire retinue, not merely the principal negotiator. Yet the easy decorum of their poses and gestures is ruptured by the facial tattooing, hairstyles, and weaponry, which hint at the inescapable difference of these people. This separation from European norms means that the weapons they brandish, coupled with their "savage" facial features, promote a display of martial prowess that is at once reassuring (as British allies) and disturbing (these people are not civilized in Europe's normative terms). The men represented here echo the "kings" of the earlier Mohawk visit in their elegant poses and their combination of actual American Indian dress and body adornment with a courtly style of clothing. This arrangement of elements sets up a tension within the visual representation that cannot be easily dissipated. The cultural distance, witnessed on the occasion of the meeting with George II, reappears here in the play of details, subverting the composition's decorous presentation with nonconformable reminders of another world. Markham's picture, in its very awkwardness, reveals the inconsistencies within the attempt to produce a language of empire, whose univocal discourse cannot entirely overwrite alternative understandings and articulations.

There is some evidence, in fact, that this inconsistency was perceived at the time. No matter how carefully stage-managed the delegations' diplomatic visits and the prints commemorating them might be, the sharp-eyed saw more than was intended. It was noted at the time that the designation of "king" was often too grand an appellation for what was, in reality, a carefully manufactured representative.[23] If some of the delegations were thus understood as somewhat theatrical in presentation, satirical commentators felt free to manipulate their meanings.

Thus, in Richard Steele's journal, the *Spectator*, of April 27, 1711, Joseph Addison tells an apocryphal tale about the uncovering of some "little Bundle of Papers" that can speak for the long since departed Indian "kings."[24] Using the "kings" as satirical mouthpieces, Addison has them comment on the bizarre artificialities of London high living. Ladies are made up so much that their true beauty is hidden, and men with elaborate wigs and neckties are considered to be the epitome of refinement. Other targets include the lack of piety among churchgoers and the general falseness of the rich and powerful. At the end of the piece, in a statement that seems a clear transposition from Montaigne's *Essais* (1580), Addison states "that we are all guilty in some Measure of the same narrow way of Thinking, which we meet with in this Abstract of the *Indian Journal*; when we fancy the Customs, Dresses, and Manners of other countries are ridiculous and extravagant, if they do not resemble those of our own."[25] Addison's satire in one sense does no more than anticipate that well-known eighteenth-century device of anatomizing society by means of an outside witness, whether native, culturally distant, or both together. In doing so, the specific delegation that had visited Queen Anne is appropriated for satire and lost to history. The Indian delegate is divested of actual political importance to become an empty vessel to make a satirical point. There is something of a degradation here, a reduction to a generic type or cipher, stripped of any of the complexity present in the circumstances of the 1710 embassy. By fitting his satirical Indians to a literary genre, little can survive of their Mohawk identity. To be Indian in this context is to be merely the antipodes of England. At the same time, Addison's concern with the artificial appearance of well-to-do London returns us to the issues of dressing up, and the awkwardness of doing so, in the images produced by Verelst and Markham. The Mohawk delegation, in effect, can be used to comment on the excesses of European fashion in a satirical account, despite having worn aspects of that same apparel in the conduct of their embassy. Addison's satire requires that the delegations be remembered not as accommodating themselves to English notions of decorum but as exotic emissaries from another culture.

The Indian as an exotic figure in the European imagination requires further investigation here. In what follows, I examine a few examples of this fictive presentation of American Indian peoples as it was manifested in the first half of the eighteenth century. The production of this exotic Indian takes place at the same time that colonial policy, diplomatic initiatives, and military strategy all acknowledged the actual inhabitants of North America. What I hope to show here is that the depictions of Indian delegations were exceptional and that the creative arts relied in the main on an Indian figure whose position in contemporary history was at best tangential and most often entirely lacking. The Indian to be habitually encountered in literature or the visual arts was a pliable figure, capable of meeting every British expectation of nobility and simplicity. In this context, the fact that some authors based their creations on travel accounts, notwithstanding the veridical status of these texts, is significant, for the same process seen in the "compliance" of the delegates with portrait conventions is at work, but more emphatically. Designated individuals, in all their cultural specificity and historical complexity, are refashioned to become less complex and ultimately symbolic figures. History and society are abstracted to leave merely a sense of character, transcending time and place.

The first instance of a Northern American tribal figure in the English drama of the eighteenth century occurs before the fateful visit of the Mohawks in the character of Ulamar in John Dennis's *Liberty Asserted* of 1704.[26] The action of the play takes place in Canada, where both French and British trading relations had been established. Dennis's intention seems to have been "to contrast English liberty with French tyranny" and to distinguish between their separate forms of colonial rule, the British version, naturally, being the more desirable.[27] In this way, Dennis's patriotic storyline can be linked to that of earlier dramatists, such as John Dryden and William Davenant, who had used drama to portray the idea that the English were better at achieving appropriate relations with the Native peoples of America. Crucially, Dryden and Howard's *The Indian Queen* (1664) and its sequel, Dryden's *The Indian Emperor* (1665), are both set in South America, and their principal Indian protagonist is the Aztec king, "Montezuma." In *Liberty Asserted*, where the setting is now the North American forests, the Iroquois man, Ulamar, has been taught the secret of the "European Arts" by a friendly English captain.[28]

In choosing to represent a North American Indian, Dennis took on a more complex characterization. Unlike the highly popular theatrical representations of South American Indian history and tales of the Spanish Conquest, North American Indian cultures exhibited different modes of religious practice, which could not be matched in the European mind with a classical equivalent. Nor could the tribal leaders be seen to command their peoples in the way that an absolute ruler or king might exert his will. North American Indian figures in dramatic roles were therefore much more shadowy and nonspecific in their function and cultural definition. Dennis's Indian character, Ulamar, is not central to the play as Montezuma had been for Dryden and Howard, but his personification foreshadows much of what subsequent authors would do with American Indian figures. More important, Ulamar is shown to combine American Indian and European experience. The ideal held out in Dennis's play, of course, is that contact with a European power will confer wisdom and humanity on an already noble but untutored individual. The reception of American Indian delegations in colonial centers or in London itself, together with developing trading relations and military alliances, can be seen as motivated by the same concerns.

Ulamar, for all his ideal blending of American Indian and European values, may owe his characterization to travel writing. The year before Dennis published *Liberty Asserted*, Baron de Lahontan's *Nouveaux Voyages* was published in English, as was a French edition of his *Dialogues curieux entre l'auteur et un sauvage de bon sens*. The main Indian character in the *Dialogues* is a chieftain named Adario. Like Ulamar, he is described as an Indian leader of a class above the rest who had met Europeans. Lahontan claimed to have met Adario, who in real life was an actual spokesman for the Huron people and had traveled to New York and Quebec in the late seventeenth century. Adario's gifts of oratory became legendary and were noted by the chronicler of the Five Nations of Iroquois, Cadwallader Colden.[29]

It is significant that during this period, there was a tendency for real individuals to inspire travel writers and, through their accounts, to inhabit fictional writing as well. What marks all these productions is the hybrid nature of the American Indian protagonists. Their function is to act as a foil to the social and moral failings of an imperfect world, and this requires them to know of and preferably experience British culture. For example, in John Shebbeare's *Lydia; or Filial Piety* (1755), the central protagonist, Cannassatego, visits Europe, examines its failings, and returns to his native land and his paramour, Yarico. Drawing on Cadwallader Colden's History of the Five Indian Nations for detail, Shebbeare models Cannassatego on Colden's "Cannassateego," or Canasatego, the Iroquois/Onondagan headman who acted historically as representative for the refugee Delawares and Shawnees.[30] This Indian leader has been interpreted recently as having inadvertently sold off land rights over the whole of the Ohio Valley to the British in the Treaty of Lancaster of 1744.[31] The Cannassatego of *Lydia*, however, loses practically all of this historical specificity to become a mouthpiece for ironic reflections on British customs and behavior. As with Addison's 1711 satire, so here in 1755 the literary Indian exists to one side of contemporary history.

In one sense, this abstraction from history can be compared to the older allegorical figure of America, discussed in chapter 1. Although these are literary figures and none of them can be read emblematically as simple representations of a landmass and its peoples, they nonetheless contribute to their narratives a symbolic rather than a historical role. For the reader, America is a place where Ulamar and Cannassatego live, and they in turn exemplify what America is and how its people behave. The models Dennis and Shebbeare may have used—Adario, the Huron, and Canasatego, the Onondagan–had an impact on history, but Ulamar and Cannassatego live in a world outside of that history.

The years between the publication of *Liberty Asserted* in 1704 and *Lydia* in 1755, as we have seen, were years in which the place of American Indians in contemporary events was becoming more and more urgent. In the second half of the eighteenth century, this trend accelerated, as the struggle for America intensified. Diplomatic initiatives and military alliances placed Indian tribes at the center of British policy in America. The French and Indian Wars of 1748 to 1766 contributed to the British and French Seven Years' War (1754–63) but took place over a longer span of time, including a major Cherokee uprising in 1760–61 and the pan-Indian "rebellion" organized by the Ottawa chief Pontiac in 1763. A relatively peaceful decade followed the cessation of hostilities, before the American Revolutionary War broke out in 1775. Whether as friend or foe, the Indian warrior achieved a new prominence in the English imagination. Precisely because the actions of Indian auxiliaries were part of a larger struggle, taking place at a time when news gathering was relatively sophisticated, Indian aggression received a great deal of attention. The potential violence of Verelst's and Markham's emissaries (figs. 2.2, 2.3) was now actualized in real events.

A useful place to begin my analysis is the monument in Westminster Abbey dedicated to Lieutenant Colonel Roger Townshend, killed at the Battle for Ticonderoga in 1759 (figs. 2.4, 2.5).[32] Designed by Robert Adam and erected in 1761, it contains the most significant eighteenth-century monumental representation of

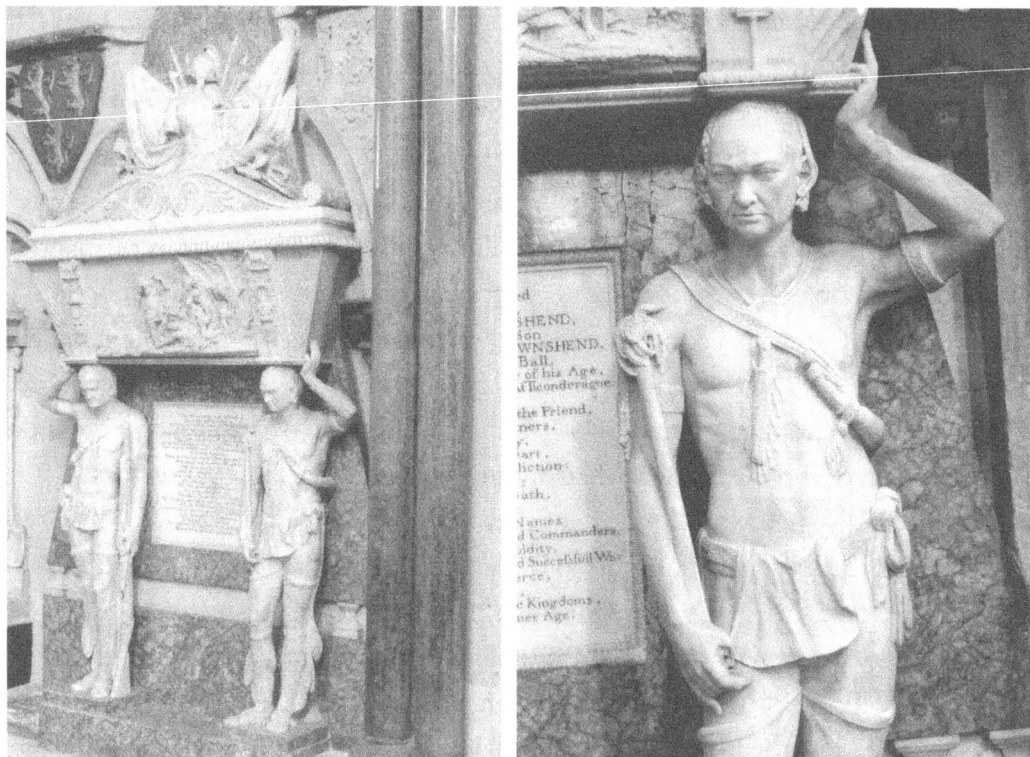

Fig. 2.4a and 2.4b (detail). Robert Adam, *Townshend Monument*, stone carving and marble relief, 1761, Westminster Abbey, London. From the Conway Library, Courtauld Institute of Art. Courtesy of the Conway Library.

an American Indian. Supporting the central relief, with the dying figure of Townshend, are two full-length Indian figures. These sculptures were taken from life, modeled on a Choctaw boy who had been captured by the British and was now in the charge of General George Townshend, the deceased's brother. Adam's detailed presentation of the Indian warriors is remarkable. One holds a hatchet, the other a musket; both have powder horns, worn at the side, and a sheathed knife dangling on their chests. They wear buckskins on their legs, and their hair is dressed in Choctaw or Cherokee style, with a plucked scalp and curled locks of hair at the back of the head. These figures, then, are emphatically contemporary in appearance, armed with modern weapons and benefiting from European trade as the French fleur-de-lis on the powder horns demonstrates.

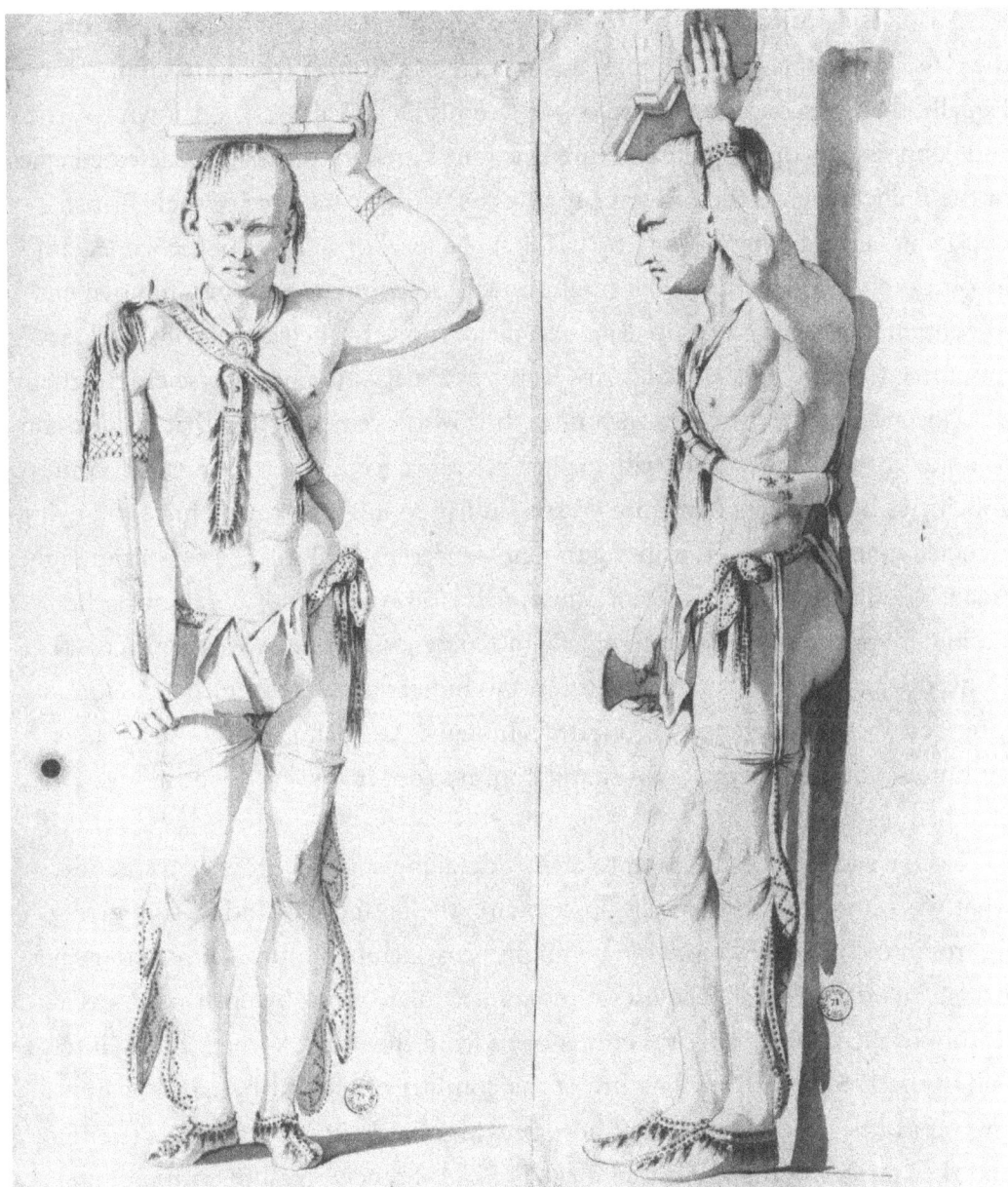

Fig. 2.5. Robert Adam, study for the American Indian support figures for the *Townshend Monument*, pen and wash, 1761, Sir John Soane's Museum, London. From the Conway Library, Courtauld Institute of Art. By courtesy of the Trustees of Sir John Soane's Museum and the Conway Library.

Adam's presentation of the warriors suggests his deliberate intention to invoke the classical use of barbarian figures as supporters in Roman triumphal architecture. Equally, their poses are suggestive of the famous Della Valle satyrs, known to artists and connoisseurs of classical sculpture since the sixteenth century. As defeated allies of the French enemy, the Indians support the patriotic sacrifice of their British opponent, acquiescing in his victory. Yet at the level of artistic coherence, Adam's invocation of classical precedent might be said to compete with his employment of contemporary references in arms and decoration. In the context of a funerary monument, where generalized forms were customary, Adam's precise employment of Choctaw accoutrement was surprising. It is worth remembering that his decision to honor Townshend's death with explicit reference to the North American context anticipates by ten years Benjamin West's similar contextual treatment of the dying General James Wolfe in his painting of that subject in 1770 (plate 4).[33] Intriguingly, Adam's design for the *Townshend Monument* is a reworking of the drawing he submitted for the commission to erect a monument to Wolfe in Westminster Abbey. In his design for the Wolfe competition, no indication was given that Adam intended a visual reference to American Indians. As Adam adapted his Wolfe's monument design for the Townshend commission, however, he must have changed his mind.[34]

Even if such minor attention to artistic detailing shows a growing awareness of what was or was not aesthetically appropriate, the presence of Indian supporting figures in the *Townshend Monument* might provoke uncomfortable reactions in a British audience as well. The use of Indian irregular troops by both sides was a feature of the struggle and was contentious from the start. As the fighting intensified in the 1750s, the brutal nature of the conduct of the war became apparent. Two episodes achieved an instant notoriety, the Battle of Monongahela (1755) and the attack on Fort William Henry (1757).[35] French pressure on the Ohio Valley trading settlements was answered with a British force under General Edward Braddock, whose orders were to repel French incursions. In July 1755 Braddock's troops were surprised on the banks of the Monongahela River by a combined French and Indian force. Surrounded and disorganized, the British incurred very heavy losses from an enemy skilled in concealment and ferocious in attack. The rout of Braddock's force was but a prelude to perhaps the most well known military debacle, the siege of Fort William Henry, when a retreating British column was decimated by Indian forces. A report published in the *Gentleman's Magazine* in September 1757 describes how the British were

> [p]ursued by the Indians 6 or 7 miles on their way to Fort Edward; All the rest were despoiled of their arms; the most were stript stark-naked; many were killed and scalped, officers not excepted. . . . The throats of most, if not all the women were cut, their bellies ript open, their bowels torn out and thrown upon the faces of their dead and dying bodies; and the children were taken by the heels, and their brains beat out against the trees and stones, and not one of them saved.[36]

The unrestrained violence of this form of warfare is compared by the writer to Braddock's defeat, underlining British vulnerability to such perfidious tactics and suggesting that the French had instigated their Indian allies to commit such acts.

Yet no matter that the British viewed these reverses with dismay and were appalled by the casualties they suffered, their strategists accepted the need to adjust their tactics to the realities of this new form of warfare. The Marquis de Montcalm, the French supreme commander, declared of the Indians, "in the midst of the woods of America one can no more do without them than without cavalry in open country."[37] On the British side, General John Forbes was equally convinced, confessing in 1758 that "in this country, wee must comply and learn the Art of Warr, from Ennemy Indians or anyone else who have seen the country and Warr carried on in itt."[38]

The supporting figures of the *Townshend Monument*, erected when memories of Indian atrocities at Monongahela and Fort William Henry were less than six years old, would have carried a heavy resonance for any British spectator. The fleur-de-lis on the powder horn made explicit what most viewers would already have understood, that these warriors, at French bidding, could become implacable enemies of the British. Subdued in pose and subordinated to Townshend's sacrificial death, they stand as frozen figures from an all-too-recent nightmare.

Understandably, the importance of forging political alliances with Indian tribes was recognized, just as it had been in 1710 and 1730 when the Mohawk and Cherokee delegations visited London. The Treaty of Lancaster of 1744 was a crucial development in these relations. The Onondaga leader, Canasatego, assigned what had been Iroquois suzerainty in the Ohio Valley to the British. This ended the Iroquois Confederacy's antipathy to the British and gave them access to the trade routes along the Ohio River and its tributaries. Whoever controlled these was in a position to dominate the fur trade and further commercial contacts with Plains and Great Lakes tribes. Trade between Europeans and Indians, with the Ohio tribes conducting transactions on the "middle ground," relied on a highly complex system of negotiation and alliance.[39] The Treaty of Lancaster attempted to introduce Britain as the dominating presence, but the diplomacy on which it rested widened the potential for conflict. Canasatego had been the Onondaga spokesman in previous negotiations, and as Iroquois group decisions were usually made at the Onondaga council fire, he was allowed to sign the treaty as paramount chief of all the Iroquois tribes and the Iroquois tutelary groups, specifically the refugee Ohio Indians.[40] These same peoples, the Delawares, Shawnees, and Mingos, as well as the Great Lakes Indians, by virtue of this arrangement, were now drawn inexorably into the struggle for control of the Ohio Valley region. After midcentury, it was these more western tribes, as well as the Southern Cherokees, who threatened to destabilize British settlement and trade, first with the Cherokee uprising of 1760–61 and then with Pontiac's Rebellion of 1763.[41]

The diplomatic relationship with certain factions of the Cherokees, resulting from the earlier visit in 1730, would play an important role in later conflicts between the British and Cherokees in the early 1760s. As might be argued for the delegation strategy as a whole, those representatives of tribal groups who had been to London naturally had a better idea of Britain's strength and numbers of people than those who had not been to the capital. In the case of one figure, Attakullakulla, the Cherokee leader present in the 1730 delegation, his experiences led him to seek peace with the British later in the century in the face of great opposition from his own confederates.[42] Conflict between the Cherokee peoples and the British colonialists had largely been avoided during the Seven Years' War, but American Indian resentment, stemming from harsh treatment meted out to certain Cherokee warriors and General Jeffrey Amherst's stringent policies on gift giving, gave cause for active aggression on the part of the Cherokees. After a two-year period of hostility in 1760 and 1761 between the British and the Cherokee settlements, during which time General James Grant had conducted a scorched earth policy on the middle towns of the Cherokees, the Cherokee upper villages sued for peace. Attakullakulla, or Little Carpenter, was among those sent to meet with General Grant at Fort Prince George in August 1761.[43] In November of the same year, a treaty was signed with some of the Cherokee upper towns on the Tennessee and Tellico rivers.[44] In order to secure this treaty, Lieutenant Henry Timberlake met certain leaders of these towns and agreed to take some men over to England to meet the colonial administration.[45] Three of the younger "warriors" had wished to see the king, according to colonial records, and they left their home in April 1762 to do so. A letter written by Virginia's governor, Francis Farquier, stated that the "Chief Warrior" traveling to London was called "Skiagusta Oconesta" and that the "chief wished to see the English king so he might judge whether the Little Carpenter told them lies concerning his visit abroad."[46] The three men making up the 1762 Cherokee delegation to London are known only by the titles of the positions they held within the tribe. The so-called chief warrior was known as Ostenaco (also Austenaco, Ustenacah, Judd's Friend, Judge Friend, and Man Killer) or, most commonly, as Outacity (also Ottassite and Otacite). The other men carried the titles Pouting Pigeon and Stalking Turkey.[47]

It seems obvious that propaganda was used to heighten interest in their visit, as a report sent to London while they were en route stated that the "Indian (Outacity) was a powerful monarch capable of raising ten thousand warriors."[48] Whether this was accurate or not, the fact remains that the British were interested in restoring peaceful trading relationships in an area of the colonies thought to be relatively amenable to the British and Anglo-Americans. As their newly earned allies, the Cherokees needed to be secured by the British as a powerful force in the field. There were, therefore, very good reasons to treat the visitors with some seriousness.

The constant use of European terminology, such as "monarch" or "king," to describe Outacity added to the impact made by the Cherokees. On top of this, we find here a repetition of the earlier construct of Indian "king" as was found in the Mohawk and Cherokee visits of 1710 and 1730. Timberlake and his British sponsors were probably well aware of the impression made by the earlier visits and took pains to make sure that this delegation of 1762 would receive the same treatment. As in 1730, the Cherokees of this delegation were given satirical treatment by contemporary journalists, with one of their supposed "letters" translated by the same "interpreter to the chiefs 'that were over here about thirty years ago.'"[49] The letter written by the "Great Warrior," Tohanohawighton (or Pouting Pigeon), to Yasoma, who apparently was acting commander of the Cherokees in the former's absence, was published in the *St. James Chronicle; or the British Evening-Post* in July. Tohanohawighton says that he wishes to stay in England "as the English are, beyond Dispute, a brave people, though undoubtedly inferior to the Cherokee Nation, and tinctured with many Follies which we are entirely free from." The usual comparisons are made in this letter between overrefinement on the part of the English and simplicity of manners and customs on the part of American Indians. A final comment that wine is much better for drinking than rum, "but, like our Brethren the English, [we would] be almost ready to sell even [our] own land for it," suggests that British readers were aware of the injurious effects of alcohol in colonial trading arrangements.[50]

Timberlake and the other colonialists emulated the earlier embassies when preparing the Cherokee men for their meetings with royalty and government ministers. The Cherokees were given courtly dress, as is shown in contemporary descriptions and in their portrait images. One account from Salisbury, as the Cherokee men and their contingent made their way to London, reports that they appeared in "shirts, trousers and mantles; their faces were painted copper colour and their heads adorned with shells, feathers, and earrings."[51] Thus, both in terms of their apparently Europeanized dress and in terms of the regal concepts applied to them, the Cherokees presented an image of American Indians that was relatively easily assimilated to an existing model, that of the representative of empire seen as early as 1710. The portraits of Tee Yee Neen Ho Ga Row and his colleagues by Verelst (figs. 2.1, 2.2) showed how the supposed gentlemanly and noble status of the Indian "Emperor" might be constructed using portrait conventions. This nobility is entailed in their stately poses and the relationship of figure to landscape, indicating "ownership" in European terms. In 1762, however, portrait painting in Britain worked within a more extensive field of operations and a sophisticated development of portrait conventions gave artists greater freedom to evoke character. The portrayal of the Cherokee delegation provides a vivid example of how Indian identity was accommodated to these new circumstances. In a sense, the opposition between European shirts, trousers, and mantles and Indian shells, feathers, and earrings is played out not only at the level of differing dress codes but in the texture of representation itself.

Francis Parsons's portrait *Cunneshote* (plate 2), also known in a mezzotint by James MacArdell, depicts one of the "chiefs" who accompanied Outacity.[52] Cunneshote is shown in a half-length pose, clutching his deadly knife with a forceful gesture. About his person are several items of accoutrement: a silver and gold peace medal at his throat, strings of small black beads and a brooch (both possibly American Indian in origin) around his neck, and a large plate gorget with the initials "G.R.III" around his neck. This gorget may have been a very recent present, given during the treaty negotiations of the preceding year. The most recent contribution to Cunneshote's appearance was British made. As noted above, the Cherokee delegation was dressed in a manner that suited European standards. The deep red cape, or coat, draped over Cunneshote's left shoulder had been provided by Timberlake, the Cherokees' go-between, who ordered scarlet garments in the English fashion to be made for them. The white shirt trimmed with lace was also manufactured in England.

Cunneshote's presence, however, offers another frame of reference. His plucked scalp, tinted skin, hair decoration, and stretched and lacerated earlobe signal his distance from the civility of Timberlake's outfitters. Indeed, one might want to read Parson's portrait as encoding a cultural clash, as the uniform red cape gives way to a medley of cultural markers on Cunneshote's chest over which he presides in all his Indian otherness. This movement between European and Indian cultural registers seems to be echoed by the placement of the exotic tropical tree on the "Indian" side of the portrait, with a more European-looking tree close to the red cape on the "English" side of the portrait.

Little is known about the circumstances of this picture's production, such as the original commission or its motive. However, when Cunneshote sat for Parsons in Queen's Square, it was clearly a popular attraction for Londoners, as a contemporary report attests: "a throng of ladies coming out of Mr. Parsons' Room from seeing the pictures of the Cherokee Chief, one of them had the misfortune to fall down the Stairs and dislocate her knee; two surgeons were sent for, and she was carried home in a Chair."[53] The "throng of ladies" hints at a gendered fascination for Cunneshote, and the sexuality of this encounter is echoed elsewhere. During their visit of 1762, it was reported that the Cherokee men caused a stir among the British ladies, who were said to be enthralled by the men's appearances.[54] Henry Howard wrote a short song entitled "A New Humorous Song, on the Cherokee Chiefs. Inscribed to the Ladies of Great Britain." Published as an undated broadsheet, it carried engraved, full-length portraits of the three men (fig. 2.6).

I.

What a Piece of Work's here, and a d——d Botheration!
Of Three famous Chiefs from the *Cherokee* Nation;
Who the Duce wou'd ha'thought, that a People polite, Sir,
Wou'd ha'stir'd out o'Doors to ha'seen Such a Sight, Sir?
Are M——rs so rare in the *British* Dominions,
That we thus shou'd run crazy for *Canada Indians*.

II.

How eager the Folks at *Vauxhall*, or elsewhere, Sir,
With high Expectation and Rapture repair, Sir;
Tho' not one of them all can produce the least Reason,
Save that M——rs of all Sorts are always in Season.
If so, let the Chiefs here awhile have their Station,
And send for the whole of the *Cherokee* Nation.

III.

The Ladies, dear Creatures, so squeamish and dainty,
Surround the great *Canada* Warriors in plenty;

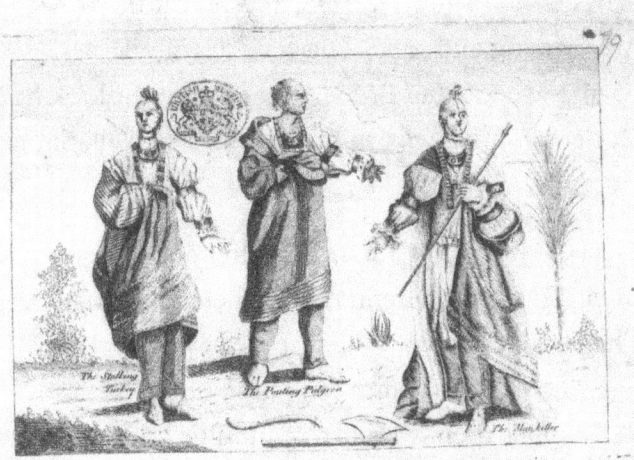

A NEW HUMOROUS SONG,

ON THE

CHEROKEE CHIEFS.

Inscribed to the LADIES of GREAT BRITAIN.

By H. HOWARD.

To the Tune of, *Cæsar and Pompey were both of them Horned.*

I.

WHAT a Piece of Work's here, and a d—d Botheration!
Of Three famous Chiefs from the *Cherokee* Nation;
Who the Duce wou'd ha' thought, that a People polite, Sir,
Wou'd ha' stir'd out o' Doors to ha' seen such a Sight, Sir?
Are M——rs so rare in the *British* Dominions,
That we thus shou'd run crazy for *Canada Indians.*
     Are M——rs so rare, &c.

II.

How eager the Folks at *Vauxhall,* or elsewhere, Sir,
With high Expectation and Rapture repair, Sir;
Tho' not one of them all can produce the least Reason,
Save that M——rs of all Sorts are always in Season.
If so, let the Chiefs here awhile have their Station,
And send for the whole of the *Cherokee* Nation.
     If so, let the Chiefs, &c.

III.

The Ladies, dear Creatures, so squeamish and dainty,
Surround the great *Canada* Warriors in plenty;
Wives, Widows and *Matrons,* and pert little *Misses,*
Are pressing and squeezing for *Cherokee* Kisses.
Each grave looking Prude, and each smart looking Belle, Sir,
Declaring, no *Englishman* e'er kiss'd so well, Sir.
     Each grave looking Prude, &c.

IV.

That *Cherokee* Lips are much softer and sweeter,
Their Touch more refin'd, and their Kisses repleter;
The fair ones agree—nay, I mean not to flatter,
For who like the Ladies can judge of the Matter?
Ye Nymphs then, who like 'm, indulge your soft Passion,
Be sw——d by the Chiefs of the *Cherokee* Nation.
     Ye Nymphs then, &c.

V.

Ye Females of *Britain,* so wanton and witty,
Who love even Monkies, and swear they are pretty;
The *Cherokee Indians,* and stranger *Shimponzees,*
By Turns, pretty Creatures, have tickl'd your Fancies;
Which proves, that the Ladies so fond are of Billing,
They'd kiss even M——rs, were M——rs as willing.
     Which proves, that, &c.

VI.

No more then these Chiefs, with their Scalping Knives dread, Sir,
Shall strip down the Skin from the *Englishman's* Head, Sir;
Let the Case be revers'd, and the Ladies prevail, Sir,
And instead of the Head, skin the *Cherokee* T—l, Sir.
Ye bold Female *Scalpers,* courageous and hearty,
Collect all your Force for a *grand Scalping Party.*
     Ye bold Female Scalpers, &c.

VII.

For Weapons, ye Fair, you've no need to petition,
No Weapons you'll want for this odd Expedition;
A soft Female Hand, the best Weapon I wean is,
To strip down the Bark of a *Cherokee* P—s.
Courageous advance then, each fair *English* Tartar.
Scalp the *Chiefs* of the *Scalpers,* and give them no Quarter.
     Courageous advance then, &c.

AUTHOR, opposite the Union Coffee-House, in the Strand, near Temple-Bar, and by all the Print and Pamphlet-sellers.
[PRICE SIX-PENCE.]
N. In a few Days will be published the *Political Bagpipe.* A new Song, with a Head-piece.

Fig. 2.6. Henry Howard, "A New Humorous Song, On the Cherokee Chiefs, inscribed to the Ladies of Great Britain," broadsheet with engraved portraits, undated, manuscript no. 1850c.10(79), the British Library, London. By permission of the British Library.

Wives, *Widows* and *Matrons*, and pert little *Misses*,
Are pressing and squeezing for *Cherokee* Kisses,
Each grave looking Prude, and each smart looking Belle, Sir,
Declaring, no *Englishman* e'er kiss'd so well, Sir.

IV.

That *Cherokee* Lips are much softer and sweeter,
Their Touch more refin'd, and their Kisses repleter,
The fair ones agree——nay, I mean not to flatter,
For who like the Ladies can judge of the Matter?
Ye Nymphs then, who like'm indulge your odd Passion,
Be sw——d by the Chiefs of the *Cherokee* Nation.

V.

Ye Females of *Britain*, so wanton and witty,
Who love even Monkies, and swear they are pretty;
The *Cherokee Indians*, and stranger *Shimpanzeys*,
By turns, pretty Creatures, have tickl'd your Fancies;
Which proves, that the Ladies so fond are of Billing,
They'd kiss even M——rs, were M——rs as willing.

VI.

No more than these Chiefs, with their scalping Knives dread, Sir,
Shall strip down the skin from the *Englishman's* Head, Sir;
Let the case be revers'd, and the Ladies prevail, Sir;
And instead of the Head, skin the *Cherokee* T—l, Sir.
Ye bold Female *Scalpers*, courageous and hearty,
Collect all your Force for a *grand Scalping party*.

VII.

For Weapons, ye Fair, you've no need to petition,
No Weapons you'll want for this odd Expedition;
A soft Female Hand, the best Weapon I wean is,
To strip down the Bark of a *Cherokee* P——s.

Courageous advance then, each fair *English* Tartar,
Scalp the *Chiefs* of the *Scalpers*, and give them no Quarter.[55]

Howard's song cost sixpence and was perhaps the most widespread image to result from the Cherokee visit of 1762. His salacious verses, satirizing the erotic appeal of the Cherokee delegation, reveals nevertheless the extent to which worries about the brutality of Indian warfare still resonated in the English imagination. Parsons's portrait of Cunneshote, similarly, makes the scalping knife a prominent part of the Cherokee's presentation.

In contrast, the image of Outacity as portrayed by Joshua Reynolds (plate 3) seems to have qualified the identification of American Indians with violence or aggression by revealing a different, more sedate image of leadership. Reynolds shows the warrior "Scyacust Ukah" in a more relaxed pose, his right arm in an open gesture and his hand holding what looks like a pipe-tomahawk of the kind manufactured in Europe from the early part of the eighteenth century until the mid-nineteenth century.[56] Outacity wears a similar shirt as that worn by Cunneshote, but in this portrait it is unbuttoned in décolleté fashion, as if the sitter was caught at an informal moment, perhaps relaxing in his quarters after the day's round of diplomatic meetings and negotiations. He, too, has been given a rich-looking coat or cloak, which drapes over one shoulder, and this article seems slightly more elaborately decorated with gold trim than does Cunneshote's. Again, a peace medal and a gorget are shown prominently displayed around the neck of the sitter and thus help to underline Outacity's connection with British affairs in the colonies. In fact, both Parsons and Reynolds seem to have emphasized the effect of costuming the Cherokee figures in such a way, for the display of their "red coats" and military-style gorgets links them to contemporary portraits of military leaders. Indeed, Outacity had recently been compared to the Marquis of Granby in appearance. (Reynolds, of course, if not Parsons, had painted such portraits during the 1750s and 1760s.) The depiction of the Cherokees is thus contextualized within a perception of them as commanders of irregular troops. Although the viewer might see a picture of a strange, even forbidding character, he or she would also be aware that this was an ally, capable of directing his men in military fashion.

Reynolds's portrait differs from Parsons's vision in the choice of a more informal moment and the emphasis on the peaceful, diplomatic, and gentle sides of the character of American Indians. The breadth of handling in the Outacity portrait, while necessarily a part of Reynolds's developing style, has in any case given to his sitter's features a softer, more approachable look and thus diminished the inherent message of violence attached to Outacity's tomahawk and to his name, Man Killer. It is fortunate that both portraits have come down to us, for what Parsons and Reynolds reveal between them are two possible interpretations of the same delegation. Parsons, perhaps through choice, perhaps through his more wooden technique, confronts the viewer with an image of power and aggression sufficiently vivid to occasion contemporary comment. Reynolds, on the other hand, opts for a more seigniorial pose, where power and rank are subtly betokened in an aloof but steady gaze and a certain studied negligence of dress. Both Cherokee men who sat for their portraits showed an awareness of the means by which an image could be deployed as a sign or representation. Before leaving his own country at the start of the delegation, Outacity had stated that he wished to see the king in person, having only been shown the portrait head of him. Cunneshote had been so pleased with his own portrait image, which was later made into an engraving, that he wanted to give the image to his family in order to remember him by when he had gone to war.[57] Outacity and Cunneshote, for their parts, appreciated the power of an image to stand for an actual individual and to represent them when absent.[58]

Several prints depicting the Cherokee chiefs were published at this time, and one of these, a group portrait, shows Outacity brandishing his tomahawk in one hand while holding a belt of wampum in the other (fig. 2.7).[59] Outacity's pose with the wampum belt is very reminiscent, however, of Verelst's portrait of Tee Yee Neen Ho Ga Row (fig. 2.1), even down to the wolf at the "Emperor's" feet. Verelst's picture shows the "Emperor of the Six Nations," an Iroquois representative, not a Cherokee, and this tendency to borrow visual elements from previously devised prints reveals how graphic imagery tended to influence the production of later images in a rather indiscriminate manner. It mirrors the recycling of the satirical mode of representing American Indians whereby words are placed in the mouths of essentially generic Indians.[60]

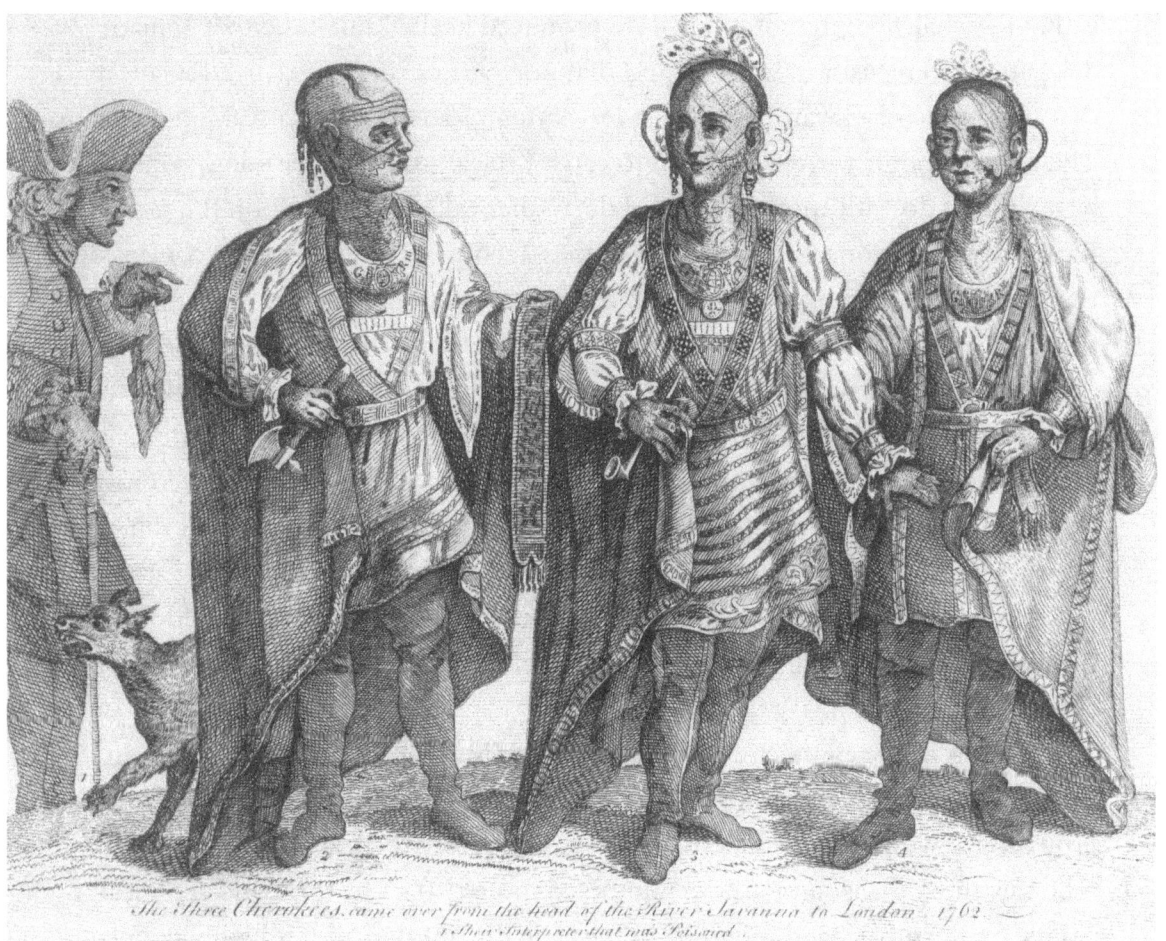

Fig. 2.7. Anon., *The Three Cherokees came over from the head of the river Savanna to London, 1762*, engraving, 1762, Colonial Williamsburg Foundation, Virginia. Courtesy of The Colonial Williamsburg Foundation.

Nowhere can this be seen more clearly than in the Indian figures included in prints concerning American political affairs in the 1760s and 1770s. In functional terms, the Indians depicted here share the same generic iconography seen in allegory, with a limited repertoire of attributes signifying Indian and thus America: a crown of feathers, a bow and quiver, and a naked torso and swarthy skin.[61] As with allegory, for the symbolic connection to hold it was essential that the image be divested of extraneous detail. Quick execution and minimal expense exaggerated the tendency to schematize typical of symbolic representation. The irony, of course, is that these clichéd presentations were produced at the same time that Indian delegations were visiting London and that portraits of them were in circulation that, for all their awkwardness, did at least attempt a likeness of a real individual. The political print, with its concern to catch topical issues on the wing, could have little to do with those niceties of detail that called into question the generic Indian of the allegorical tradition. If the message was to be successfully conveyed, the reader/viewer must read through the representational devices without distraction. A departure from the standard allegorical image is thus not to be expected. Yet granted the necessity for graphic satire to operate with clichés, its presentation of American Indians could not but diminish the reality of tribal involvement in military events and diplomatic maneuvers. Instead of differentiated communities, one individual is offered; instead of male warriors or diplomats, one half-nude woman; instead of contemporary involvement in war and negotiation, timeless symbolism. American Indians, in short, are removed from history and current affairs and restored to the signifying function of the old allegorical tradition.

In terms of the eighteenth century's construction of an image of the Indian, this is a notable development. Despite the crush at Parsons's rooms or the large crowds who witnessed the Cherokee delegation at Vauxhall and Ranelagh, those who saw the Indians cannot have numbered more that a few thousand. Political prints, on the other hand, often had very wide distribution and, if highly popular, massive print runs. An extremely popular work such as *The Repeal, Or, the Funeral of Miss Americ- Stamp*, published on March 18, 1766, sold 2,000 copies in four days and stimulated the production of four pirated editions, two of which amounted to a total of 16,000 prints.[62] Such widespread distribution of visual imagery meant that its iconography and stark symbolic configurations would become the visual currency of most of the public, either through purchase or by seeing engravings displayed in print sellers' windows.[63]

The first appearance of a figure of America in political prints of the last half of the eighteenth century begins with the Stamp Act (1765) and its consequences. This notorious act of Parliament was created in order to raise funds to help with the defense of the American colonies. It drew censure in the colonies and led to

60

the first intercolonial congress, which called the act unconstitutional. After wide-spread refusal to pay the tax and an American blockade of British merchant shipping to the colonies, William Pitt and his ministers repealed the act the following year. As with the Derby porcelain figure group celebrating Pitt, discussed below (see fig. 2.11), so here the feather-garbed Indian princess of allegory stands for the colonies and their grievances. In contrast to its usual passive placement as one of the four parts of the world, the figure becomes a protagonist in the theater of allegory, acting on and reacting to the other symbolic characters depicted. Thus, whereas the older allegorical figure of America was always compliant with European notions of order, knowledge, and control, the figure of America in political prints is capable of taking on a subversive role. Although the Indian princess works within a symbolic space and is thus removed from the actuality of tribal contributions to commerce, war, and diplomacy, her presence does offer an attenuated notion of America as a site of conflict.[64]

In a print of 1765 entitled "The Great Financier" (fig. 2.8), the figure symbolizing America appears kneeling with one arm raised in protest and a yoke used in the slave trade placed around her neck. The yoke is labeled "taxation without representation," and the accompanying verse reads:

America groans and petitions in vain,
Her Grief is his Toy and her Loss is his Gain;
For ways and means curious his Brain he ne'er racks,
He stops all her wealth and then lays on his Tax.

The figure of America is pleading with the ministers, who seem to be deciding her fate with a large set of scales that are set at an extreme imbalance. America's facial features are undefined here and quickly drawn. Appearing as an indeterminate shadowy type, she is given only the minimum of detail to provide referents for the character she is portraying. The basic symbolic content of the allegorical figure has changed from the cosmologically to the economically significant. She is no longer the sovereign of an entire continent (in spite of her "crown" of feathers) but has become the figurehead for a commercial and economic entity.

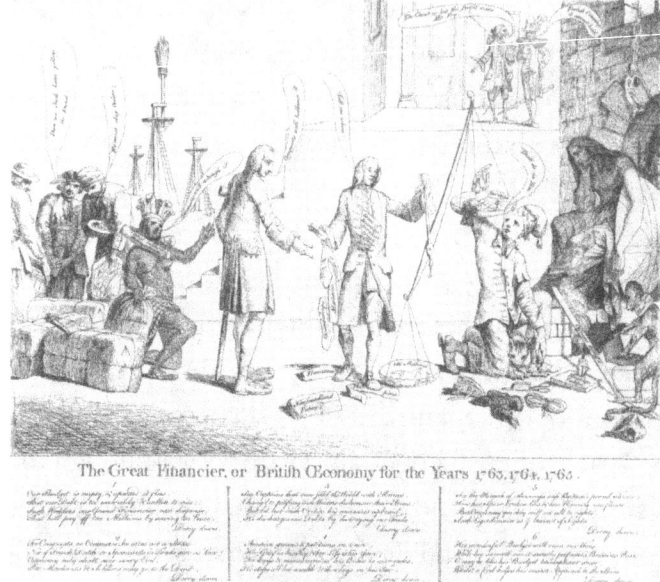

The Great Financier, or British Œconomy for the Years 1763,1764,1765.

Fig. 2.8. Anon., "The Great Financier," engraving, 1765, The British Museum, London. Photo © Copyright The British Museum.

The changes of allegory's meaning within the genre of the political print meant that the figure of America could be exploited graphically for purposes outside her original representation as a spirit of the continent. Her actual purpose within prints such as "The Great Financier" is to call to mind the more elaborate decorative depictions of the continent that had displayed America in her finery and surrounded her with items of wealth and fecundity. America in this particular print kneels next to large parcels of material wealth that are given monetary value by the label "dollars," which she grasps in her right hand. Wealth of a majestic kind was present in versions of the four continents, such as that of the ceiling decorations in the dining hall at the Greenwich Naval College, painted by James Thornhill (plate 1). When the graphic artist wished to make a similar point about the colonies' wealth, however, the bounty has been realized and reduced to hard cash.

A similar alteration occurs with respect to the perception of America herself. In place of the regal figure of allegory, the America of the political print is more vulnerable. Her ethnicity and gender now suggest an innocent victim rather than a powerful queen. In its allusion to the practice of slavery, the yoke placed around the neck of America locates her within a wider area of restrictions. She is bound economically, but the use of a slave's yoke to indicate this is surely derived from general knowledge of the treatment of subject races. In this sense, America's situation becomes overdramatized, as her plea for freedom of commerce is equated with the slave's plea for personal freedom.

In a further response to the Stamp Act, America, again given the features of an Indian princess, holds center stage in a drama being enacted for the viewer. "The Deplorable State of America or SC—H Government" (fig. 2.9) of January 2, 1765, shows seven allegorical characters arranged about the tree of Liberty. Seated on the right, Britannia hands America the "Pandora's Box" of the Stamp Act. George III looks on, summoning the emblem of Lord Bute and proposing, "Take this and let thy banefull influence be poured down on upon them." Mercury flees the scene, "with reluctance." To the left of America a reclining Liberty declares, "It is all over with me"; a philosopher hopes that heaven will allow the tree of Liberty to stand; while Minerva, symbolizing wisdom, advises the figure of America not to accept Britannia's gift. In the center, the figure of America appeals to Minerva, "Secure me, O Goddess, by thy Wisdom, for I abhor it as death." Echoing the well-known composition *The Choice of Hercules,* America in this print must choose not between virtue and vice but between independence and financial distress or dependency and wealth.[65] As the central character in this print, the American figure's association with American Indians and their perceived lifestyle as free and independent agents would not have gone unnoticed by its viewers.[66] America is cleverly devised in that she is an object of sympathy, surrounded and defenseless. Her American Indian attributes only enhance this feeling.[67] The figure of America no longer reacts to the Stamp Act alone but to a general restriction of freedom, a situation abhorrent to her perceived nature.

We can see a similar politicization of allegory in the production of porcelain figurines. Allegorical sets of the four continents were produced by many porcelain manufacturers after midcentury. Sometimes the figure of America in these sets of figurines appeared as a cherub or putto dressed in feather garments and sporting a bow and arrows, as seen in sets produced at the Duesbury, Derby, and Chelsea potteries in the 1750s.[68] At other times, the figure appeared in the more classicizing vein as a partial and draped nude woman wearing her "crown" of feathers and

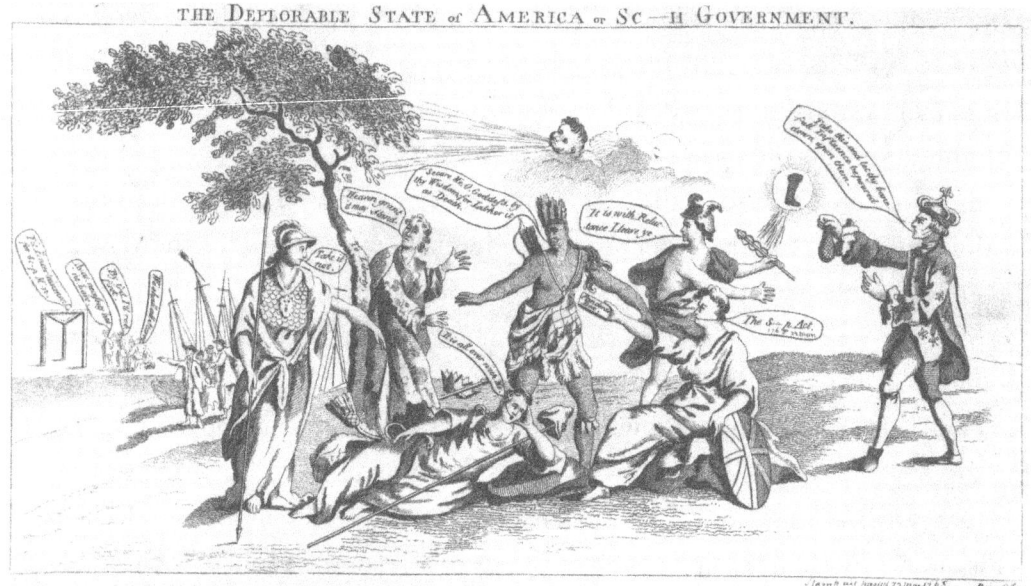

Fig. 2.9. Anon., "The Deplorable State of America or SC—H Government," engraving, 1765, The British Museum, London. Photo © Copyright The British Museum.

seated or standing next to the animal that had become associated with the continent of America, the alligator or caiman. The figure of America appears in this latter mode in a set of porcelain manufactured by the Plymouth Pottery between about 1768 and 1770, when the design was probably sold to Bristol.[69] This set of figures was produced under technically difficult conditions, as they are large in scale and worked in the hard-paste material, the first of its kind produced in England. America, as a personage, differs from the other continents only in the variations of her attributes in this set of figurines. More noticeable is her skin color, which is indistinguishable from the figures of Asia and Europe as opposed to the figure of Africa, whose skin is completely blackened (fig. 2.10). The prominence usually given to her native animal attribute has also been played down, as she stands next to a broken tree stump at the base of which cowers a small furry animal, perhaps a fox. Thus, while there were strata in society that paid attention to the Indian delegations arriving in London, others perhaps far from the capital would have formed some of their perceptions of American Indians around these older and allegorical renditions.

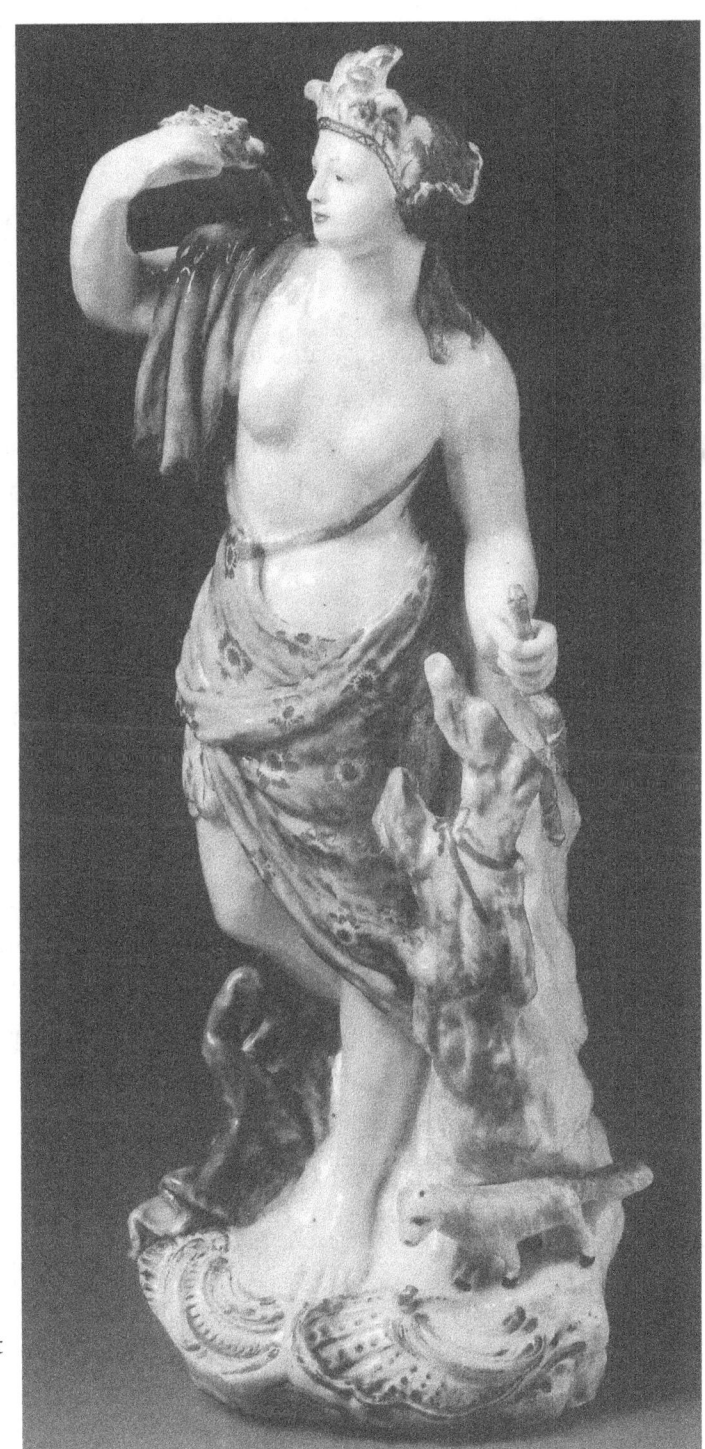

Fig. 2.10. Plymouth Pottery,
figurine *America* of *The
Four Continents*, porcelain,
1768–70, Victoria and Albert
Museum, London. Photo ©
Copyright V&A Images,
London.

In keeping with this tendency to view American Indians within both an allegorizing and politicizing context, the image of William Pitt, supported by the small figure of a putto, America, signals the combined and complex nature of the presentation of American Indians in this period (fig. 2.11). Called "America's Champion," this porcelain ceramic group is probably from the Derby factory and has been dated to around 1766, the time of Pitt's elevation to Earl of Chatham.[70] The arrangement shows Pitt "protecting" an allegorical America, who kneels next to him and is accompanied by an alligator. This American Indian figure amalgamates the two modes mentioned above in having both the child attributes, tiny and cherublike, and those of the adult figure, womanly breasts and draped, classical garments. The use of a childlike figure certainly underlines the dependant relationship, which was pertaining at the time in America, particularly after the Seven Years' War and the defeat of the American Indians in several battles of the 1760s. However, Pitt had recently commended the American colonists for refusing to submit to the taxation levied by the Stamp Act of 1765. The American figure thus stands for colonial interests rather than Indian peoples. The Indian, in other words, is merely a geographical sign rather than a representative of a non-European culture.

Throughout the era of the Stamp Act, the overall trend in the depiction of the figure of America was to portray her as the Indian princess of the traditional allegory. This tradition allows the perception of the continent in terms of an exoticism, insofar as the highly symbolic language of allegory admits the perception of differing cultures at all. But admission of the existence of a group of people who inhabit such lands and who are separate from oneself was not a comfortable awareness for those who sought American Indians' dispossession. As the century continued, the figure of America underwent a gradual metamorphosis, which began to deny the realization of her original ethnicity, and the "ethnic princess" figure was replaced by new symbols for the continent.[71] The revolutionary period was a critical time for the representation of the figure of America. A gradual change took place in the arena of political satire, where America, the personage, assumed a variety of roles inspired by human relationships. The age-old conflicts between parents and their offspring were adopted to explain and comment on the state of things

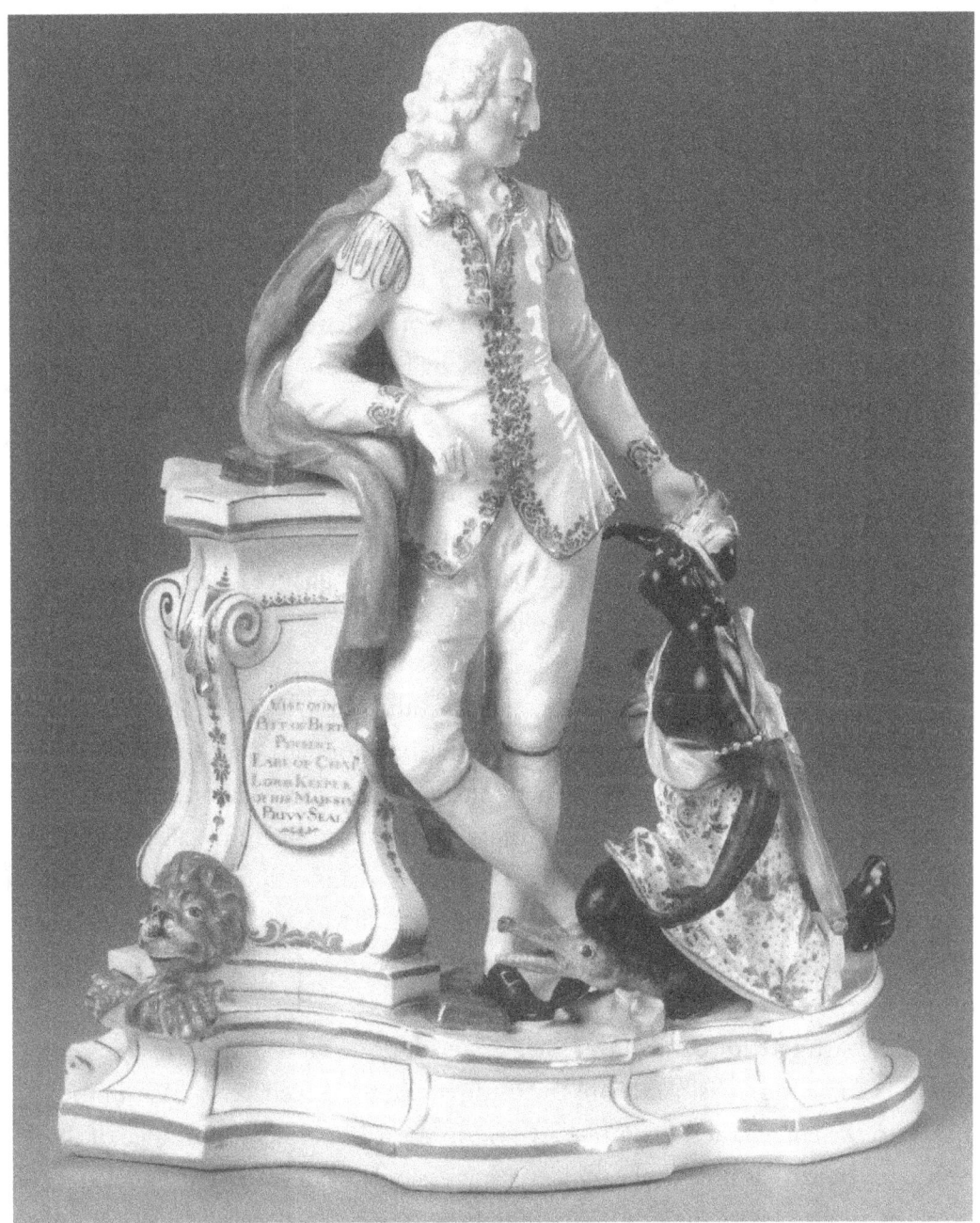

Fig. 2.11. Derby Factory, *America's Champion*, porcelain, 1766, Victoria and Albert Museum, London. Photo © Copyright V&A Images, London.

during and after the war.[72] America's ethnic features that were still retained were advantageously used to great effect in order to show the appropriate visage of an angry young rebel or unsophisticated child. Both of these roles could be filled by American Indians, in that written descriptions of their cultures were often composed in just these terms.[73] Increasingly, however, many elements of the traditional American Indian figure were discarded, such as the darkened skin and feathered accoutrement, in favor of new enthusiasms for the classical figure of Liberty. The United States, in its symbolic representation, would henceforward be imaged by the representation of an ideal, based on ancient European culture. The suggestion in the older allegorical tradition of a culture beyond European understanding was no longer pertinent. This transition from one symbol to another is thus itself symbolic. While the competing parties used Indian alliances to advance their war aims, so the Indian figure remained active in the political prints of the time. With the United States triumphant and the need for Indian alliances over, so the Indian figure is discarded from the realm of allegory.

What I have hoped to show in this chapter is the existence of a tension between two perceptions of America and its peoples. On the one hand, colonial strategy required diplomatic and military alliances with the tribes adjacent to British settlements and influential in trade. Here there was every reason to deal with the Indians as military, economic, and political partners. In contrast, with the exception of the portrayal of Indian delegations, the treatment of Indians in literary and visual culture relied on their abstraction from contemporary history and even their submergence in a transcendent allegory from which all specific cultural markers had been effaced.

As the struggle for control of North America grew more bitter, this tension would become more visible. From the outbreak of the Seven Years' War in the 1750s to the end of the Revolutionary War in the 1780s, the importance of American Indians as historical agents was increasingly evident. These circumstances brought about a more nuanced representation, especially in the early 1770s. Likewise, Britain's defeat in the Revolutionary War occasioned a return to a more complacent view of Indian peoples. It seems fair to say, then, that the representation of American Indians is not stable during the eighteenth century and that the entry of Indians into visual consciousness owes much to the pressure of political events. To escape their signification as "exotic," a people need to act, to be seen as protagonists on the world stage, to be taken seriously.

3   *History Painting and American Indians*

Benjamin West and Others, 1760–1804

THE ORIGIN OF Robert Adam's *Townshend Monument* design in the competition for a James Wolfe memorial reminds us that the artistic response to the death of Wolfe produced the most memorable engagements with American subject matter in British eighteenth-century art. As is well known, the commemoration of Wolfe's patriotic sacrifice also extended to painting, in particular in the works of Benjamin West and James Barry, who depicted the dying general on the heights of Abraham, near Quebec, at the very moment when news of his spectacular victory reached him. Although several painters attempted the scene, it is only in West's and Barry's paintings that an American Indian figure is included to suggest the use of Indian fighters during the battles for control of North America.

Benjamin West's *The Death of General Wolfe*, painted in 1770 and shown at the Royal Academy in 1771, is the most significant of all his major works (plate 4). The painting was very successful. It was engraved by William Woolett in 1776, and his print after West's painting became so commercially viable that some have described it as the most successful ever printed.[1] West himself painted four copies, obviously wishing to capitalize on its popular success. When first exhibited, the painting caused something of a sensation and, famously, helped to reinvigorate the practice of history painting in England during the latter part of the eighteenth century by demonstrating the possibility of depicting contemporary events without recourse to classical motifs. West asserted that his approach was accurate, for "that same truth that guides the pen of the historian should govern the pencil of the artist" and that, perhaps even more important, North American warfare took place "in a region of the world unknown to the Greeks and Romans, and at a period of time when no such nations, nor heroes in their costume, any longer existed."[2]

To take West at his word, one might presume that historical accuracy was the sine qua non of the image. Yet a moment's reflection would dispel this assumption. Although Greek and Roman costume have been excluded, the refinement of pose in the figures and the nobility of behavior expressed by West's protagonists are evidently modeled on classical prototypes. Similarly, as Charles Mitchell has demonstrated, the figure group surrounding Wolfe is reminiscent of a seventeenth-century deposition of Christ from the cross.[3] Historical accuracy thus finds accord with the history of art. West's "mitigated realism," to use Edgar Wind's phrase, might still be reconciled with his pronouncements on truth, however, for the truth that guides the pen of the historian is, in the age of Hume and Gibbon, more than merely documentary report.[4] Historical events, properly understood, provoke reflections in the mind of the historian that move away from accuracy of detail to wider considerations of statecraft, morality, and the course of empire. It is precisely because the historical evidence is accurate that these reflections can be established on a firm base, but the base alone is chronicle, not history. West's truth, then, insofar as the artist's pencil is equivalent to the historian's pen, will be both particular and general, using properly observed detail to stimulate the mature reflections that historiography requires. It should thus occasion no surprise that the identity of some of the officers is still problematic, some of them not being present at the battle at all but associated instead with the overall campaign or with the region. In like manner, the American Indian figure cannot be justified on documentary grounds, for the British assault made no use of Indian irregular forces at Quebec. West's enigmatic warrior is here as a token of something else.

West's inclusion of an American Indian figure in this picture is widely considered to be one of its most striking features, and the function of his Indian "brave" has been the subject of much analysis. The Indian warrior dominates the left foreground, midway below a group of five officers who make up a third of the composition. He is seated on the ground, his legs bent toward the right, in an informal pose that is qualified by his contemplative attitude as he rests his chin on the loosely clenched fingers of his right hand. The diagonal of his back and legs, moving from left to right, is thus checked by the vertical of his head and arm, echoing in his own pose the contrast between the left-hand figures of the group, rushing in from the side, with their upright companions, recoiling from the sight of Wolfe's imminent death.

There is more to this Indian figure than a compositional device, however. Because he is turning toward the scene of the death of the general, we see displayed on his back and right shoulder the tattooed markings of two snakes and a bear's claw, respectively.[5] There are other tattoos whose geometric and linear patterns are less easy to interpret on both his forearms and his legs. His scalp is plucked and painted red; he has feathers and other ornaments in his hair; and his weapons, dress, and accoutrement are all insistently American Indian. West seems to have intended a deliberate comparison between the stock of the Indian's musket, customized with ornamental markings, and its unadorned equivalent lying at Wolfe's feet. At once, West's Indian warrior can be seen as a device that is part and parcel of the artist's desire for accuracy. Once such a figure is included, it becomes impossible for any of the other figures to be clothed in classicizing dress. Indeed, one might claim that the Indian figure, above all, is a guarantor of the realism West wished to promote. The care taken to detail these features is quite emphatic and is made even more so by the figure's presentation to the viewer. By separating the warrior from the others, he alone, even more than Wolfe, exists self-sufficiently, emotionally detached and disentangled from other bodies and other gestures, as though inviting our most minute examination. His body becomes a screen onto which is projected West's declaration of truth.

This register of ethnographic accuracy coincides, however, with an older reading of this figure as a symbol of the New World. In Robert Anthony Bromley's *A*

Philosophical and Critical History of the Fine Arts (1793), West's Indian in *The Death of General Wolfe* occasions the following comment.

> No sooner does the eye fix on the collateral circumstances, but we know that the scene of action was foreign from Britain, . . . and that this scene must be North America for the savage warrior shews us that the country was his. In allegory, can any thing speak more correctly than these? . . . And is not the savage-warrior every way as just as the crocodile on the Nile? Without him no imagination would have found it easy to acquaint us by any other symbol what was the country, at least no symbol that could speak with so much precision, and so much in tone with the subject, as that which has been chosen.[6]

This reading of the painting demonstrates that contemporary audiences in the late eighteenth century well understood West's ambitions in *The Death of General Wolfe* to produce historical truth as a complex mixture of documentation, narrative, and allegory. The functional and symbolic status of the Indian figure is thus an appropriate vehicle for West's larger intentions concerning the representation of colonial events. The fact that he deployed his Indian figure in this painting as a bearer of metaphorical rather than literal meaning should be noted, for the representations of American Indians in most of the images with which this chapter is concerned share the same ambiguity. Even when depicted as accurately as possible in terms of appearance, their iconographical function pulls them away from historical reality toward the realm of allegory.

This is also true of James Barry's *The Death of General Wolfe* (1775; exhibited 1776), which represents an entirely different vision of the last moments of the general but also contains a figure of an American Indian warrior (plate 5). When Barry painted this event, all the figures were given contemporary costumes rather than more generalizing classicized attire, which is somewhat surprising given Barry's objections to West's version. West's choices had been controversial by the doctrines of the Royal Academy, and certain academicians had objected at the time to the use of contemporary dress in West's picture. Barry was one of these.

73

Barry's painted version of Wolfe's death is arranged, compositionally, in a much simpler form than the earlier picture by West. There are fewer figures grouped around the dying general, and they are shown in closer proximity to the viewer. Barry, in fact, wished to be even more accurate than West and to follow the reports of survivors of the Battle for Quebec, who stated that only a few were actually present at Wolfe's death.[7] Barry's attention to historical truth and firsthand reports is interesting in light of his representation of an Indian auxiliary. In Barry's picture, the American Indian figure is incidental to the composition, almost invisible in the lower portion of the painting. Barry's interviewees would surely have informed him that the presence of an Indian figure at the scene was not justified by the historical record, but it is a measure of the association of Indians with American campaigns that Barry felt impelled to include one. That said, however, this fallen warrior, drenched in shadow, face down, and presumably killed in the conflict, is presented trophylike, as a vanquished enemy rather than an ally. Barry's Indian, then, is a throwaway gesture, akin to a discarded musket or a broken sword, whose presence discreetly signifies America without compromising the idealized representation of Wolfe's death. The signs of exotic otherness that West isolates and emphasizes are here effaced. Even had Barry been able to include such details, their particularity would have violated the generalizing sentiment he wished to impart.[8]

West's use of Indian figures is singular in the context of British art.[9] It is, of course, likely that his colonial upbringing allowed him to stake a very particular claim for understanding the American situation, giving him a specialism by which to differentiate his practice from others. This professional niche-market was best secured by asserting his firsthand experience of the frontier, and that experience was most pungently signaled by knowing something of the indigenous peoples. In John Galt's biography of Benjamin West (1820), there are various references to American Indians throughout. In one extraordinary example, Galt tells of an incident in West's youth when a group of Indians (tribes unspecified) visit Springfield, Pennsylvania, and view West's early essays in black charcoal and pencil of local birds and flowers. They teach him how to prepare their traditional pigments of red and yellow ochre, and with the indigo dye given him by his mother, the artist can complete his basic palette.[10] The American Indians, the forests and landscapes of America, and thus American particularities can be mustered and contrasted with what West, via his biographer, views as European sophistication and overdevelopment. Whether it was comparing the Apollo Belvedere to a Mohawk or painting Indians with an authenticity no English artist could hope to match, West was able to present himself as supremely able to make sense of American Indian reality.

The period 1761–71 might be characterized as West's Indian decade, with at least six such subjects executed as paintings or designs for engraving. The first evidence of such concerns can be seen in a painting of about 1761, *The Indian Family*, painted in Italy (plate 6). West was commissioned to produce this painting by John Murray, the British Resident in Venice, as a contribution to a projected picture of the four parts of the world. Given Bromley's reaction to the death of General Wolfe in terms of a continental allegory, it is significant that West's earliest Indian painting also melded allegorical and documentary functions. The image was subsequently engraved by Francesco Bartolozzi to serve as the frontispiece for the Italian translation of William Burke and Edmund Burke's *Account of the European Settlements in America* (1763).[11] The picture was intended to show an Indian chief setting out for war, leaving his family behind to look after their home until his return. Following Murray's instructions, West was required to paint the figures at least eighteen inches high so that details of dress, ornament, and weapons would all be clearly distinguishable. In the Italian text accompanying the engraving, many of these details are pointed out and described.[12] Here, then, there is a specific intention to provide an authentic image by means of ethnographic detail. The viewer is expected to mine the image for the accurate information it contains. West, meanwhile, elides his knowledge of Indians with his understanding of the history of art, most obviously in the chief's pose, indebted as it is to the classical sculpture of a Roman orator, such as the figure of Tiberius in the Louvre, a source that has also been identified in British portraits painted in the 1740s and 1750s.[13]

West left Italy for England in 1763. His success in complying with Murray's instructions may have prompted him to attempt a more specific employment of the "proper dress and accoutrement" he had supplied for *The Indian Family*.

General Johnson Saving a Wounded French Officer from the Tomahawk of a North American Indian (plate 7) was probably begun shortly after his arrival in London and seems to follow logically from the preparations for war seen in *The Indian Family*. But whereas the Italian picture was generic, this new composition was intended as a record of a recent incident in the American conflict. Major General William Johnson was in charge of a mixed force of Mohawk and New England militia in the campaign of 1755. He repulsed a French attack while encamped at Lake George, defeating his adversary, Baron Ludwig von Dieskau, and later protecting him from the Mohawks who wanted revenge for their fallen kinsmen.[14] The subject represents Johnson disciplining the aggressive actions of one of his auxiliaries, elevating European standards of honorable conduct in warfare over the ferocity of uncivilized peoples.

The Seven Years' and Revolutionary wars of the mid-1750s to the mid-1770s had brought fresh instances of heroism and tragedy to the attention of the public. These wars also introduced some anxieties over the use of American Indian irregulars in the fighting of major military campaigns. Light infantry tactics had become a feature of warfare in America since the Battle of Monongahela (1755), but it was the employment of American Indian irregulars in battles on the frontier that created the greatest debates. Back in England in 1777, both Houses of Parliament debated over their use in warfare. The Earl of Chatham's speech in the House of Lords (November 20, 1777) suggests the abhorrence many felt toward extraordinary acts of violence perpetrated on "innocents" such as women and children, and Chatham was particularly forceful in showing his disgust at the practice of cannibalism on the part of the "savages."[15]

The worries occasioned by such atrocities in the American campaigns played some part in the genesis of a later picture, John Vanderlyn's *The Death of Jane MacCrea*, first exhibited in the Salon of 1804 (plate 8). The story of the genesis of Vanderlyn's picture, however, suggests that while these debates of the 1770s about American Indian auxiliaries were an element in the creation of the painting, there were other reasons why he chose to produce such a work. Vanderlyn had been commissioned by the poet Joel Barlow to illustrate his epic poem concerning the founding of America, *The Columbiad* (1807).[16] During the execution of this task, Vanderlyn became so intrigued by one of its subjects, the murder of Lucinda at the hands of the Indian braves who had captured her, that he wanted to work exclusively on it and found it impossible to continue the commission.[17] Vanderlyn instead went on to create *The Death of Jane MacCrea* based on a well-known frontier incident that occurred in 1777.[18] Jane MacCrea, an American Tory, was on her way to meet her fiancé, a British officer named David Jones, when the Indians who were escorting her through the lines apparently decided instead to kill her to gain the bounty that the British offered for American scalps. Despite its deep resonance within the American psyche at the time and MacCrea's instant elevation into the ranks of a heroine of the Revolutionary War, the details of her murder and the certainty that it ever took place are still questionable.[19] In terms of a propagandist tale, however, her death at the hands of those who should have protected her, her vulnerability and exposure to the most horrific excesses of savage warfare, exacerbated by colonial demands, gave the story an almost unbearable poignancy. Barlow, in his *Columbiad*, alluded to this real-life episode in the murder of Lucinda. Vanderlyn, in choosing to paint Jane MacCrea rather than the fictional Lucinda, evidently wished to ground his picture in supposed real events.

The arrangement of the figures in *The Death of Jane MacCrea* emphasizes her weakness and submission to the forces of brutality and viciousness, which are beyond her control. Her hair is caught up in the left hand of the Indian figure moving in from the right-hand side and clutching his tomahawk in his right hand, while the second Indian figure holds her outstretched right arm in his left hand and raises the glinting blade of his tomahawk with his right hand.[20]

Compared to the Mohawk in *General Johnson Saving a Wounded French Officer*, Vanderlyn's American Indian figures have a more dominant role to play. Unrestrained by European authority, they grasp the frightened victim and expose her face to the merciless blade of the tomahawk. The contrite expression of West's Mohawk is far removed from Vanderlyn's moment of violence, as the two warriors set about their task with forceful and uncompromising determination. Vanderlyn gives these Indians, who were no longer subordinate to European control, a pictorial domination that overwhelms the white woman. Some scholars have suggested that the figure group in Vanderlyn's picture may owe something to Jacques-Louis

David's *The Sabine Women* of 1799.[21] Vanderlyn was working in Paris, and it is certainly possible that he might look to David for inspiration. But Vanderlyn's emphasis on cruelty and violence is all his own, a grim portrayal of an assassination that is bereft of redeeming heroic features. Unadulterated savagery is far removed from the principled combat of David's canvases. As such, Vanderlyn's picture throws something of a raking light on West's treatment of Indian subjects a generation earlier.

The Death of General Wolfe in 1770 and *William Penn's Treaty with the Indians When He Founded the Province of Pennsylvania in North America* (1771–72; plate 9) complete West's pattern of engagement with American Indian figures. *William Penn's Treaty with the Indians* was West's interpretation of an important historical meeting said to have taken place in 1682 between the Lenni Lenape, or Delaware, tribe of Indian peoples, living in what was then the colony of Pennsylvania, and the founder of the colony, William Penn. During that meeting, a treaty was signed between the Lenni Lenape and William Penn's Quaker proprietors establishing peaceful relations and offering gifts to the Indians in payment for lands soon to be occupied by white settlers. The historicity of this meeting is problematic. It was first committed to print by the Indian agent Thomas Clarkson in 1813, but there is no other historical evidence to suggest that such a meeting ever took place.[22] However, the attitudes of peaceful relations with others and a nonaggressive stance toward the Indians would accord with Quaker sentiments generally and would reinforce the association of Pennsylvania with humane Indian-white relations. Its members' perceived peaceful attitudes to the Indians living nearby the settlements was one of the initiatory myths of the colony, reinforced perhaps by the Quakers in Philadelphia arming themselves to defend Christianized Moravian Indians from genocidal attack by the Paxton Boys in the winter of 1763–64.[23]

A Pennsylvania native son, Benjamin West was born in Chester County and, although close enough to Philadelphia to travel there early in his career, considered himself to have been born on the frontier and therefore molded by it. As mentioned, West used his background early in his career to help him to stand out from other painters, and he included portraits of his father and half brother, and perhaps his own self-portrait, in *William Penn's Treaty with the Indians*.[24] In his biography of West, Galt also spends a few pages detailing the scene of the annual visits of the Indians to the Quaker plantations. For West, it offered a contrast "to the systematic morality of the new inhabitants. . . . The Indians, who mingled safe and harmless among the Friends . . . raised their huts in the fields and orchards without asking leave, nor were they ever molested." Galt concludes that, according to Voltaire,

> the treaty which was signed between the Indians and William Penn was the first public contract which connected the inhabitants of the Old and New world together, and, though not ratified by oaths, and without invoking the Trinity, is still the only treaty that has never been broken. In may be further said, that Pennsylvania is the first country which has not been subdued by the sword, for the inhabitants were conquered by the force of Christian benevolence.[25]

Galt's long discussion of Penn's treaty and its significance cannot be taken at face value, however, especially in its unproblematic description of the picture's historical accuracy. As Ann Uhry Abrams has argued, the picture is inflected by the political situation of the colony in the 1760s. William Penn's son, Thomas, was in nominal control of Pennsylvania, but he had delegated responsibility to a proprietary government whose opponents criticized the political and economic governance of the territory. Indian-white hostilities, which had been bad during most of the colony's recent existence, were resolved with the Fort Stanwix peace treaty of 1768, but some of the ceded Indian lands east of the Ohio River enriched the Penn family, stirring up more criticism.[26] In these circumstances, William Penn's legacy, especially his pacifism and his honorable treatment of the Indians, was a means to refocus debate on the colony's current status by remembering its original ideals. It was Thomas Penn who requested West to paint his father's treaty with the Indians, and this commission might thus be seen as a forcible reminder of the colony's founding myth at a time of political uncertainty.[27] West's picture, celebrating William Penn's benevolent rule and the blessings of prosperity, can be seen as a legitimation of Penn family interests and an answer to those who criticized the family's control.

We can see immediately that West composed the picture to contrast the Quakers and their way of life with that of the Lenni Lenape.[28] In effect, West has divided the picture in half, with the Quakers and their associated symbols of peaceful activity and brotherhood on the left side, contrasted with the American Indian groups on the right. The light flooding in from the left bathes the Quakers, their cleared land, and their settlement as though divinely blessed. It only begins to fade out in the thick forest beyond the settlement, the place where the Native peoples dwell. This movement from light to dark is echoed in the different stages of completion in the background buildings. Closest to the river stands a finished house, with tiled roof and glazed windows. To the right are additional houses being built, ladders and scaffolding in evidence, workmen occupied. These give way, in their turn, to the "crude" shelters of the Lenni Lenape, whose natural materials and coloring make them only just perceptible in the thick darkness of the forest setting. Tokens of trade (ships, goods), industry (portering, building), and Christian brotherhood are on the Quaker side of the picture, while their opposites, intertribal aggression (weapons) and idleness (passivity), associated with the Lenni Lenape, largely occupy the right-hand side of the picture.

We know from a letter of 1805, as well as references to the Quakers from his biography, that West specifically intended that a comparison would be made between the two groups such that their actions could become symbolic of the whole colonial enterprise, the one group civilizing the other. "The great object I had in forming that composition was to express savages brought into harmony and peace by justice and benevolence, by not withholding from them what was their right, and giving to them what they were in want of, as well as a wish to give by that art a conquest made over native people without sword or dagger."[29] West seems to be confirming here in this letter that his picture is about the teaching of a colonial lesson, which can be stated thus: it is unwise to use the sword or dagger to gain power over the Indians but much better to convince them with kindness, benevolence, and the truth of the Christian message. The Indian figures in this picture have been quelled in this sense, their weapons discarded on the ground.

The main groups of Indian men are circling the trade goods, questioning and debating the positive things to be gained by treating with these new arrivals on the scene. In the right foreground, a young Indian mother breast-feeds her infant in the pose of a Madonna, an image highly symbolic of peace and happiness. In terms of Thomas Penn's commission, the picture can be seen as a synopsis of Quaker justification for the settlement of Pennsylvania, almost literally lightening the darkness of unredeemed savages through the exemplification of peace, justice, and industry in the Quaker faith.

For all his readiness to document aspects of the American frontier in peace and war, however, West's success in doing so was limited. Indeed, if we look at West's painted images of Indians, it is evident that their production never generated the public interest that might have encouraged him to extend such activities. *The Indian Family* and *William Penn's Treaty with the Indians* were commissions for very specific purposes, unlikely to find an echo in the art-loving public. His major public success to include an Indian figure, *The Death of General Wolfe*, was chiefly concerned with a British national hero in a particularly well remembered campaign. The Indian warrior may have added an exotic note, but he was incidental to the picture's general reception and the production of copies for other collectors. *General Johnson Saving a Wounded French Officer*, on the other hand, does not appear to have been commissioned and failed to find a purchaser. It was never exhibited and remained in West's possession until his death.[30] This lack of success may have a bearing on West's decision to abandon another picture based on events that had occurred during colonial times. In this case, its subject concerned an episode from the Seven Years' War. The Battle of Monongahela, fought in July 1755, concerned the military defeat of General Edward Braddock and his men as they were making their way toward Fort Duquesne. Surprised by a group of French soldiers and Indian irregulars, who took advantage of the surrounding woods, Braddock's men were tactically disadvantaged and fell into complete disarray. Reports of the disaster were sent back from the frontier and reached London within a month.[31] The impact of Braddock's defeat was significant, for it called into question traditional methods of fighting and laid the foundations for a more modern guerrilla style of warfare. West's identity as a Pennsylvanian again comes to the fore, as that colony felt most exposed to Indian incursions once the French had begun to build their forts in the Ohio Valley regions and nothing seemed able to stop them.

Given West's investigations of American colonial history, the Monongahela battlefield might well have seemed to have the makings of an appropriate addition to his expanding oeuvre of frontier paintings. West himself had been in Lancaster, Pennsylvania, at the time of the battle and is supposed to have served in the local militia. His elder brother, Samuel, helped recover for Christian burial the remains of those lost in battle. This subject, mingling morbid detail with patriotic emotion, would have constituted West's picture. In the biography of West, again, several pages are spent describing the saddest of details for the soldiers and the sorrows they felt at actually running across decaying skeletons in the woods. Major Sir Peter Halket accompanied the detachment and was taken aback at eventually finding the bodies of his father and brother who had died in battle there. Later, in conversation with Lord Grosvenor, who had purchased *The Death of Wolfe*, West related to him that such an event as was witnessed by his brother "undoubtedly furnished topics capable of every effect which the pencil could bestow, or the imagination require in the treatment of so sublime a scene." In response, his "Lordship admitted, that in possessing so effecting an incident as the discovery of the bones of the Halkets, it was superior even to that of the search for the remains of the army of Varus."[32] However, the project was entirely abandoned, and West's decision to discard the topic is partly explained in a discussion he had with Joseph Farington.

> West told us a story of the death of Colonel Sir Peter Hacket [*sic*] who, with one of his sons, was killed in America by the Indians, when General Braddock fell. Another son of the Colonel's was wounded but recovered. The bodies of the slain were left unburied. Four or Five years after Fort Pitt as it is now called was taken by the English. It was only a few miles from the field of battle where the bones of the slain still lay. Those of the Colonel were found being known by a remarkable tooth. His Son, who had been wounded, was present at the discovery. The Scene was interesting and had it been generally known West said He would have painted it.[33]

West's hesitation at depicting what he evidently thought to be a fascinating and yet little known event was probably a well-judged response. Whatever the public feeling had been in 1755, in the 1760s and afterward only the most major events and personalities seemed able to secure widespread enthusiasm or recognition. West's failure to sell *General Johnson Saving a Wounded French Officer* is thus of a piece with his decision to abandon the battlefield at Monongahela as a potential subject. Only events that were "generally known" could expect to find purchasers and add to his reputation. In fact, it was only in book illustrations that West was able to extend his Indian repertoire to include contemporary events. Shortly after completing *General Johnson Saving a Wounded French Officer*, West made two designs for William Smith's book, *An Historical Account of the Expedition against the Ohio Indians in the Year 1764 under the Command of Henry Bouquet* (1766).[34] These modest illustrations seem to have drawn on West's knowledge of tribes in Pennsylvania, for they share the same plucked scalp and feather adornment seen in his *The Indian Family* and *General Johnson Saving a Wounded French Officer*.

This realization must, to some extent, color our view of West's attempt at historical truth in such pictures, for West understood that merely relating authentic events was no passport to success. A subject picture had to attract if it was to succeed, and that attraction necessarily required embellishment of the original. I have already noted the lack of documentary record in *The Death of General Wolfe* and the special pleading in *William Penn's Treaty with the Indians*. *General Johnson Saving a Wounded French Officer*, likewise, conflates different incidents to produce a moral exemplum concerning civilization and savagery. In these pictures, the presence of Indians is significant, but it would be surprising if West felt impelled to record them more scrupulously than other elements in the narrative. That they are depicted fastidiously is not in doubt, however. As indicated above, the amount of detail shown and its obvious differentiation from European experience is one way in which West can signify his authoritative position with respect to American subject matter. But this detail, in and of itself, does not need to discriminate further between the clothes, weapons, tattoos, or hairstyles of different tribes. It is enough that it is "authentically" Indian, and this "authenticity" is signaled by the sharp-focus, realist treatment of skin tone, beadwork, face paint, ornaments, and weapons. Such details, West proposes, could not have been invented and so must be reliable.

There is a sense, then, that the putative ethnographic accuracy of *The Indian Family* justifies West's using it as a storehouse of motifs to deploy on a variety of Indian groups represented in his other frontier paintings. We know that West later obtained American Indian artifacts from an important donor whose identity is still uncertain. The most likely candidate suggested is the superintendent of Indian Affairs, William Johnson. West must have acquired these twelve items in order to be able to clothe his Indian figures in specimens of dress and accoutrement that would appear authentic.[35] Even in this case, however, when the provenance of these items has been passed down to us from the eighteenth century, it is still impossible to give them a precise tribal origin. Several of them can only be described loosely as Iroquois or Algonquian, that is, items from the northeastern woodlands areas. This lack of secure identification makes the process of deciding on the authenticity, or lack of it, in West's Indian figures that much more complicated. Indeed, to this day, when art historians try to identify the Indians in West's pictures, they receive contrasting answers from anthropologists and ethnohistorians. Mohawk, Delaware (Lenni Lenape), Iroquois, and Pennsylvania Indians have all been put forward as West's subjects.[36]

It is possible that a search for precise tribal affiliations is, in fact, wrongheaded and misunderstands West's intentions. The Indians appearing in West's paintings of the 1760s to 1770s might be described instead as variants of one distinct figure-type who was first represented in *The Indian Family*. This male warrior may be seen as the template for West's "generic Indian." A plucked scalp and topknot of hair decorated with feathers, a beaded pouch, a blanket or animal skin, and body paint appear here for the first time as the markers of the figure's identity and will reappear on other figures of Indian males in subsequent designs. A young Indian man dressed in many of the same items of clothing as the departing warrior in *The Indian Family* appears again as the Mohawk in *General Johnson Saving a Wounded French Officer*. In effect, what is essentially the same individual moves from the senatorial dignity of the first picture to the violence of the second, but it is of a piece with those eighteenth-century accounts of Indians that stressed the coexistence of qualities that Europeans thought were incompatible.

In this respect, it is significant that when West made a comparison between the image of a Mohawk warrior and that of the Apollo Belvedere when he was in Rome in 1760, the Italians were initially unable to understand him. Only when West's interpreter went on to further explain West's comment on seeing the ancient statue, "My God! . . . How like it is to a Mohawk Warrior," that by this he meant the Indians' "dexterity with the bow and arrow, the elasticity of their limbs," did the Italians become satisfied and pleased with his response.[37] The visualization of the Mohawk as an Apollo-like figure in his *The Indian Family* of 1760 brought this comparison to fruition.[38]

The Indian in *The Death of General Wolfe* seems to share some of the features seen in the Indian warrior of *The Indian Family* and *General Johnson Saving a Wounded French Officer*. His plucked scalp with feather and beaded adornment attached to the lock of hair left unplucked at the back of his head, his beaded pouch, and his blue decorated blanket are all reminiscent of similar details in the earlier pictures. Now, however, West's depiction seems more detailed, and it is possible to make out precise patterns in the beadwork on the pouch the Indian man carries and to see the distinctive tattoos that he displays on his back, shoulder, forehead, arms, and legs. It is likely, therefore, that West's collection of American Indian artifacts became a deciding factor in his compositions toward the end of the 1760s. West's precision of focus here may be tied into his desire to paint accurate history. Ironically, therefore, whereas the episode in *General Johnson Saving a Wounded French Officer* was connected to a real event, West painted it as an *exemplum virtutis* as much as a historical episode, and the protagonists lack scrupulous definition of uniforms and weapons.[39] In *The Death of General Wolfe*, on the other hand, the more emphatic historicity of the painting ensures that an imaginary Indian is fully realized in terms of ethnographic detail. From being a loosely described, generic type, the Indian in *The Death of General Wolfe* has become a historically situated protagonist, akin to the other figures who need differentiation from each other, the soldiers and officers, rangers and other auxiliaries, who were all part of the epic contest.

A further move toward differentiation is made in West's next painting with Indian figures, *William Penn's Treaty with the Indians*. In this picture, there are whole groups and differing ages and roles to be described within the Indian portion of the painting. Here several elements from *The Indian Family* reappear. The Indian woman and baby are recycled, and West's Indian "brave" is adapted in part for several male figures. The major change, however, concerns the variety of dress and accoutrement West now has at his disposal: feather headdresses decorated with bulls' horns, an eagle feather fan, beaded and decorated headbands, a pipe decorated with quillwork, and a skirt and shawl decorated with a distinctive floral pattern. West's Indian warrior, although not present in his totality, is echoed in the three most prominently depicted Indian men, the two seated figures listening to Penn's proposal of peace and the standing gesturing Indian man behind them whose plucked scalp, lacerated auricles of the ear, and topknot of hair decorated with bright red feathers are reminiscent of the earlier figure in *The Indian Family*. This standing and gesturing male figure also bears some relation to the Indian man giving his harangue in one of the engravings West made to accompany Provost Smith's *Historical Account of the Expedition Against the Ohio Indians*.[40]

Thus, although one can see moves toward differentiation in the representation of Indians within the body of West's work as he proceeded from his early and initial development of a generic Indian type to a more complex and complicated image such as the one presented in *William Penn's Treaty with the Indians*, there exists throughout this growing body of work a stock figure whose musculature and idealized anatomy remain essentially the same. West sought to deploy this figure in a number of ways, causing it to appear in several works and showing it adopting different poses and positions to suit the dictates of the commission and the subject. However, the Indian man/warrior/chief is less an ethnographically studied and documented personage than a lay figure clothed and accoutred according to the narrative or underlying theme of the work. West's refinement of ethnographic detail, as his collection of artifacts took shape in the 1760s, can therefore be seen as part of a more general tendency to prepare the ground for properly researched history painting. In an overall sense, however, West's habitual depiction of a generic type of Indian brave to stand for all American Indian peoples on the frontier accords with a habit of mind that restricts Indians to the symbolic realm. The Indian as a token of savagery opposes the gentlemanly refinement and humane qualities exhibited by Johnson, Wolfe, and Penn.

If West's Indian is ultimately a generic type, as opposed to a representative of an individuated tribe or people, that generalizing tendency extends also to the roles West's Indians play in these paintings. One might even go so far as to suggest that a catalog of responses to the entire Indian question and the problems of the frontier in America was being worked through and developed by West during these years. This catalog of responses begins with *The Indian Family*, where the father must leave to fight an opposing tribe or serve as an auxiliary soldier. It progresses through *General Johnson Saving a Wounded French Officer*, where a similar figure is seen in his role as auxiliary, attempting to scalp an enemy on the field of battle. West reveals the nature of American Indian warfare as it is conducted on the frontier and shows the Indian man in the throes of a "barbarous" act, which is only repressed by the steadying hand of the British colonial representative, William Johnson, who long before this picture was executed had been made one of the first Indian superintendents of the northern colonies. In *The Death of General Wolfe*, the Indian figure suggests a quiescent American Indian presence—mute, controlled, and contemplative in the face of events grander and on a scale he might never have dreamed possible before the European conquest of North America. Whereas American Indians had been central to the point of the earlier pictures, in *The Death of General Wolfe* the Indian man's subordinate position and contemplative pose place him outside the action of the picture. In one sense, this could be seen as the American Indians' most proper alignment with respect to the whole question of control of North America, for by the time this was painted in 1770, many tribal groups had lost the "middle ground" roles they had played in the preceding decades. Pantribal resistances such as Pontiac's Rebellion of 1763 had been quashed, and the dividing line between white settlement and "free" Indian country was moving westward at an extremely rapid rate.[41] As well as deactivating his warrior figure in this way, West has come close to revivifying allegory, as Bromley's reading quoted earlier suggests.[42]

The final picture of frontier history within West's group of Indian subjects is *William Penn's Treaty with the Indians*. If this is to be viewed as the end piece to a greater narrative of colonial events, it, too, places the American Indian figures in a position of vulnerability and quiescence. Here, Penn's settlers and traders move into the landscape and transform it. There is very little place of retreat for this group of Lenni Lenape; they either join the Quakers in building a new society in the wilderness or they retreat to the dark woods, shunning progress and moving outside history.

After his decade of painting Indian subjects, West was never to devote such sustained attention to this area of his practice again; one could argue that he mined that particular vein of inspiration for all that it could produce. The epic proportions of a war for empire and the Christianization of so-called savage peoples were the historic events that gave these pictures their topical relevance. British interest in the Native populations of America in such events as these was over to all intents and purposes by 1783, and other concerns regarding the English and/or British national past would assume a much more important place in public consciousness. However, as with Vanderlyn's *The Death of Jane MacCrea*, it was possible after 1783 to create scenes of violence taking place on the American frontier and to manage a kind of transition from the explicitly historicizing pictures of Benjamin West to another sort of image, one that might be labeled "serious genre." This is not to suggest that Vanderlyn initiated such a maneuver because certain of West's compositions might also fall within the bounds of such a category. Indeed, West's *The Indian Family* and *General Johnson Saving a Wounded French Officer* are similarly modest pictures in terms of actual size, and they likewise concentrate on minor military episodes grounded in historical accounts. As such, they lack the epic, generalizing, and grandiose ambitions of West's Indian subjects exhibited in *The Death of Wolfe* and *William Penn's Treaty with the Indians*.

Benjamin West's *The Indian Family* is an early example of this genrelike interpretation of American Indians. Here, in spite of the care in representing objects and Indian peoples with a degree of ethnographic verisimilitude, the classically derived poses and the garments that function like drapery, together with the restrained and dignified facial expressions of the Indian man and woman, position them in a world of universal sentiment where Woodlands Indians share the same feelings as Ulysses and Penelope. The idea of universal sentiments, of course, allowed Europeans to imagine a common humanity linking them with American Indians at the level of feelings and emotions. While Indian culture might be distinctive and, in certain respects, difficult to comprehend, this otherness could be mitigated, if not fully overcome, by aligning their behavior with more familiar European modes of personal expression. West's *The Indian Family* could thus find a parallel in European understandings of familial obligations, paternal and maternal roles, and the importance of the family to social life.

From the outset, American Indians appear as devices for the exemplification of parental or familial devotion, loyalty to one's own race or creed, or epitomes of violence as located in the American landscape. Notwithstanding attempts to realize these subjects with reference to ethnographically correct information, their "universalist" function and containment within European discourses of knowledge ensured that the older symbolic and allegorical presentations of America were never far from the surface. The allegories of America considered in chapter 1 speak through these individuated figures, and just as the four parts of the world cosmological system only made sense as a Eurocentric structure, so here these depicted Indians are to be understood as representatives of European concerns. To put this another way, we might speculate on the likelihood of a European artist attempting to produce an American Indian figure who embodied a strong and powerful presence, self-sufficiently distinct from European understandings. By definition, such an image would be conceptually impossible for a European artist. American Indians entered a kind of negotiation with the European imagination if they were to be represented at all, a negotiation that required the detection and emphasis of enough common ground for a sympathetic portrayal to be possible. Alas, the price of this sympathy was often that the power and aggressive self-assertion of American Indians had to be replaced by a concentration on their less alienating characteristics. The Indian subdued or under control (West) or vicious (Vanderlyn) seems to have been the most acceptable image.

The American Indian figure in actuality was a frontier menace too unheroic and too emotionally unaffecting to merit treatment by serious history painters, unless in the almost demonic guise of Vanderlyn's *The Death of Jane MacCrea*. In general, the Indian figure who participates in paintings of European battle scenes, a real and active agent no matter how tokenlike his presence may be, is progressively replaced by the passive and stoically enduring Indian whose existence is usually perceived outside of a specific historical context.

4 *Secret Diplomacy and Uneasy Alliances*

The British and American Indian Relationships in the Revolutionary and Post–Revolutionary War Periods, 1774–1815

THE IMAGES OF American Indians that were produced in England during and after the Revolutionary War have an oblique relation to the work of the 1760s and early 1770s. As we might expect, the image of American Indians in British art after the loss of the colonies on the eastern seaboard did not simply extend the repertoire elaborated during the early eighteenth century. The new political settlement of the 1780s and afterward called forth responses that betray these altered circumstances.

Unlike the struggle for control of North America in the middle of the eighteenth century, the use of American Indian forces in the Revolutionary War was becoming less tactical. The colonial wars had made clear the need to adapt European and American armies to the conditions of war in the forest. As American Indian ways of combat had not changed much since the seventeenth-century conflicts, by the late eighteenth and early nineteenth centuries the elements of surprise and the "skulking way of war" accomplished by the Indians were well known and often taken into account.[1] For the British, the need for large groups of Indian auxiliaries to fight in the skirmishes was becoming less pressing and was, in any case, difficult to control and coordinate effectively. Instead, more organized groups of rangers and scouts, which might include American Indians, became the method whereby the British had attempted to gain advantage over their enemies. General John Burgoyne's use of American Indian auxiliaries in 1777, which failed in its purpose, was perhaps a significant turning point.

The status of American Indians as military allies of a European power had helped to promote artistic responses to their culture. These circumstances were no longer in play, especially with the victorious United States now constituted in its own right. As a result, the portrayal of diplomatic delegations and the selection of Indian warriors for topics suitable for history painting are not features of British responses to the Revolutionary conflict. Indeed, the only major history painting from this period to make use of an American Indian figure was painted by John Trumbull to commemorate an American attack on Quebec in 1778. *The Death of General Montgomery in the Attack on Quebec* was produced in London in 1786 while Trumbull was working in Benjamin West's studio. As in West's *The Death of General Wolfe* of 1771, Trumbull included an American Indian, identified in a print of 1789 as the Oneida warrior Colonel Joseph Lewis.[2] Trumbull's inclusion of an Oneida man, like West's inclusion of a Mohawk, was not supported by contemporary accounts of this battle. It seems that Trumbull owed much to his older American mentor in his melding of symbolism and history to produce an image of American conflict.

The years following the American Revolution saw British and American Indian relations decline and are marked by "uneasy" or failed alliances, particularly from the American Indian perspective. The twenty years separating the Versailles Treaty of 1783 from the conflict of 1812–13 did not bring peace to North America. Although Britain and the United States were no longer formally at war, Indian resistance to European settlement did not abate. Also, a new movement for pan-tribal unity appeared, revivifying Pontiac's earlier message and led by the Shawnee brothers Tenskwatawa (the Shawnee Prophet) and Tecumseh. These two leaders of the Shawnees, from 1805 to their defeats in 1811 and 1813, respectively, were the most important figures to stand against any accommodation to Anglo-American culture in this period.[3] The border conflicts of the early 1790s and those between Tecumseh's forces and the U.S. troops at Fallen Timbers and at Moraviantown showed that the American Indians could still muster large forces in the field. American Indians of the nativist persuasion maintained their vigorous resistance and outright hostility to encroachment on their lands by westward-moving settlers and land developers.[4] Unfortunately for the Indians of the southern Great Lakes areas, including the Shawnees, Britain had ceded extensive lands in their regions in the Treaty of Versailles, despite the fact that some of them had fought for the British during the Revolutionary War. Fatefully, it was these same lands, west of the Appalachians, that had been identified in George III's Proclamation of 1763 as distinct Indian territory and therefore unassailable. The Americans, of course, saw the situation very differently; they had won the war against Britain and would remain implacably opposed to any further negotiation. The Versailles Treaty's blatant ignoring of the American Indian presence and their claims to the land within the law was bound to result in conflict. From 1786 until the conclusion of the British and American conflict in the 1814 Treaty of Ghent, the hope existed that American Indians, united with a common aim, might overthrow the Americans. This belief was partly fueled by the British in the figures of certain colonial leaders, such as the governors of Upper and Lower Canada, John Graves Simcoe, and Sir Guy Carleton, Lord Dorchester, respectively. Both men had their own reasons for encouraging the American Indian resistance, for a protracted United States-Indian war would delay, if not completely frustrate, the American takeover of a highly strategic area in the southern Great Lakes area around Forts Detroit and Niagara.[5] Overall, however, one might argue that compared to the earlier eighteenth century, the British public had a much reduced exposure to representations of American Indian military and diplomatic leadership in this period. Figures who would become prominent in the fight for the Old Northwest, south of the Great Lakes, such as Little Turtle, the Miami chief, and Tecumseh, the Shawnee pan-tribalist, were not given the same amount of publicity and press coverage as had the earlier delegations of Mohawk and Cherokee peoples, whose presence in London had made such an impression. It might be simply that once the American colonies had become the United States, a large portion of the public at home in

Britain viewed any continuing North American conflicts and territorial squabbles as outside the concerns of the British Empire. However, in terms of the strategic diplomatic agendas facing the colonial governors in Canada and these men's concerns over the economics of trade and industry involving American Indian peoples, Britain had every right to protect its association with peoples and places over which it had held sway up until the end of hostilities.

In this regard, it is instructive to pay attention to Britain's remaining territories in North America. In the Treaty of Paris in 1783, a plan for the handing over of the Northwest forts held by the British had been put in place. These frontier posts were located at strategic points (Detroit, Michilimackinac, and Niagara) and were crucial to fur trading and other contacts with the American Indians in these areas. To some extent, one might argue that from a Canadian perspective, Britain held some claim to areas around the Great Lakes in the 1790s, as there had as yet been no drafting of a forty-ninth parallel acting to officially separate the United States from Canada.[6] In American Indian eyes, too, there was no legal spatial division to separate them from their claims to these areas; neither had any less formal agreement been reached. In this light, it seems logical that disputes and conflicts would arise in an area still deemed largely unconquered and outside national boundaries.

In order to highlight the changes that had taken place in British and American Indian relations since the ending of the Seven Years' War and the eventual founding of a new nation, the United States, it is useful to examine the relationship between the first lieutenant governor of Upper Canada, John Graves Simcoe, and the Mohawk Indian leader Joseph Brant, or Thayendanegea. In its way, this relationship signals the changing fortunes and circumstances of North American Indian groups on the continent as they had to contend with shifts in colonial policies and leading colonial personalities. John Graves Simcoe had an important role to play at the end of the eighteenth century in establishing relations with the American Indian peoples living within the boundaries of present-day Ontario and the upper Great Lakes region. For his part, Joseph Brant represents one of those essential figures emerging from colonial interrelations who have latterly been called cultural mediators or brokers.[7] The relationship between these two men could thus stand for a whole set of colonial connections that existed in North America

94

at this time and which included personal relationships extending beyond the niceties of diplomatic or military negotiation.

One such style of intercultural relations was that established by Teoniahigarawe, known as "King Hendrick," the Mohawk leader who visited Britain in 1710, and William Johnson in the 1740s and 1750s. Johnson was perhaps a unique figure among his contemporaries in that both the British government and the local Indian peoples in the Mohawk Valley claimed his allegiance. Johnson had, by the middle 1750s, already built up a distinguished career in Indian diplomacy since his early days in office as the New York colony's Indian agent from 1746. Throughout his career in the Indian service, he was instrumental in maintaining American Indian allies for the British due to his intimate understanding of Iroquois politics and diplomacy.[8] His home in the Mohawk Valley region was a center for treaty making and negotiation as well as trade.[9] Under his wing, and soon to develop as a leader in his own right, was the young Joseph Brant. Brant's family was in fact related to William Johnson, as Brant's sister, Molly, was Johnson's common-law wife. The young Joseph Brant would eventually become a noted warrior involved in several raids during the Revolutionary War when he commanded a small contingent of his own men, known as Brant's Volunteers.[10] The span of Joseph Brant's life thus takes in many significant occurrences and developments in the history of British and American colonial relations with the American Indians.

No other American Indian figure of the English-speaking eighteenth-century world, except perhaps Hendrick/Teoniahigarawe, is as memorable as Joseph Brant. He made a name for himself in the 1770s and 1780s and occasioned deeply divided views on his achievement. To his enemies, he was associated with the notorious Wyoming Valley Massacre of 1778, and as late as 1809 the poet Thomas Campbell referred him to as the "Monster Brant."[11] To his admirers, he was the epitome of the valorous Indian warrior, leading European and Indian troops against the enemies of Britain. He visited England in 1776 and again in 1786 on diplomatic missions. As had his Mohawk predecessors before him, he had his likeness taken on both occasions as a witness of his embassy. In the aftermath of the Revolutionary War, Brant was allowed to settle on his own lands along the Grand River in Canada, and it was there in the 1790s that he developed his relationship with Simcoe.

By the time of the outbreak of the Revolutionary War in 1775, Joseph Brant had long been acting as a cultural mediator. Formerly a student at Eleazor Wheelock's school for young Indian men, Moor's Charity School in Lebanon, Connecticut, he had achieved preeminence in his role as a Christianized American Indian. He was also the inheritor of his grandfather's role as friend and ally to the English. Brant's adopted grandfather, known historically by the name placed on his portrait by John Verelst, Sa Ga Yeath Qua Pieth Tow, was a member of the Mohawk delegation of 1710 and thus associated with Hendrick/Teoniahigarawe (see fig. 2.2).[12] As we have seen, Brant also had personal connections with one of the most powerful of colonialists, the superintendent of Indian Affairs for the northern colonies, William Johnson, who had been appointed to the post in 1755. All of these connections between Brant and his Anglo-American friends and sponsors worked to reinforce his exemplary reputation.

The reasons for Brant's visits to England in 1776 and 1786 were mostly to do with securing the promise of the restitution of Mohawk lands for the members of his clan in recompense for their allegiance to England. This Mohawk of the Wolf Clan, an adopted grandson to one of the "kings" who had visited England and thus in English eyes, at least, of royal or distinguished connection, created perhaps the greatest impact on the English at the turn of the century. Through his efforts to make direct contact with leading members of British society, he became a friend to a number of English gentlemen and members of the nobility, was accepted into the Masons, and was distinguished as an officer and secretary to Sir Guy Johnson, who succeeded his uncle, William, as superintendent of Indian affairs in 1774.[13] Traveling to England at two important historical junctures for the Mohawks, Brant's impact was certainly felt abroad. His claims for recognition of and compensation for Mohawk support of the British were listened to at the highest levels. During his first visit to England in 1776, he became a friend of James Boswell's, who commissioned his portrait. (The picture is now known only as an engraved portrait in the *London Magazine* of July 1776.)[14] Boswell also related that Brant told him of his ancestor who had visited England in 1710 and been received by Queen Anne.[15]

In addition to his appealing personality, not only could Brant converse in English, he had also spent time translating into Mohawk the Gospel of St. Mark as well as the Book of Common Prayer. He could thus be regarded as educated above his peers. His ethnic traits, such as skin tone and Indian speech and mannerisms, might all be disregarded as colorful or quaint idiosyncrasies if one kept in mind that he was the beneficiary of a European and Christian education. The friendships of James Boswell; Lord Francis Rawdon, the Earl of Moira; and Lord Hugh Percy, Duke of Northumberland bear witness to his acceptance within English literary and aristocratic society.[16]

The Earl of Warwick commissioned George Romney to paint Brant's portrait during his first visit of 1776 (plate 10). Brant is depicted in a three-quarter-length pose, wearing American Indian dress, which consists of a pink shirt or blouse overlaid with elements pertaining both to his membership in the Mohawk tribe and to his allegiance to George III. Like the earlier Cherokee portraits of 1762, Brant is shown wearing a combined style of dress that makes articles of European manufacture, such as the shirt and breeches, act as the backdrop to brighter and more colorful additions. Contemporaries often described frontier fighters, such as Brant, as dressing in "Indian fashion." Brant's European garments combined with American Indian accoutrements, such as feathers, decorated weaponry, and beads or shells define his figure as a warrior, rather than a leading sachem. If he wanted to be seen as the latter according to the colonial customs of the 1740s to 1760s, he would sport a tailored coat, and possibly lace collar and cuffs, in the manner of an English gentleman.[17] His overall costume, in its combination of English and Woodlands elements, speaks of Brant's own position between two worlds. The feathers in his headband and the decorative chains of metal loops or studs that fall across his left shoulder appear all the more exotic because of their combination with more familiar styles of dress. Yet this seeming eclecticism, we should remember, would not have been especially noteworthy in the "middle ground" of negotiation that Brant inhabited. Traded fabric and metal items, combined with local materials, together constitute an apparel that made every sense in the Ohio Valley but would have appeared unmistakably exotic in England. Yet Romney was a skillful enough artist to unify these elements convincingly, such that Brant's appearance is singular but not discordant. At a time when well-traveled sitters might be portrayed dressed in Oriental or Pacific costume, or when a figure like John Caldwell had his portrait painted in Ojibwa regalia, Romney's picture of Brant is relatively urbane.[18] What distinguishes Romney's picture is its cultural location within Mohawk attitudes to England. As with his predecessors in 1710, Brant's figure combines items of European manufacture such as guns, hatchets, or pipes alongside the more American Indian accoutrement such as earrings and headdresses, not as a costumier's miscellany but as tokens of trade and good relations. Brant thus recapitulates the older and established mode of the delegation portrait and reestablishes his role as cultural mediator. The silver gorget with the pendant cross, which Brant wears alongside his other marks of distinction, is engraved with the royal coat of arms and cipher and reminds the viewer that this man is a loyal and spiritually enlightened individual whose allegiance is to be condoned. Although he carries what is probably a pipe-tomahawk in his right hand, this element is entirely played down and pushed to the margins of the picture, with the blade of the tomahawk only barely distinguishable. Brant's relaxed and informal pose is reminiscent of Reynolds's earlier treatment of the Cherokee Outacity (plate 3). Both poses help to resolve the ambiguity of the pipe-tomahawk, an item that could signify peace (the sharing of tobacco) or war (its use as a hatchet), by portraying the sitters as men of dignity and integrity, a reading that no doubt appealed to their patrons or sponsors.

This more painterly and freely executed model is further developed in the two official portrait commissions made to capture Brant's likeness during his second and final trip to England in 1786. Both patrons, the Duke of Northumberland, Hugh Percy, and the Earl of Moira, Francis Rawdon, arranged for the American portrait painter Gilbert Stuart to paint the likeness of Joseph Brant when both Americans were in London. As Brant had fought with the young Lord Rawdon, later the Earl of Moira, in Sir Henry Clinton's regiment in the Revolutionary War, this portrait may have been commissioned as a memento of their comradeship. The two men were to remain friends all of their lives.[19] The Duke of Northumberland, Hugh Percy, must have thought highly of Brant also, as his painting of the Mohawk leader remains in the family's possession today (plate 11).

The underlying reasons for Brant's initial trip to Britain in 1776 remain somewhat obscure, but surely the death of his patron, William Johnson, two years earlier must have caused some concern to Brant as to how the British might handle the situation without Johnson's negotiating skill with the Indians. Johnson's nephew, Colonel Guy Johnson, accompanied Brant on his first visit to England. Brant's sympathies had perhaps always remained with the British side, but at the outbreak of the American Revolution in 1775, the most pressing thing on his mind was to support Guy Johnson and to seek protection for and restitution of his homelands in the Mohawk Valley. On his trip to London in 1776, he made clear his choice of battlefield allies, and it was in his role as leader of Indian and combined troops that he distinguished himself for the British colonialists.[20] In 1786, however, the circumstances had changed radically. In the Paris conference of 1783, American Indian claims to the lands west of the Appalachians were ignored, and the "American negotiators . . . asserted their sovereignty over the lands of the interior."[21] Brant and his people, having backed the losing side in the Revolutionary War, had seen their lands signed away at the Treaty of Versailles and were faced with the options of acquiescing in the new U.S. policy or removing to Canada. Stuart's painting, perhaps, suggests that Brant's achievements now lie behind him.

Yet the period between the end of the Revolutionary War and the end of the War of 1812 represents a crucial last attempt by many American Indian groups to throw out the land-hungry and usurping forces on the North American continent. They were aided and abetted in these desires by some British colonials in Canada and were likewise spurred on by a nostalgia for the older associations of the "middle ground" of the seventeenth and early eighteenth centuries that had established a practicable model of negotiation and exchange for all parties concerned.[22] One of the reasons that many American Indian groups had sided with the British was due to the promises of continued trade and presents to loyal allies.[23] After the American Revolution, the ability to maintain the sources of trade goods was still largely associated with British mercantile concerns, and it was natural that American Indians dependent on such goods would seek out the British and try to retain their friendship. The British, for their part, wished to retain control of the trade with those Indians who lived to the west of the new United States. Guilt at what had taken place immediately after the cessation of the Revolutionary War caused certain members of the British colonial government to make appeals on behalf of their former Indian allies for their settlement within the provinces of Canada.

As late as the 1790s, General Frederick Haldimand, governor of Quebec, delayed the transition of frontier forts from British to U.S. control and thereby helped to support American Indian claims on the frontier territory. There is also evidence that the administration in England was sympathetic. The prime minister, Lord North, wrote, "These People are justly entitled to our Peculiar attention and it would be far from either generous or just in us, after our cession of their Territories and Hunting grounds, to forsake them."[24] It was into this somewhat unstable and developing situation, after 1790, that John Graves Simcoe, the new lieutenant governor of Upper Canada, began his tenancy in the region.

Simcoe was one of these colonial officials who believed the American Indians, particularly staunch British allies such as the Mohawks, should be resettled.[25] His governorship lasted for four years, from 1792 to 1796. His main historical significance is having founded the city of Toronto, but he is also noted for his road building and issuing of land settlements to Anglo-Americans and American Indians in Upper Canada after the war. He eventually returned to rural Devon in England, where he and his wife owned an estate and where he died in 1806. It is perhaps entirely in keeping with his actions in Canada that, on his death, his wife commissioned a sculptural monument to be erected in Exeter Cathedral, which contains the figure of an American Indian. In turning to a single work commissioned by the Simcoe family for Exeter Cathedral, many of the earlier strands in the history of visual representations of American Indians in the eighteenth century are brought together. John Flaxman's memorial to the first lieutenant governor of Upper Canada can be seen as a fitting tribute to intercultural affairs in the post-Revolutionary period (fig. 4.1a, 4.1b).

Simcoe was well aware, during his time in Upper Canada, of the strategic use of American Indian allies in the wars over North American territories. As a military commander himself, he had been a distinguished leader during the Revolutionary War and would evidently have been aware of the deteriorating situation that held in the Old Northwest. Just prior to his appointment as lieutenant governor, the U.S. military had suffered defeats by the Indians in 1790–91, essentially a continuation of the border warfare that had been a part of the American Revolutionary conflict. In such circumstances, Simcoe would have been responsible for keeping

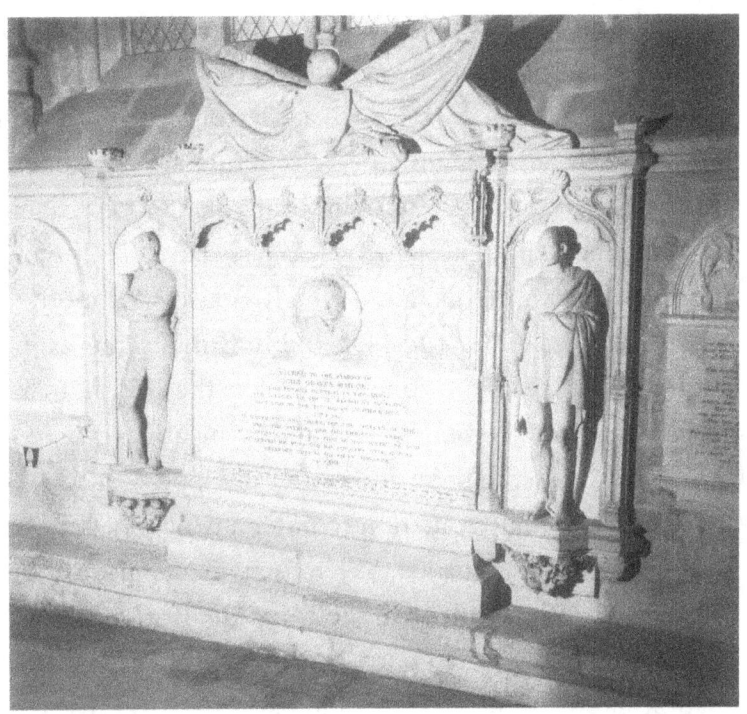

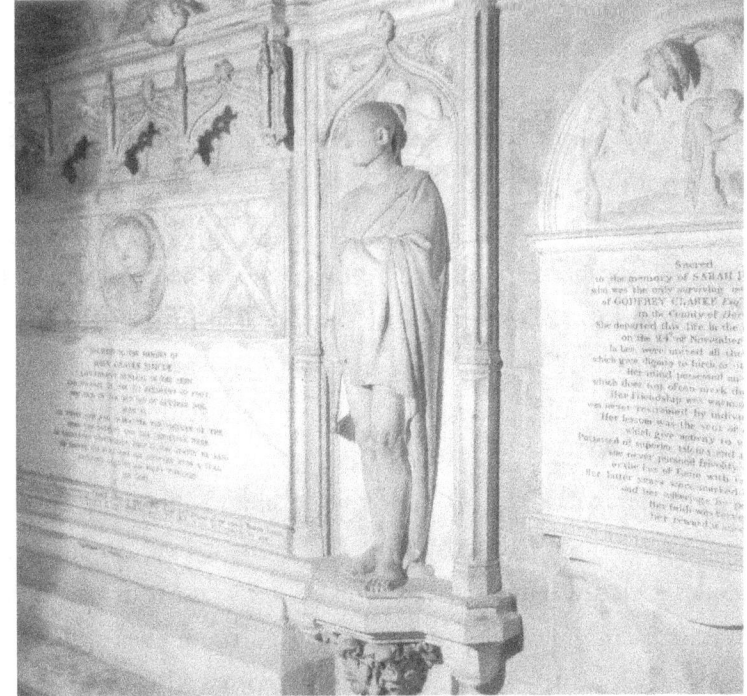

Fig. 4.1a and 4.1b
(detail). John Flaxman,
Simcoe Memorial, stone
and marble sculpture,
1815, Exeter Cathedral,
Exeter. Photo by Bruce
A. Bailey, from the
Conway Library,
Courtauld Institute of
Art, London. Courtesy
of the Conway Library.

good relations with the local and regional Indian groups in Upper Canada, but he would also have been aware of British policies to delay the handing over of British posts in the Old Northwest, such as Detroit, Michilimackinac, and Niagara.[26] The role played by Simcoe in the peaceful settlement of Upper Canada and parts of the Old Northwest was crucial in these volatile circumstances.

On his appointment, Simcoe was introduced to Joseph Brant by the Duke of Northumberland, and Simcoe would later assess the motives of the Mohawk Indian leader in this way: "He considers the Indian interests as the first Object—that as a second, tho' very inferior one, He prefers the British, in a certain degree, to the people of the United States."[27] Brant's sympathies would lie with his own people and his need to settle them adequately in Upper Canada. To do this, it was imperative that he use his reputation to enter any negotiations as a major player. In this, he seems to have succeeded. Several statements made about Brant at the time of his introduction to Simcoe suggest that the British, at least, saw him as a preeminent leader for the Six Nations in their totality.[28] This attitude recapitulates older relationships with the Iroquois and harks back to those earlier diplomatic ties that had been created nearly a century previously in 1710.

Flaxman may have been aware of Simcoe's relationship with Brant, but in one sense the American Indian presence on the North American continent had again come into public consciousness during the time the monument to Simcoe had been commissioned. The war with the United States during 1812–13 had once more seen the involvement of American Indian groups in the fighting around the frontier and border regions. Some of the same groups that had supported the British in the 1770s again fought alongside British troops in battles up and down the continent. Flaxman would have been aware of the role they played in campaigns in Canada, and their relevance for a sculptural work of this kind was thus not only symbolic but topical.

In the iconography of late medieval and Renaissance altarpieces, the side panels flanking the central scene traditionally held the images of saints or the high-ranking clergy, which sanctity and religious custom had demanded. In Flaxman's medievalizing monument, the figures in the niches act more as witnesses to the governor's achievements, giving testimony to his policies of appeasement and humanitarian ideals. Their calm and dignified poses are in keeping with this function, and as a result, the American Indian figure achieves a monumental gravitas quite different from the figures in the earlier *Townshend Monument* (see fig. 2.4). Indeed, the two figures on each side of the central portrait bust of Simcoe almost assume a greater importance than the governor himself as they are much larger and nearly carved in the round. Comparison of Flaxman's *Simcoe Memorial* with the *Townshend Monument* is crucial to this discussion, as the monument is a work Flaxman knew and admired yet evidently chose not to follow. In *Nollekens and His Times* (1828), J. T. Smith quotes an anecdote that "Flaxman used to say he would give something for the possession of the name of the artist who executed the sculptural parts of this monument which he considered to be one of the finest productions of art in the Abbey."[29] As the Abbey's *Townshend Monument* had included figures symbolic of the involvement of American Indians in the Canadian wars, it may have been influential in Flaxman's decision to include such a figure in his own work. But whereas Adam's Choctaws on the *Townshend Monument* are subjected in defeat, supporting their British victor, in Flaxman's *Simcoe Memorial* the Mohawk is given an equivalent importance to the figure of the Ranger in the opposite niche. Here, then, we seem to witness a direct reference to Brant's people, perhaps even to Brant himself, whose loyalty to the British cause is commemorated at Exeter.

Flaxman's original design for the monument portrays the Mohawk figure with more detail then the sculpted image possesses (fig. 4.2). The most notable difference in the Flaxman design after its transformation to marble is the toning down and deletion of ethnographic details in the Indian figure's dress and costume. The head and neck ornamentation has been relinquished in order to present a more classicizing bare head and shoulders. The plaited hair hanging behind his head is only noticeable when close to the memorial and viewed from the side. Technical concerns may have prompted the deletion of the feather headdress, but this cannot be the entire reason for the elimination of detail. Flaxman, as a neoclassical sculptor, could not admit a superfluity of cultural markers that would have detracted from a clear uncluttered line and the use of smooth modeling.

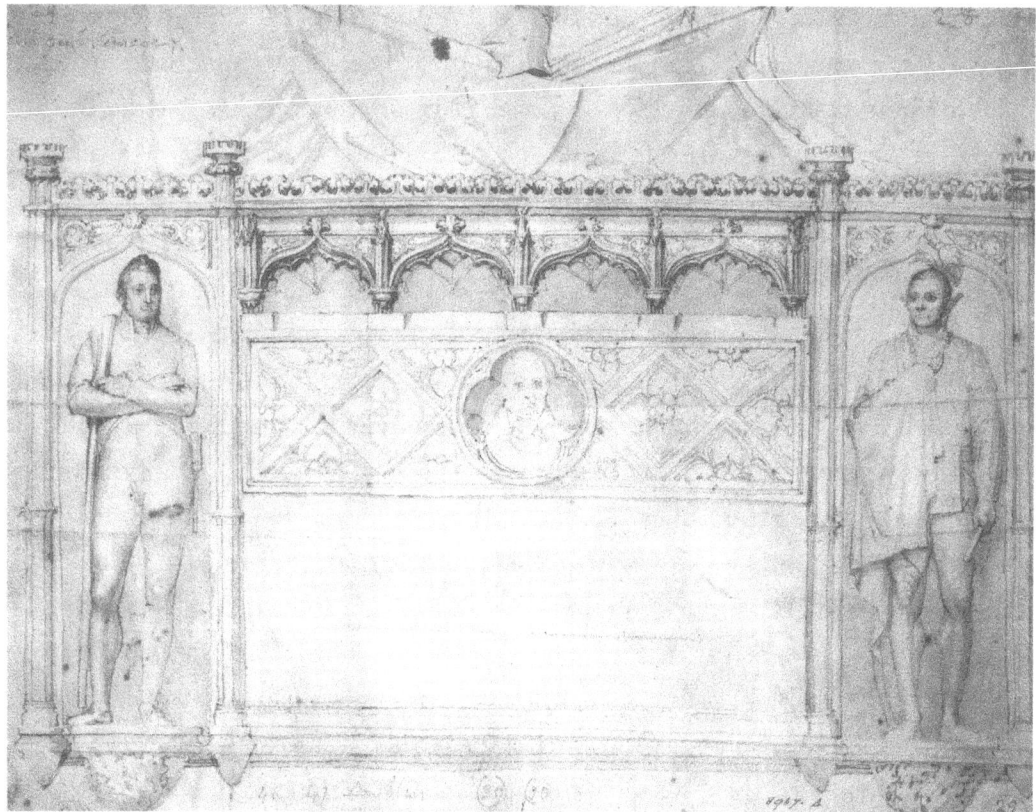

Fig. 4.2. John Flaxman, "Simcoe Memorial," study, pen and ink on paper, ca. 1814, Victoria and Albert Museum, London. Photo © Copyright V&A Images, London.

What has been lost in the reduction of the Northeastern Woodlands Indian's detailed finery, and thus the "exotic" quality of the work, has been gained in the impact of the sculpture as a whole. Flaxman's use of the intervening space between the figures and the background gives harmony to the work. The American Indian figure occupies an important role in this sense in that he balances the composition and invites comparison with his compatriot, the Ranger, in the opposite niche. He stands alongside the other figure in companionship and mutual respect, just as he had done in life when he fought beside the British. In this respect, the Simcoe Memorial is a unique early-nineteenth-century celebration of the strategic importance of American Indians. At a time when most contemporary representations of Indians showed them as victims of the inevitable progress of European settlement, bringing cultural disintegration or even death in its wake, Flaxman's monument recalls the last moment when British and American Indian interests made common cause.

Another region that was drawn into conflict was the southern frontier along the borders with Tennessee, the Carolinas, and Georgia. Both the Cherokee and Creek nations who still occupied these regions were to a great extent forced by the new U.S. policies and actions away from "accommodationist" positions toward the pantribal and nativist forces growing in the northern areas and centered in the Shawnee polities.[30] The years 1790 and 1791 saw outbreaks of frontier aggression by several groups, and this unsettlement would find a driving force in the inter-tribal developments that led to a huge council at Glaize in present-day Ohio in 1792. The 1790s were further complicated by competition between Britain and Spain over residual colonial territories. Disputes between Spain and Britain in 1790–91 over the Northwest coast territories eventually led to another signed treaty between the European powers. However, Spain also held territories in the southern border areas stemming from its claims to Florida. Spanish colonialists worked to secure influence over the Creek Nation through contacts with Creek representatives such as Alexander MacGillivray.[31] Thus it seems clear that American Indian groups in this early post-Revolutionary period had a number of factors influencing their decisions and attitudes toward conflict. Loyalties in this scenario would inevitably become divided and insecure. This situation should be kept in mind when turning to a later instance of an American Indian "delegation" who presented themselves in Britain in 1790 as representatives and leaders of the Creek and Cherokee nations. A man named William Augustus Bowles, a British-born expatriate living in America who came to style himself as the commander in chief of the Creek and Cherokee nations, headed up this unofficial delegation. The delegation probably would not have received as much attention historically if their visit had not occasioned the production of several important and well-known examples of portraiture by distinguished artists of the day.

William Hodges, best known today for the work he produced as one of Captain Cook's artists, has had the portraits of two members of this Cherokee and Creek delegation that visited London in 1790 attributed to him (plate 12; fig. 4.3).[32]

The reasons for the visit were less based on frontier diplomacy of the kind seen in the delegations of 1710, 1730, and 1762 and more in terms of supplication for assistance. The American Indians in this party, led by Bowles, had been mobilized to defend their lands from encroachment and to assert American Indian land rights. "The avowed purpose of [the] . . . mission . . . was to solicit a supply of arms and ammunition for the PRESENT purpose of effectually repelling the inroads of some troublesome neighbors."[33] The phrase "troublesome neighbors" most likely refers to the Americans and not to any nearby British or Spanish enclaves. Bowles's main objective, and those of his Creek and Cherokee compatriots, was to "attempt the reduction of Mexico," according to contemporary accounts. In return, the Indian men promised they could raise several tens of thousands of warriors and that if England would help them, "the new world would be a certain conquest, and open a source of trade and wealth to this nation, that will more than compensate for the loss of America."[34] Perhaps some of these factors may have been in the mind of Lord Dorchester, the governor of Lower Canada, when he arranged a safe passage for the group from his power base along the St. Lawrence River. Contemporary reports of a sudden "sharp contest" between the Creeks and the Americans and Spanish over boundaries, which curtailed the delegation's visit and sent them racing home to fight, are indicative of the volatility of the frontier in the early 1790s.[35] More specifically, however, the Creek Nation may have been aware of the calls sent out by Shawnee leaders at Glaize in Ohio country for a great council (held eventually in 1792) to unify all Indian peoples north to south along one boundary line.[36]

Bowles's arrival in London with five companions, listed in contemporary accounts as Unatoy, Kuohtekiske, Seponejah, Luskeniah, and Wassoe, attempted to reenact some of the elements that had gone into the earlier diplomatic Indian visits. The group attended the theater at Covent Garden and viewed St. Paul's Cathedral with "curiosity and amazement." It has long been thought that two members of the delegation had their portraits painted by the distinguished artist and royal academician William Hodges.[37] In addition, in some of the documents related to this group, Bowles is referred to as "Commander-in-Chief of the Creek and Cherokee nations," a phrase that calls to mind the earlier delegation language

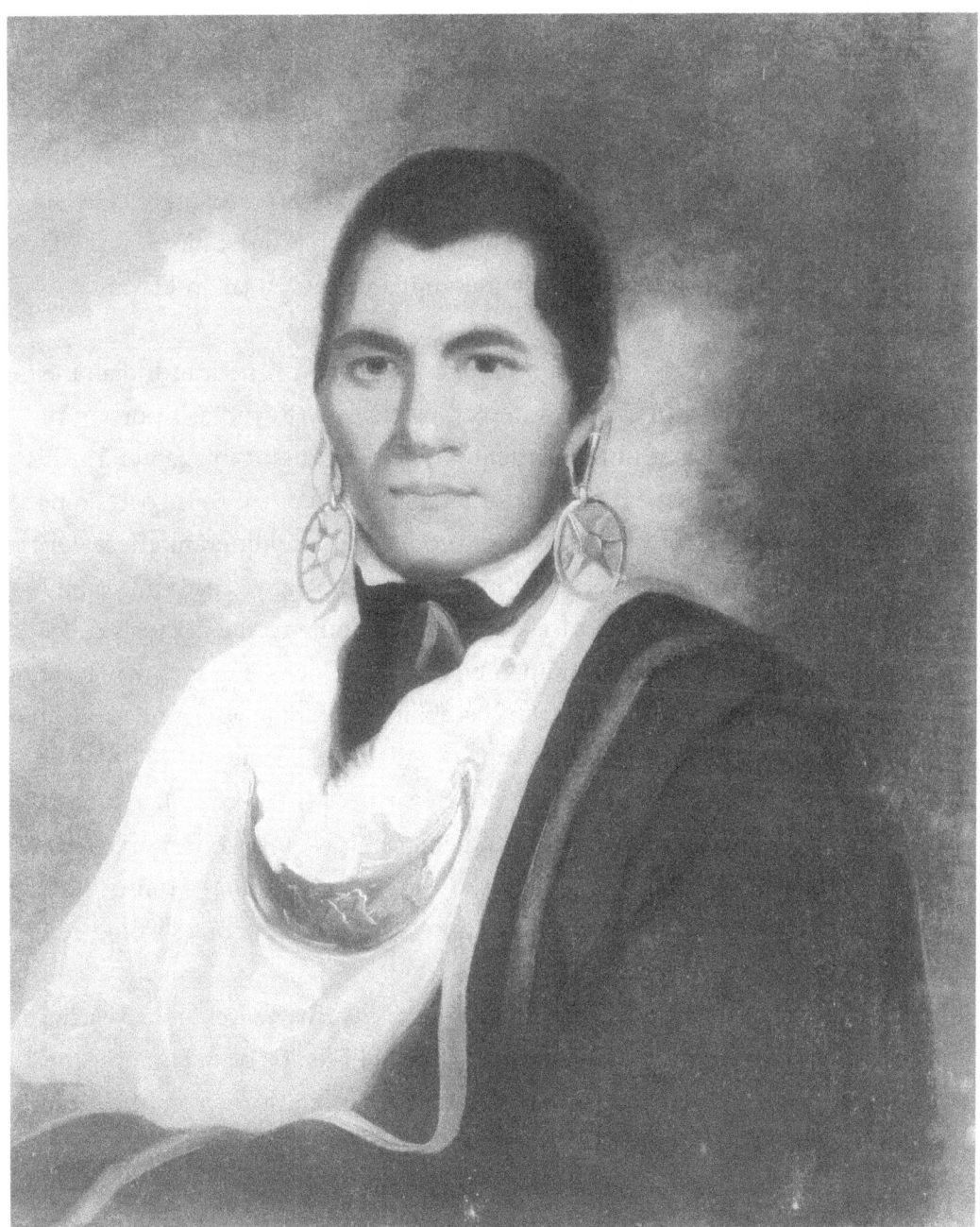

Fig. 4.3. William Hodges, *A Cherokee Man*, oil on canvas, 1790–91, Hunterian collection, the Royal College of Surgeons, London. Reproduced by the kind permission of the President and Council of the Royal College of Surgeons of England.

and the honorific references to the Indian leaders in them. However, King George IV did not receive the Cherokee and Creek delegates; neither were they allotted the title and status of king, emperor, or *miko*.[38] Statements made at the time of their visit suggest that Bowles was merely an adventurist and intriguer who had somehow inveigled his way into the Creek and Cherokee communities. (He had married a Creek headman's daughter.) The American opinion of him was highly critical and negative, and his later arrest and imprisonment in jail in Havana brought on an early death in 1805.

The portraits attributed to William Hodges of the two American Indian men have much in common with earlier examples, particularly Reynolds's portrait of Outacity, whose relaxed and unthreatening pose was discussed in chapter 2. This commission, however, stems from quite different interests than those pertaining to Reynolds's work, which was intended to produce a quite different effect. Dr. John Hunter, a surgeon with a particular interest in comparative anatomy, commissioned the paintings. Hodges's portraits would contribute to the doctor's collection of representative examples of human types as specimens. Hodges may have been awarded the commission because of his ability to work in a scientific context, as he had demonstrated on Cook's second voyage to the Pacific in 1772–74. Bowles's group met Hunter at a party given by Sir Joseph Banks; as Banks had accompanied Hodges on Cook's second expedition, it is quite conceivable that Banks recommended Hodges to Hunter as the artist for the job.[39] Hunter would have reckoned that Hodges's experience in portraying Pacific peoples would equip him well to work on the Cherokee portraits.

Both Cherokee men exhibit similar details of dress, such as silver looped earrings, a gorget, white European-made shirts, and draped cloaks (or blankets) over their left shoulders. In this way, the two portraits do not differ greatly from the earlier examples that combined American Indian dress with European fashions and represented an acceptable costume in which to be presented at court and in society. Despite the overall similarity of pose and appearance, the two sitters are distinguished from one another in facial expression and physiognomy. Of course, this was also true of the men in the 1762 Cherokee delegation whose portraits were painted by Reynolds (Outacity) and Parsons (Cunneshote). But the crucial distinction lies in the fact that Reynolds and Parsons were painting portraits of named individuals, whereas Hodges was painting members of a tribe. Significantly, neither of the sitters is identified, and the portraits are referred to today only as Cherokee and Creek representatives. The distinctions to be drawn between the sitters are effectively physiological rather psychological. Hodges was to record bone structure and skin tone and to demonstrate its variety in one American community. That each individual possessed a name, a history, and a political ambition was not, for Hunter, an essential consideration. Yet Hodges was no servile artist, as his work in the Pacific attests, and within the strictures of comparative anatomy he manages to express something more than a generic type. The use of a formal portrait mode and a skilled deployment of painterly modeling confer on both sitters a personalized presence somewhat at odds with Hunter's scientific needs. The interrogative gaze of one of the sitters, in particular, seems to ask a question of his viewers and in this regard, at least, forces the spectator to engage with him as an individual rather than merely inspecting him as would be the case were he only an ethnographical specimen (see fig. 4.3). Nonetheless, this individuation only goes so far. The sitter has no name and is painted as a representative of an anatomical and even prototypical racial type.[40] Hodges did not exhibit his two portraits, but portraits of William Augustus Bowles by Samuel Drummond and Thomas Hardy were exhibited at the Royal Academy in 1792. Bowles at least secured the recognition he sought, but if he received the major share of attention during their visit, one picture at least records the Cherokee men as part of the general fashionable London scene of that year.

Peter Francis Bourgeois's *The Inside of a Rotunda in The Bank of England with Several Portraits of Polish Noblemen and Ladies, the Cherokee Chiefs and other figures* was exhibited at the Royal Academy in 1791 (fig. 4.4). The picture shows two American Indian figures to the right of the doorway leading into the rotunda of the Bank of England, where several elaborately dressed figures promenade among some distinguished bystanders. The setting of the bank may refer to preliminaries to the negotiations for the financial aid the delegation required. It seems likely that these two figures are the same men whose portraits were painted by Hodges, although they appear here to be more elaborately accoutred than on that occasion.

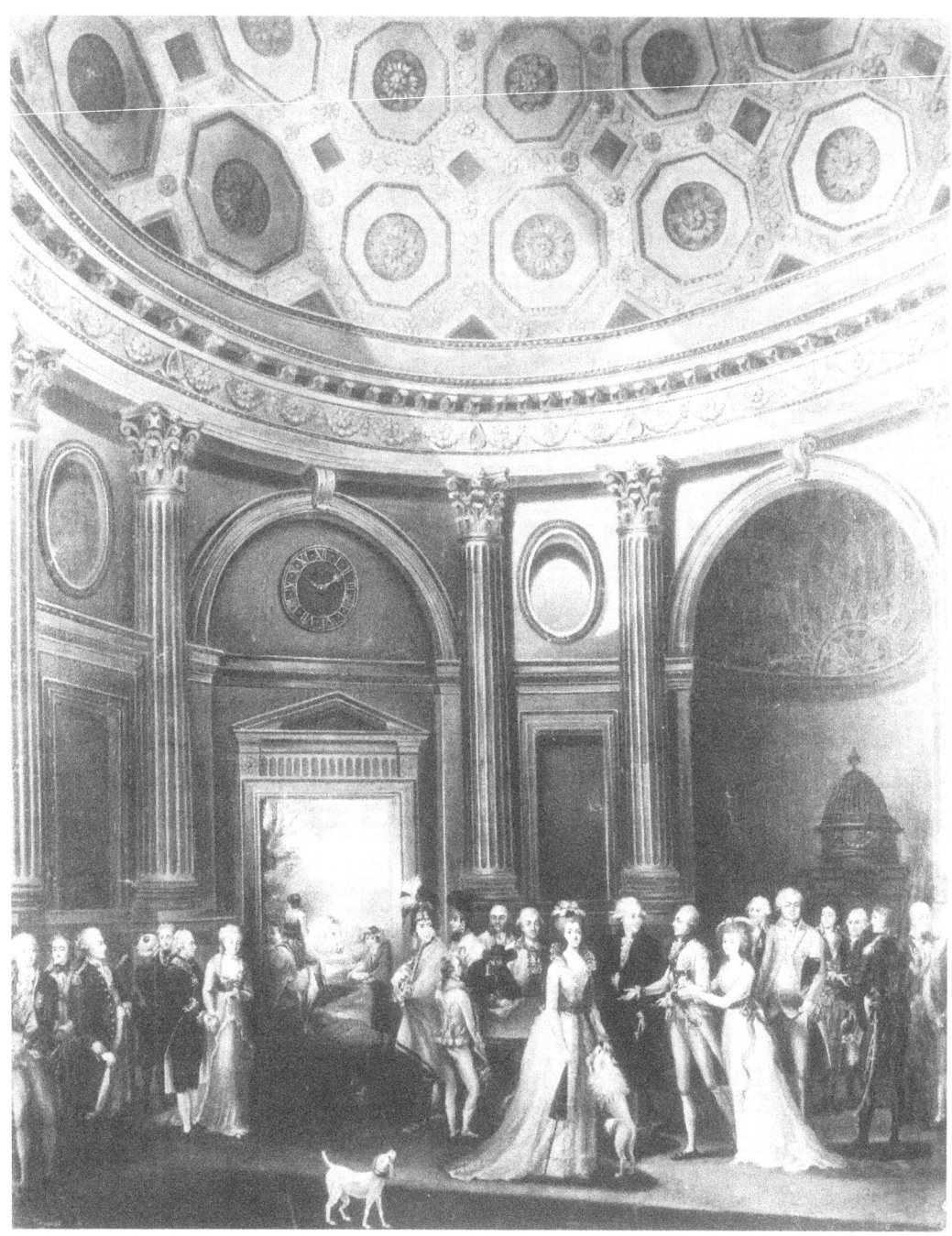

Fig. 4.4. Peter Francis Bourgeois, *The Inside of a Rotunda in The Bank of England with Several Portraits of Polish Noblemen and Ladies, the Cherokee Chiefs and other figures*, oil on canvas, 1790–91, National Museum in Warsaw, Poland. Courtesy of the National Museum of Warsaw.

Linking the two sets of images are the earrings, worn by the Indian figure on the left in Bourgeois's group portrait and prominently displayed on both figures in Hodges's work.

Bourgeois's picture brings to mind an earlier painting by Willem Verelst, *The Common Council of Georgia Receiving the Indian Chiefs* of 1734–35, in which James Edward Oglethorpe, first governor of Georgia, is shown presenting a group of Yamacraw Indians (or possibly Yuchi and Cherokee) to the trustees of that colony (plate 13).[41] Both the Verelst and the Bourgeois paintings give some indication of the public attention paid to these delegations and at once indicate the difference between an artist's presentation of a public spectacle and the private face recorded by Hodges. But significantly, the Verelst painting is a record of a diplomatic success, which helped secure a lasting alliance between the British and one division of the local Native people living near Savannah in the colony of Georgia. In contrast to this, Bowles did not have the overall consent of the entire Creek and Cherokee nations that he claimed to have for his mission. Thus the party occasioned interest more as a "curiosity" than as a serious diplomatic initiative. This lack of serious or officially sanctioned treatment was consistent with the post-Versailles situation of American Indians, who were no longer at the center of diplomatic and military concerns in Britain.

There is a certain incongruity to Bourgeois's scene in the rotunda of the Bank of England, with the Cherokees and Creeks being both distinguishable and yet pushed to the edges of the fashionable groups being represented. It is as if the artist was captivated by the obvious contrast between the European nobility, as represented by the Polish prince and others, and those whose supposed nobility came from another source, far removed and different to that existing in Europe. The French Revolution had toppled the ancien régime in 1789, and the effects of such a turnaround in hierarchies were only beginning to be felt two years later. American Indian leadership, which Europeans supposed arose from a natural consensus and derived from innate personal abilities, was seen as a powerful alternative to the idea of inherited nobility. Consider, for example, the introductory comments in William Bartram's "On Their Government and Civil Society" in his *Travels Through North and South Carolina, Georgia . . .*, first published in 1791. He states that the constitution or system of their police is simply natural, and as little complicated as that which is supposed to direct or rule the approved economy of the ant and the bee; and seems to be nothing more than the simple dictates of natural reason, plain to every one, yet recommended to them by their wise and virtuous elders as divine, because necessary for securing mutual happiness: equally binding and effectual, as being proposed and assented to in the general combination: every one's conscience being a sufficient conviction (the golden rule, do as you would be done by) instantly presents to view, and produces a society of peace and love, which in effect better maintains human happiness, than the most complicated system of modern politics, or sumptuary laws, enforced by coercive means: for here the people are all on an equality, as to the possession and enjoyments of the common necessaries and conveniences of life, for luxuries and superfluities they have none.[42]

Bartram's comments both recapitulate the old primitivist tradition, discussed in the introduction, and acknowledge a new understanding of American Indians. Those peoples who had been seen precisely as military and political allies in the circumstances of the Seven Years' War are now to be regarded as innocent children of nature. For all their enlightened example offered to modern Europe, Bartram's Indians are not conceived as a modern people who might negotiate with governments and fight alongside regular troops. Instead, they are relegated to the confines of history and a growing sense of archaeology, whereby one could step back in time on viewing their example and see a case of living history, showing the viewer from whence modern people had come and how the new modern world was very different to that which had existed in the past.

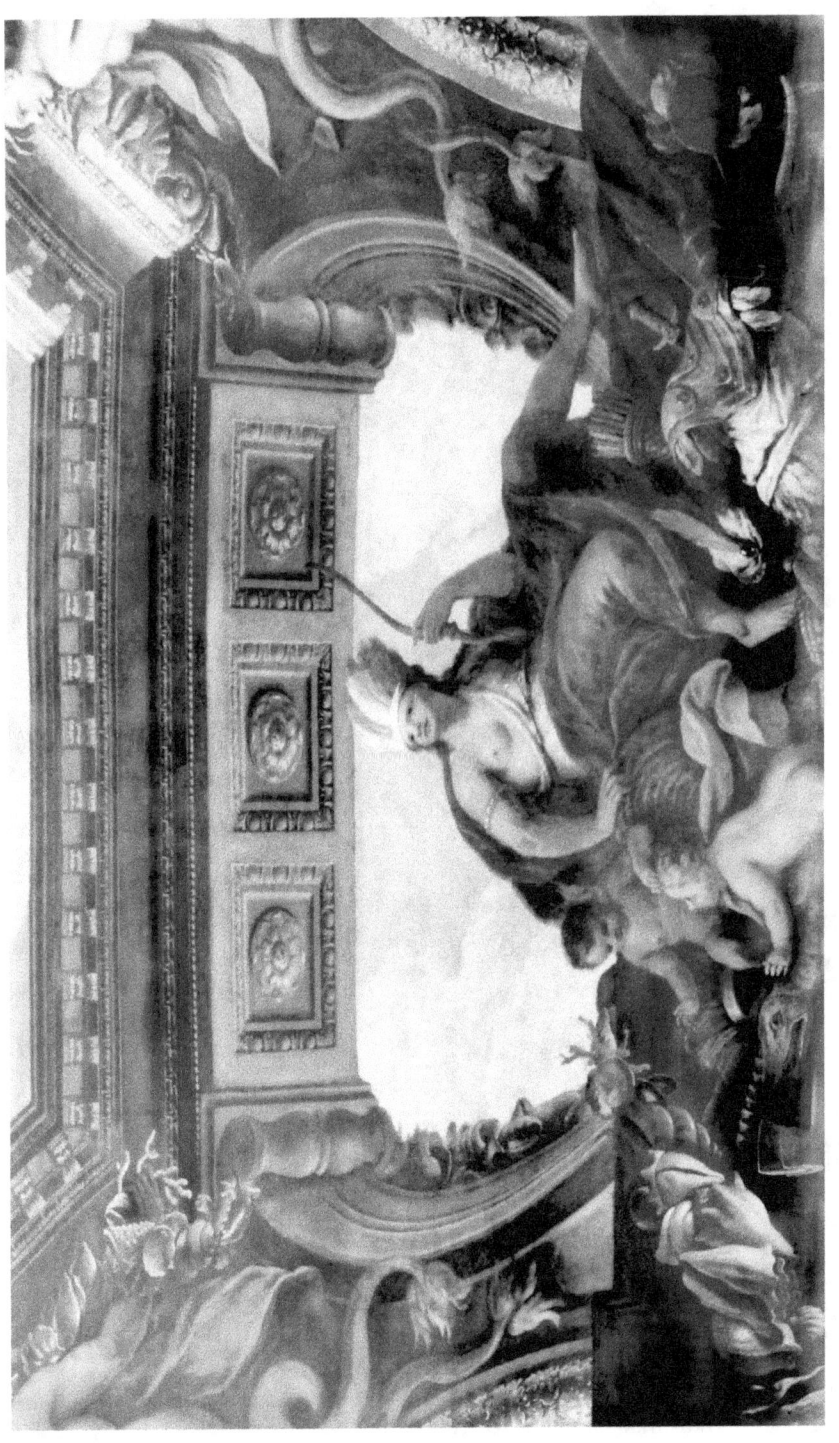

Plate 1. Sir James Thornhill, *America*, part of the painted ceiling with the *Four Continents Paying Tribute*, oil on plaster, 1718–25, cove, Upper Hall, Painted Hall, Royal Naval College, Greenwich, Kent. Photo by Ian Wood.

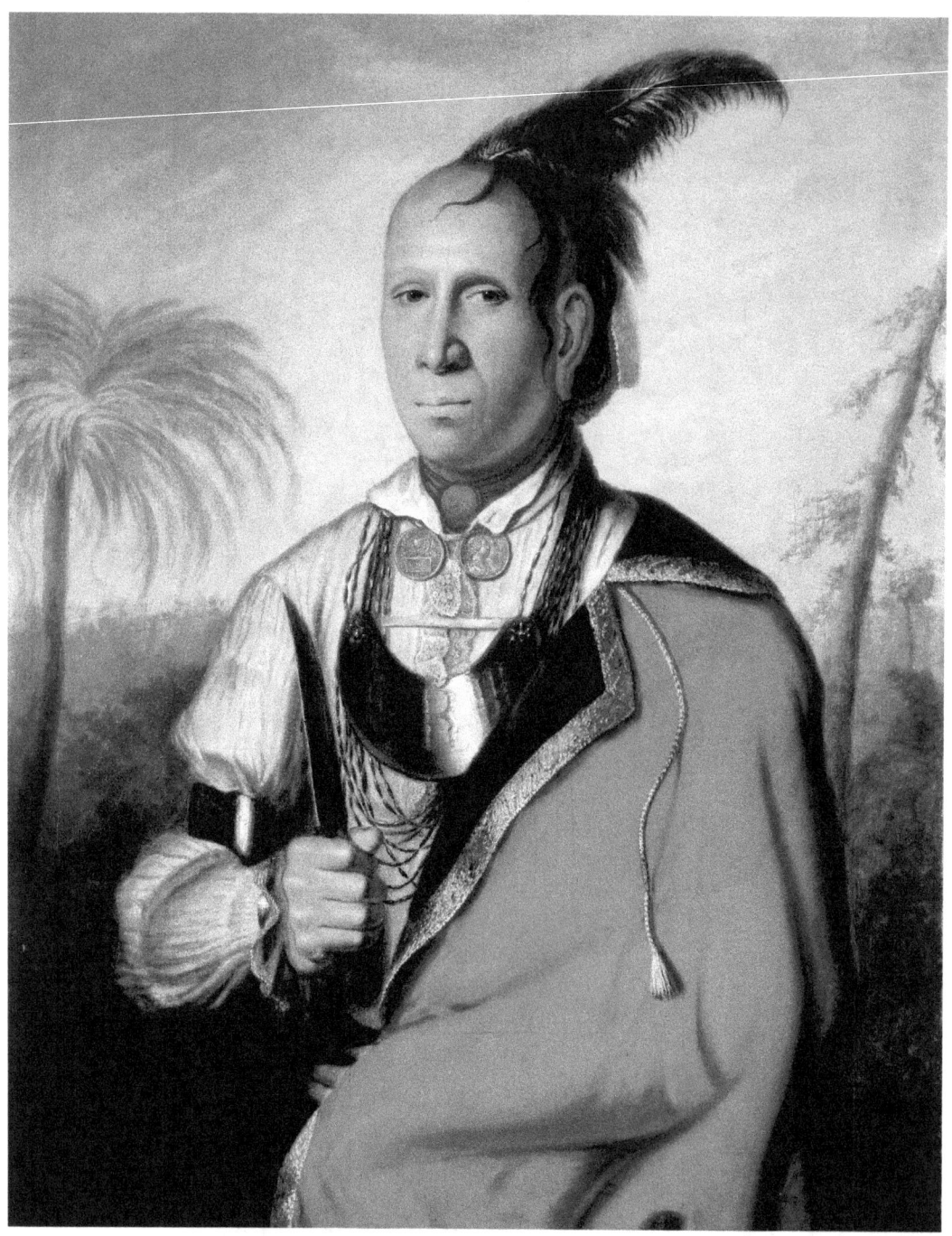

Plate 2. Francis Parsons, *Cunneshote*, oil on canvas, 1762, from the collection of the Gilcrease Museum, Tulsa, Oklahoma. Courtesy of the Gilcrease Museum.

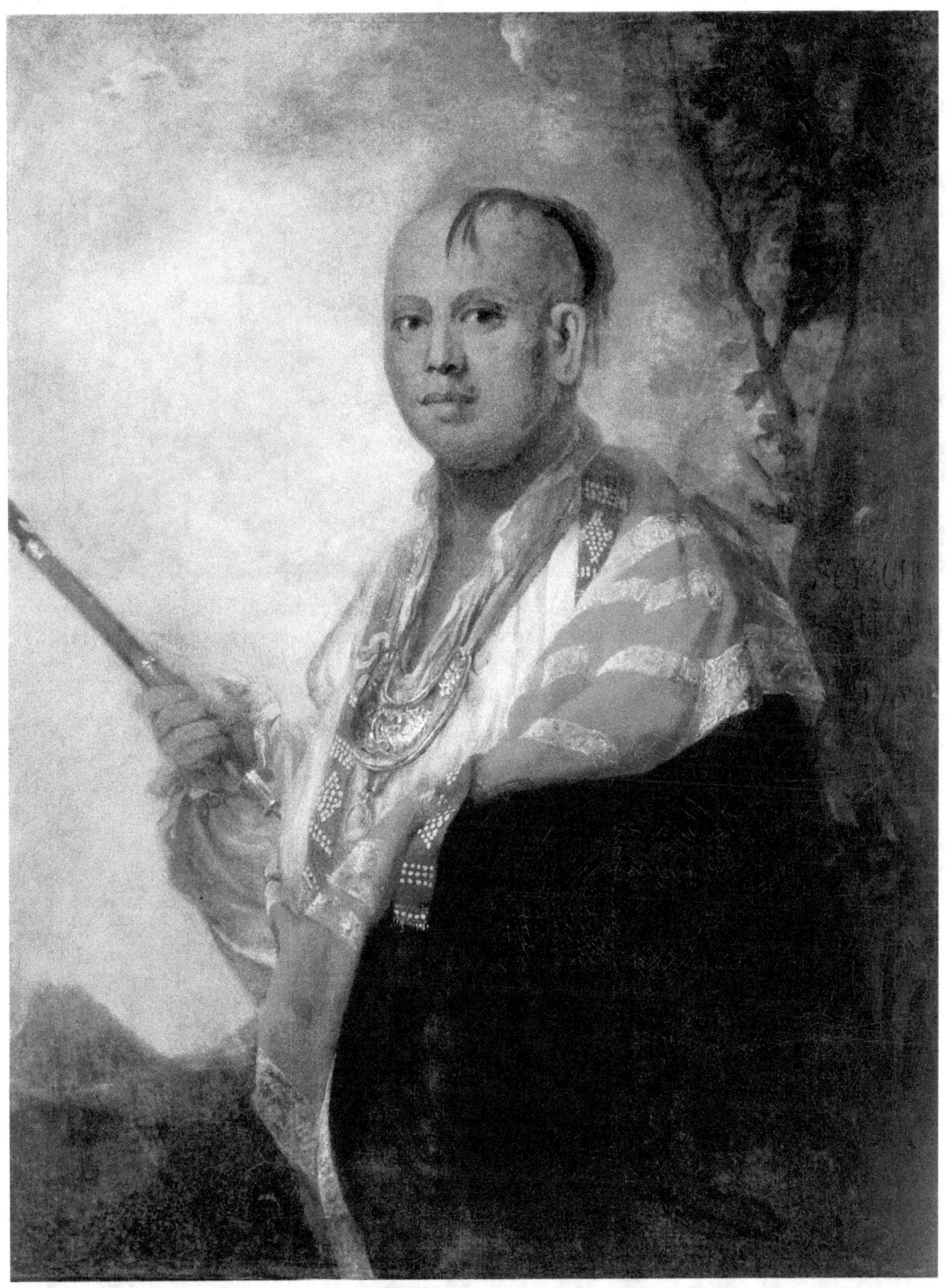

Plate 3. Joshua Reynolds, *Scyacust Ukah*, oil on canvas, 1762, from the collection of the Gilcrease Museum, Tulsa, Oklahoma, Courtesy of the Gilcrease Museum.

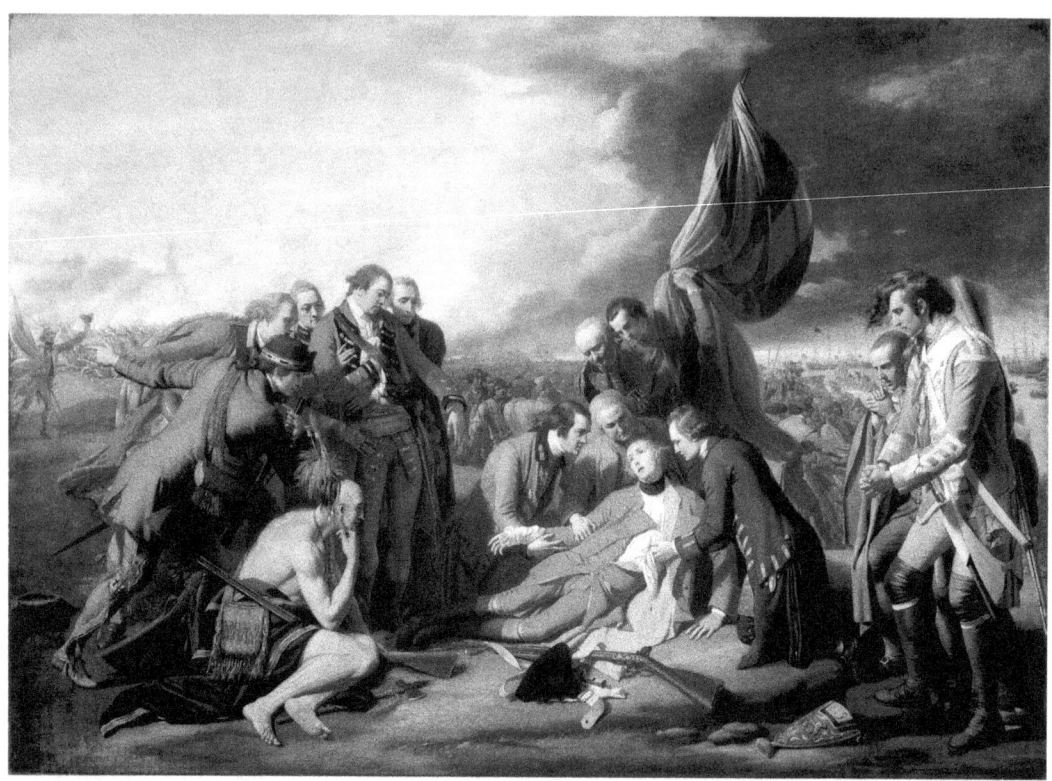

Plate 4. Benjamin West, *The Death of General Wolfe*, oil on canvas, 1770–71, the National Gallery of Canada, Ottawa, gift of the Duke of Westminster. Courtesy of the National Gallery of Canada.

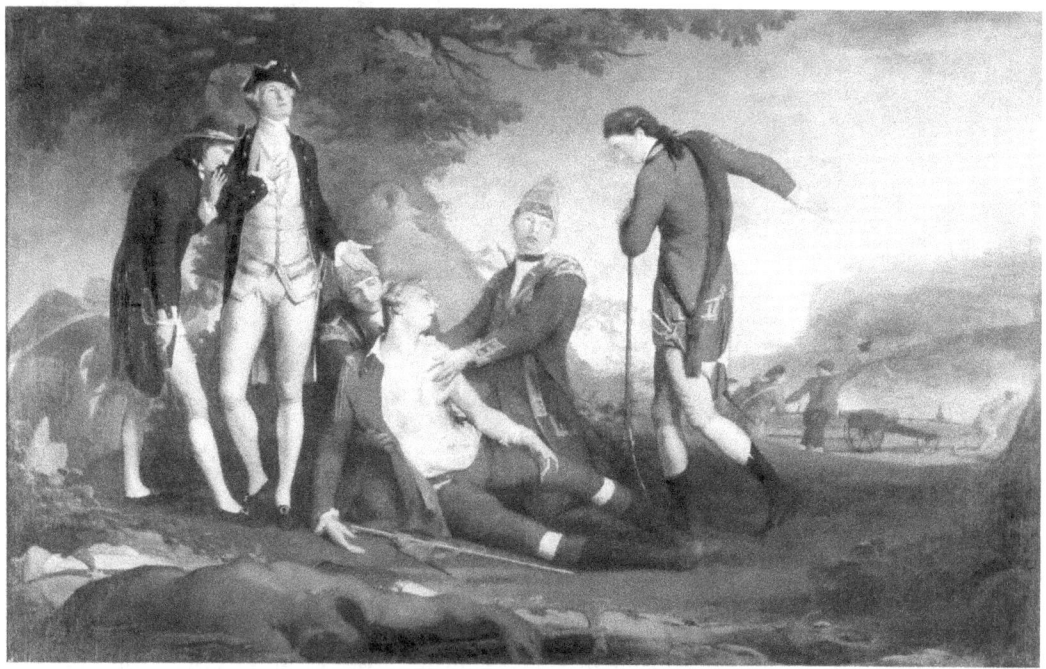

Plate 5. James Barry, *The Death of General Wolfe*, oil on canvas, 1776, John C. Webster Collection W1987, New Brunswick Museum, St. John, New Brunswick. Courtesy of the New Brunswick Museum.

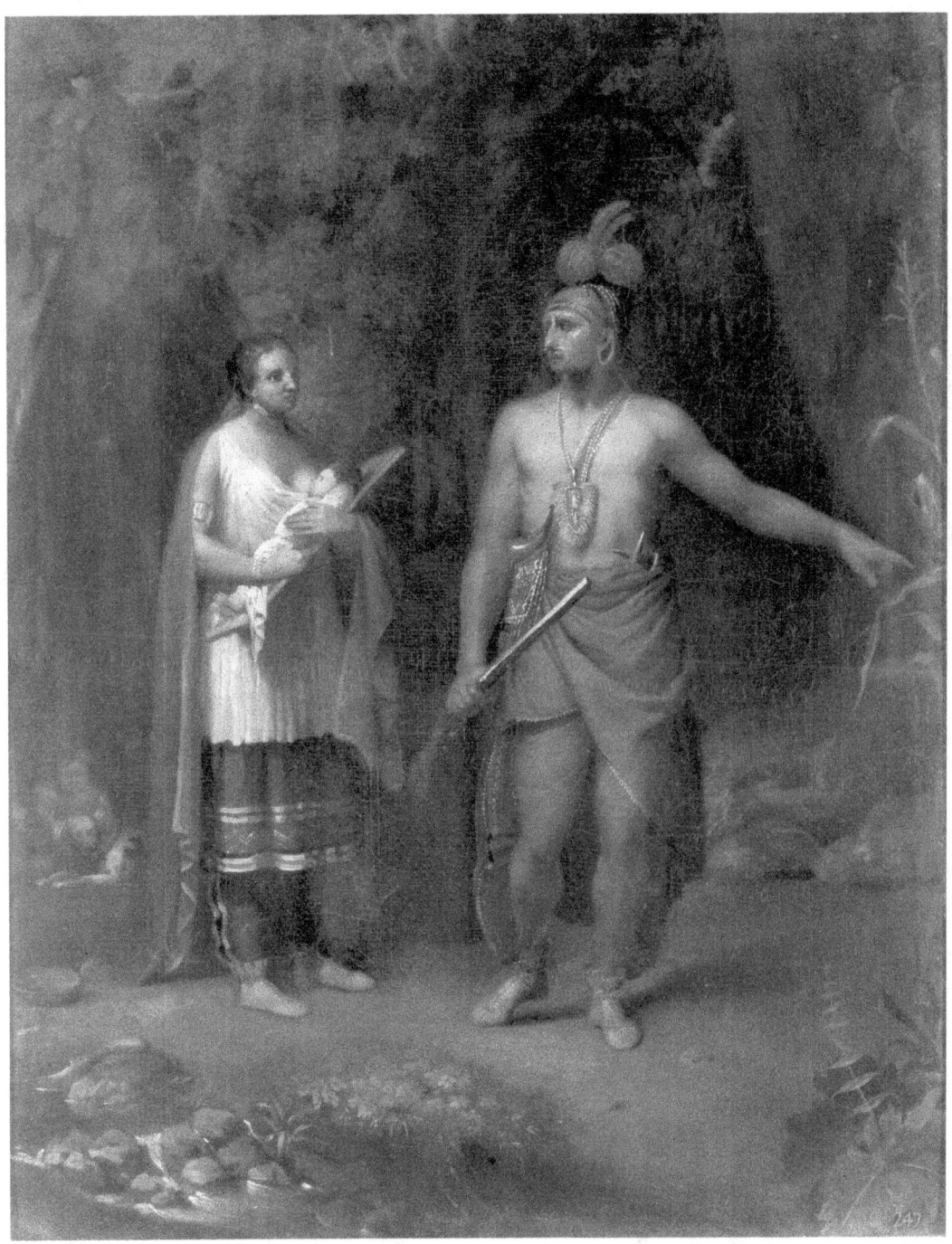

Plate 6. Benjamin West, *The Indian Family*, oil on canvas, ca. 1761, Hunterian Collection, the Royal College of Surgeons of England, London. Reproduced by the kind permission of the president and council of the Royal College of Surgeons of England.

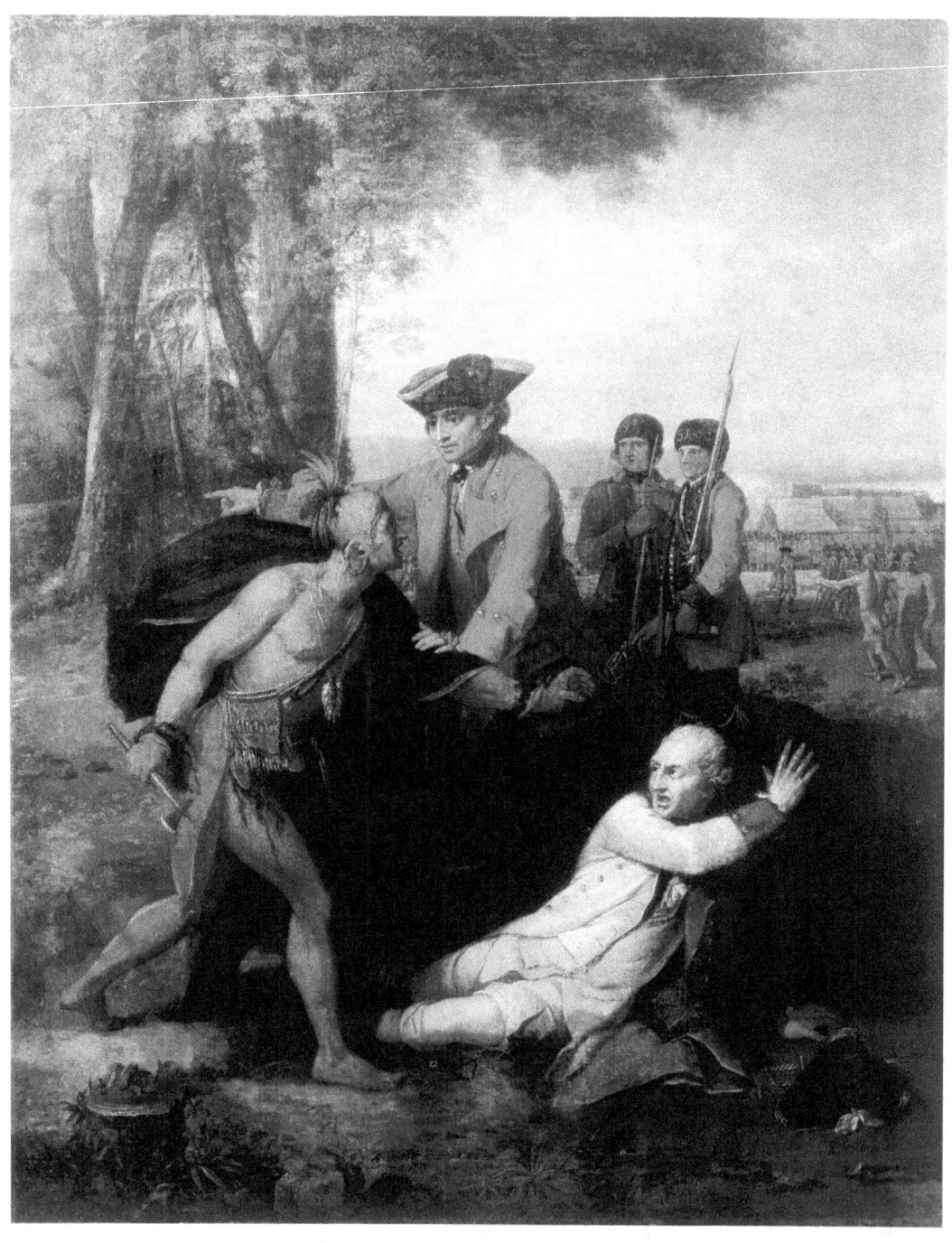

Plate 7. Benjamin West, *General Johnson Saving a Wounded French Officer from the Tomahawk of a North American Indian*, oil on canvas, 1762–65, Derby Museum and Art Gallery, Derby, United Kingdom. Photo © Copyright the Derby Museum and Art Gallery.

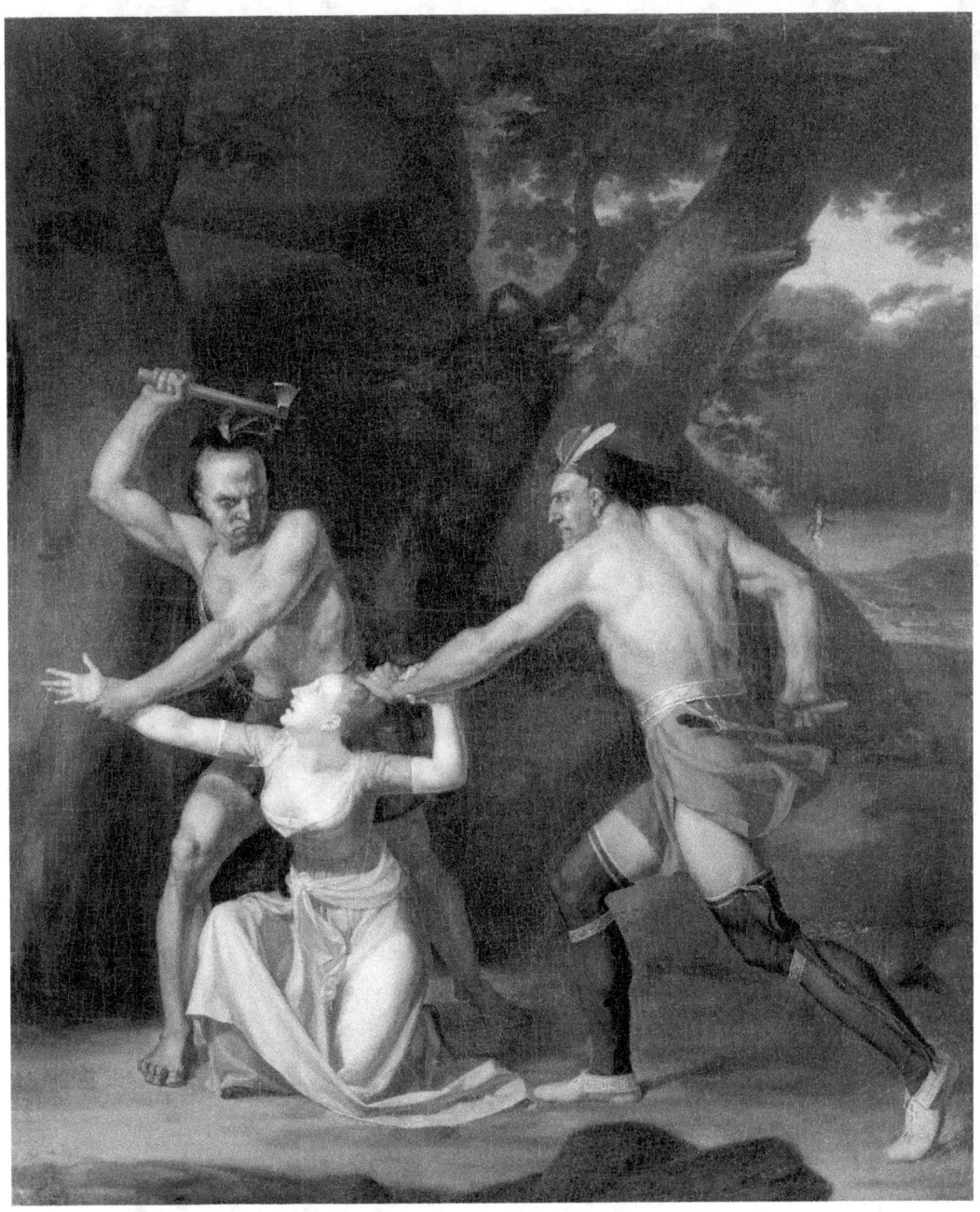

Plate 8. John Vanderlyn, *The Death of Jane MacCrea*, oil on canvas, 1803–4, accession # 1855.4, Wadsworth Atheneum, Hartford. Purchased by the Wadsworth Atheneum. Courtesy of the Wadsworth Atheneum.

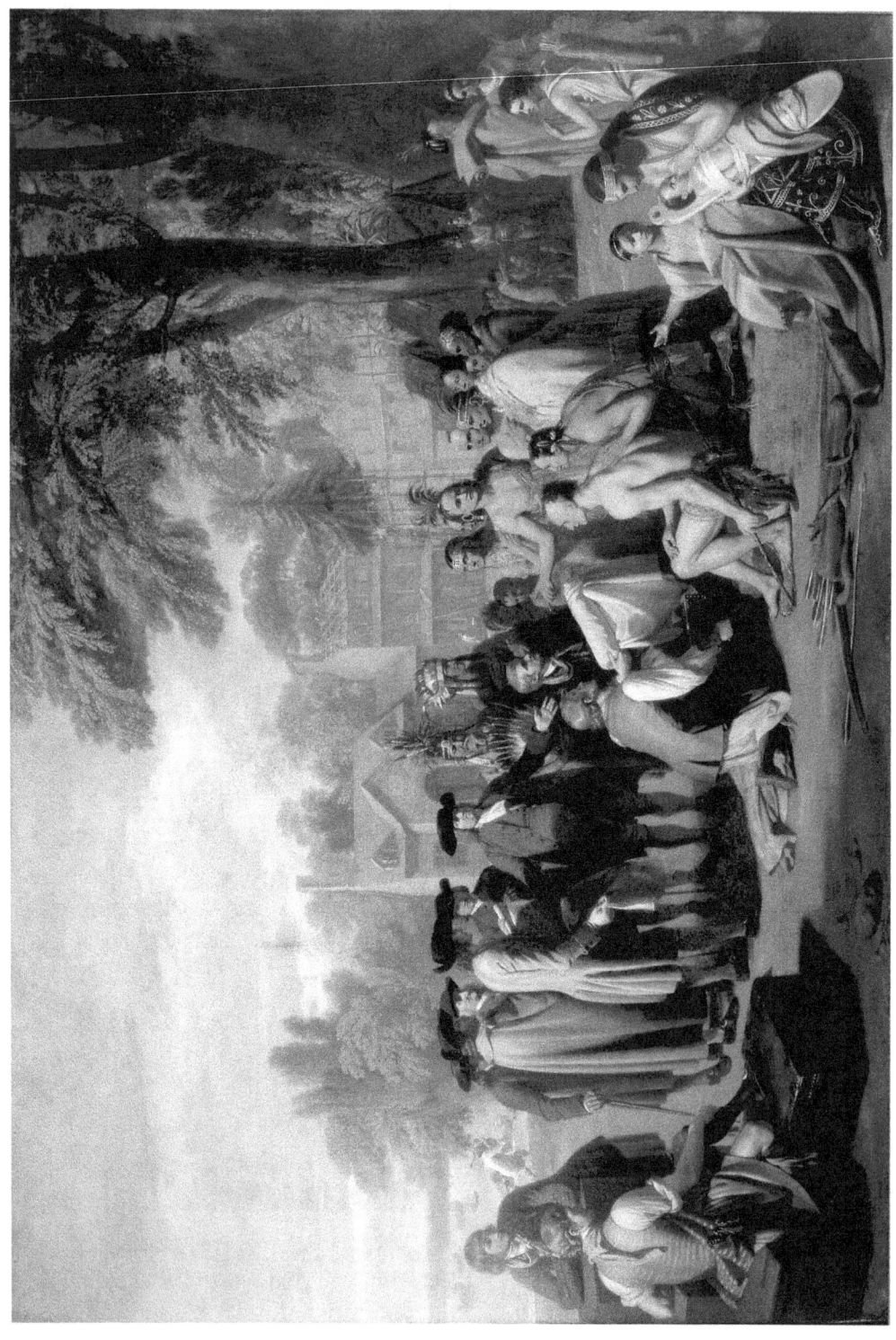

Plate 9. Benjamin West, *Penn's Treaty with the Indians*, oil on canvas, 1771–72, the Pennsylvania Academy of the Fine Arts, Philadelphia. Courtesy of the Pennsylvania Academy of the Fine Arts, Philadelphia. Gift of Mrs. Sarah Harrison (the Joseph Harrison, Jr., Collection).

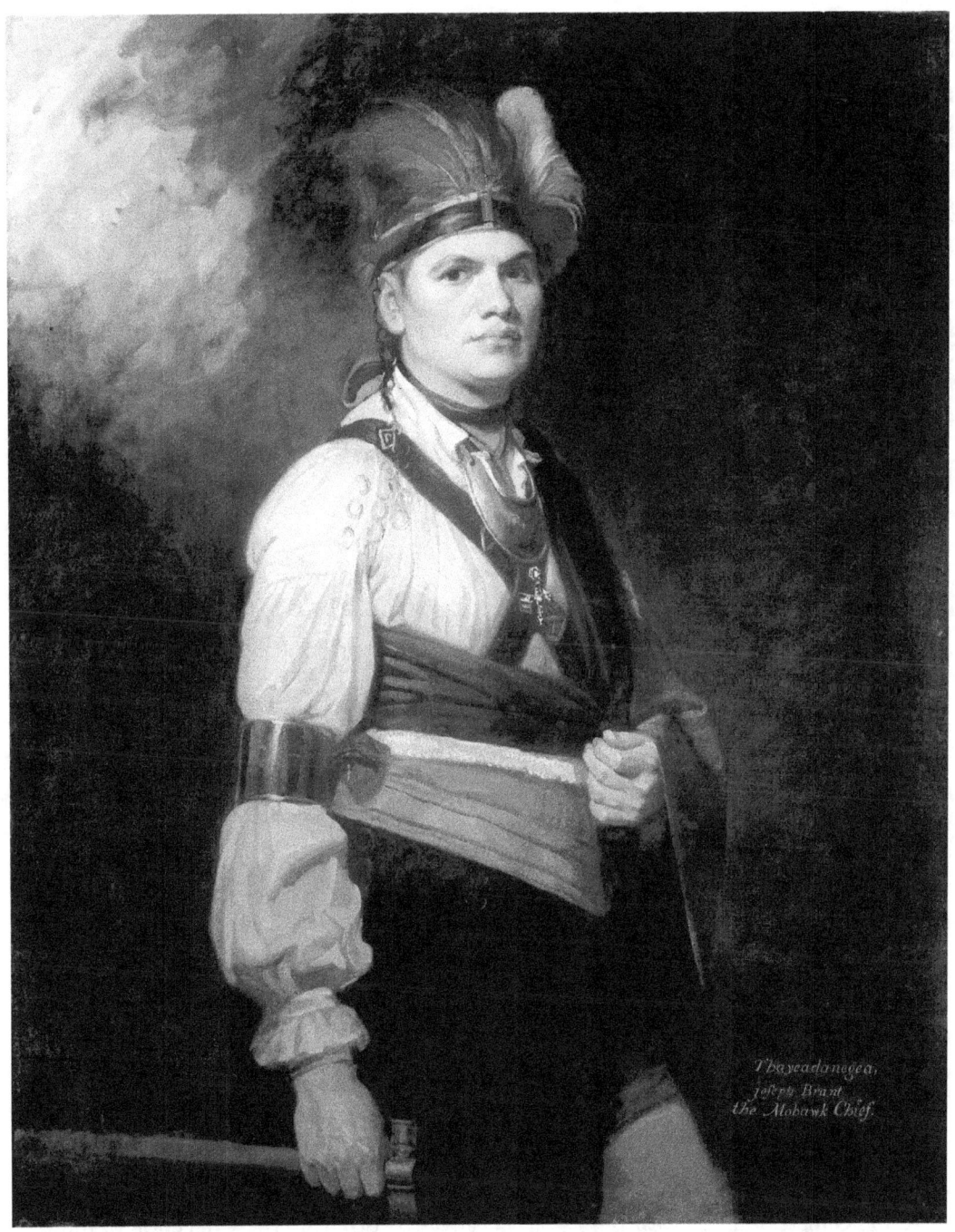

Thayeadanegea,
joseph Brant
the Mohawk Chief.

Plate 10. George Romney, *Joseph Brant—Thayendanegea*, oil on canvas, 1776, the National Gallery of Canada, Ottawa. Courtesy of the National Gallery of Canada.

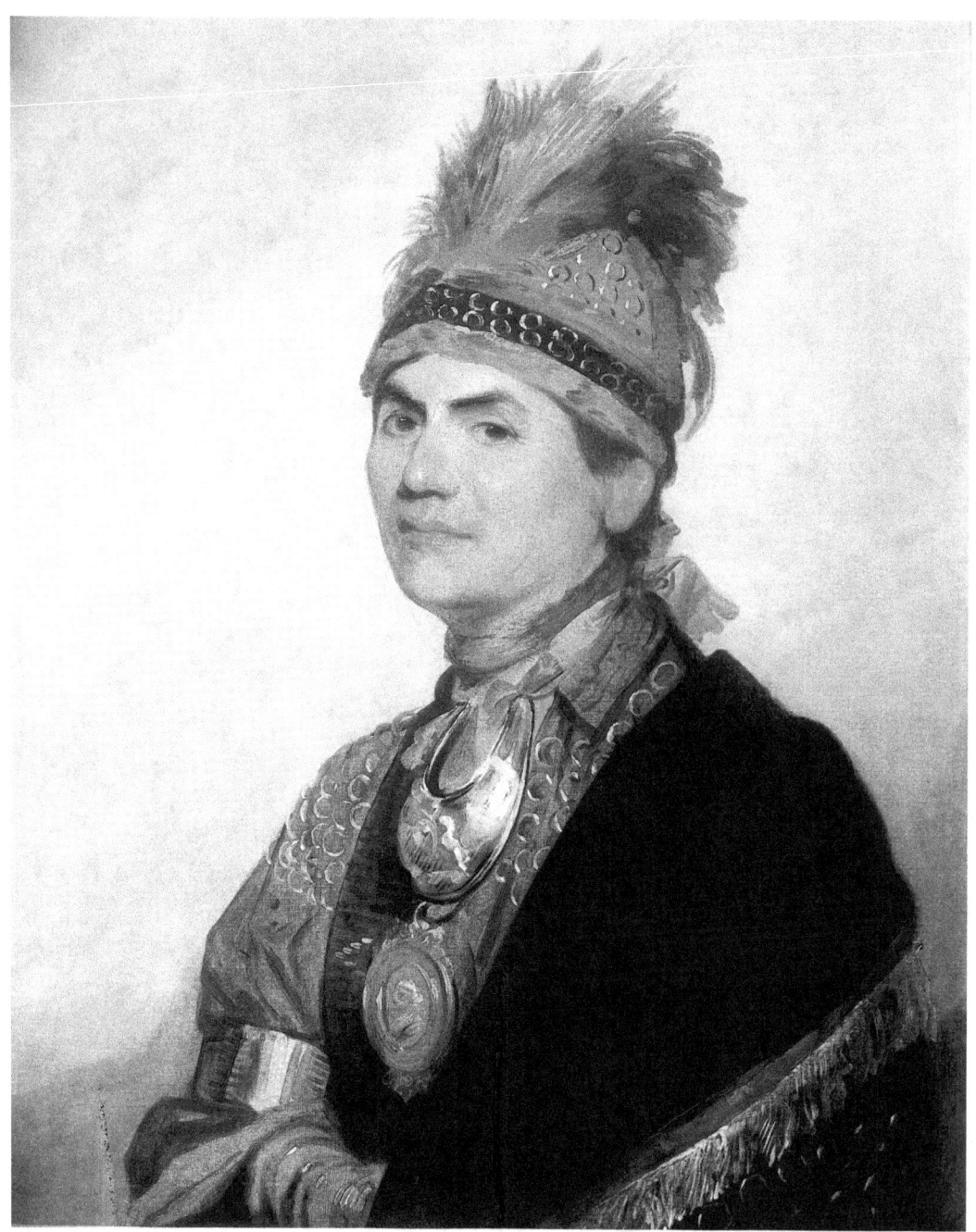

Plate 11. Gilbert Stuart, *Joseph Brant*, oil on canvas, 1786, from the Collection of the Duke of Northumberland, Syon House, London. Courtesy of Syon Park.

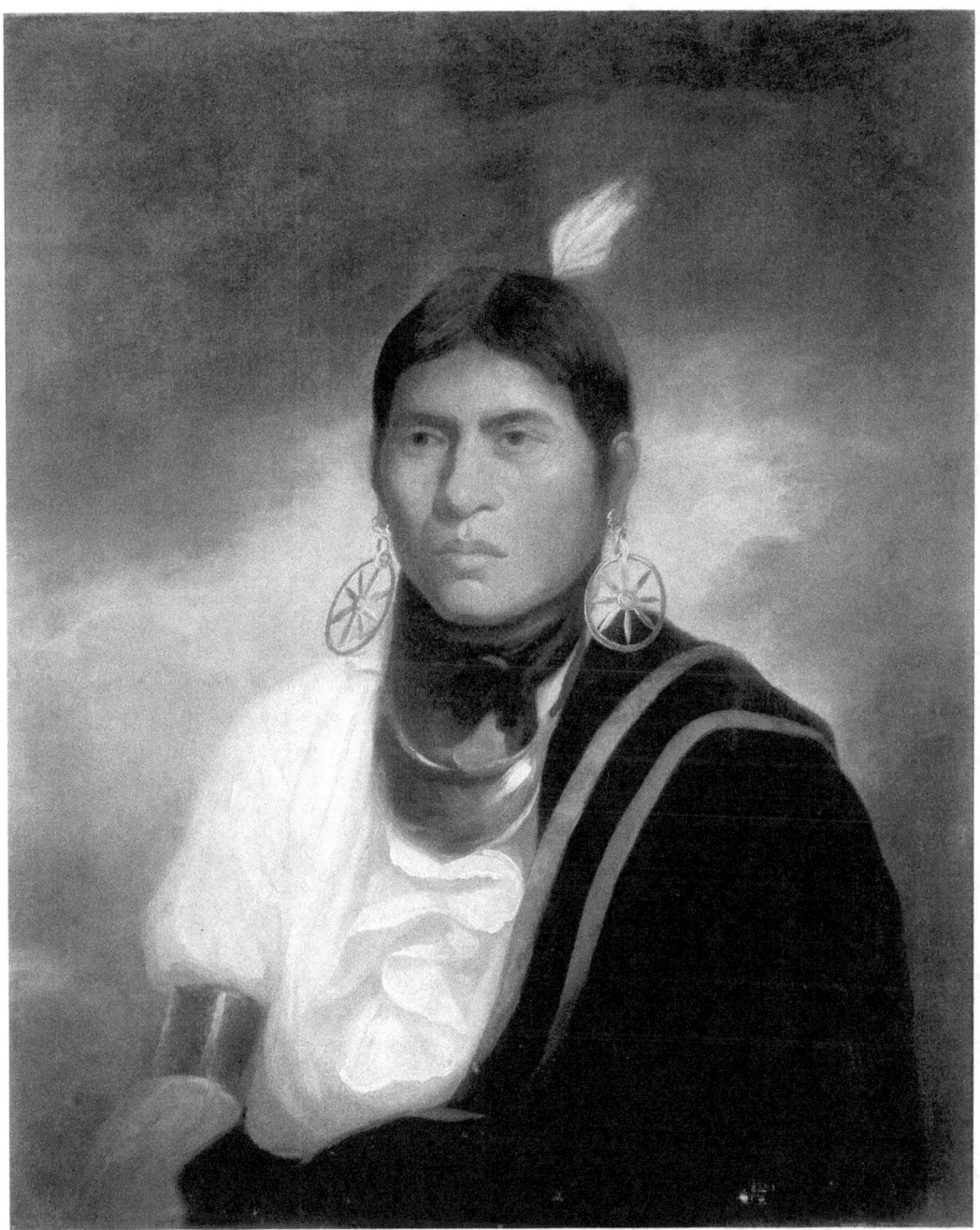

Plate 12. William Hodges, *A Cherokee (or Creek) Man*, oil on canvas, 1790–91, Hunterian Collection, the Royal College of Surgeons, London. Reproduced by the kind permission of the president and council of the Royal College of Surgeons of England.

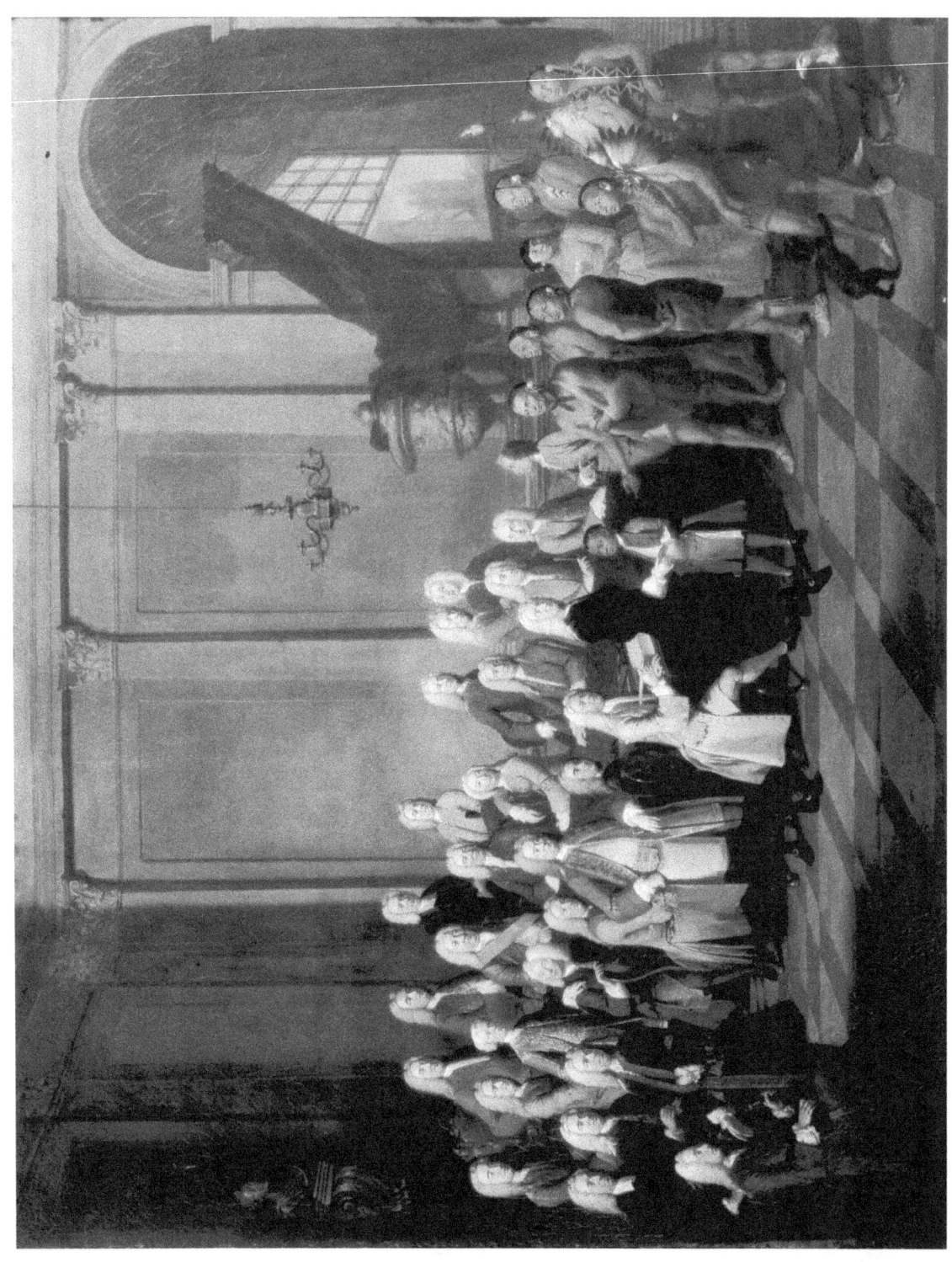

Plate 13. Willem Verelst , *The Common Council of Georgia Receiving the Indian Chiefs*, oil on canvas, 1734–35, a gift of Henry Francis Du Pont to the Winterthur Museum, Delaware. Courtesy of the Winterthur Museum.

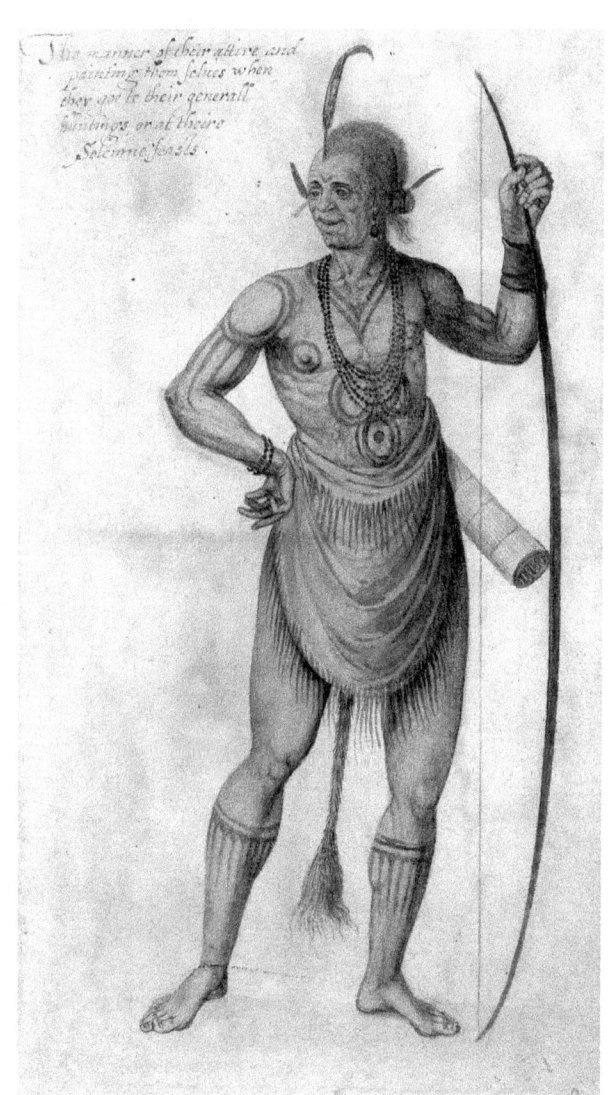

Plate 14. John White, *An Indian in Body Paint*, pen, ink, and watercolor, 1585, Prints and Drawings, The British Museum, London. Photo © Copyright The British Museum.

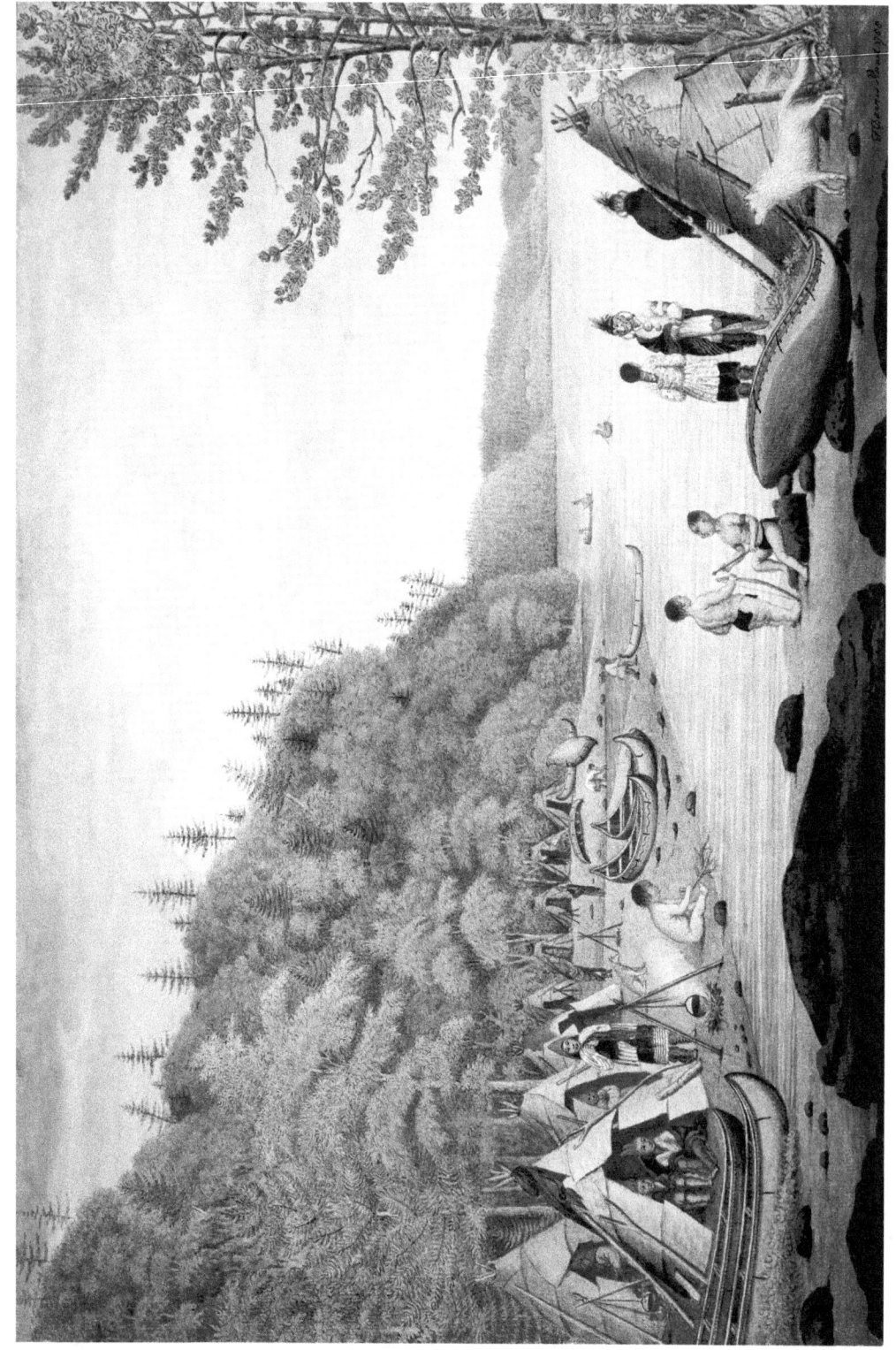

Plate 15. Thomas Davies, *A View near Point Levy Opposite Quebec with an Indian Encampment*, oil on canvas, 1788, the National Gallery of Canada, Ottawa. Courtesy of the National Gallery of Canada.

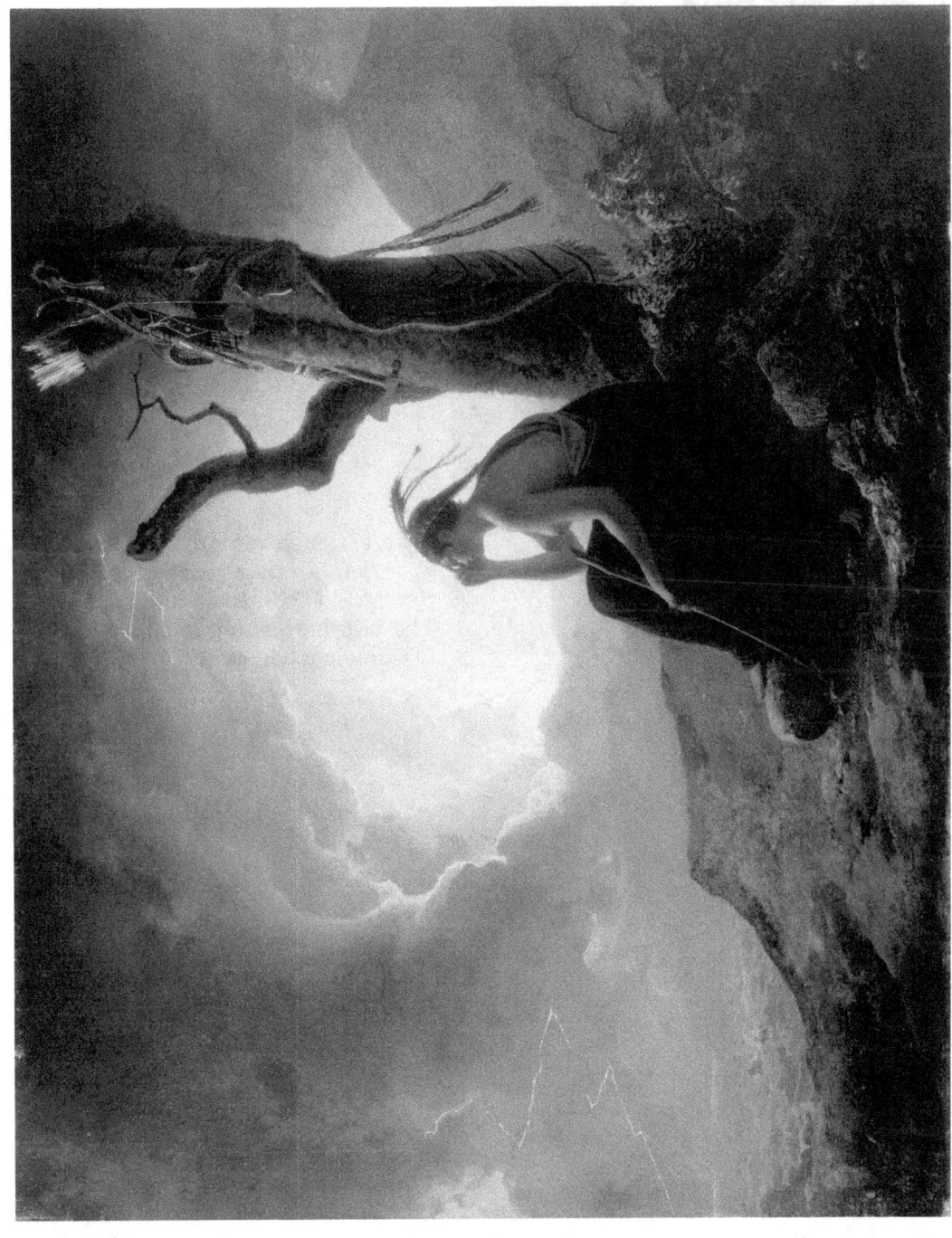

Plate 16. Joseph Wright of Derby, *The Indian Widow*, oil on canvas, 1783–85, Derby Museum and Art Gallery, Derby, United Kingdom. Photo © Copyright the Derby Museum and Art Gallery.

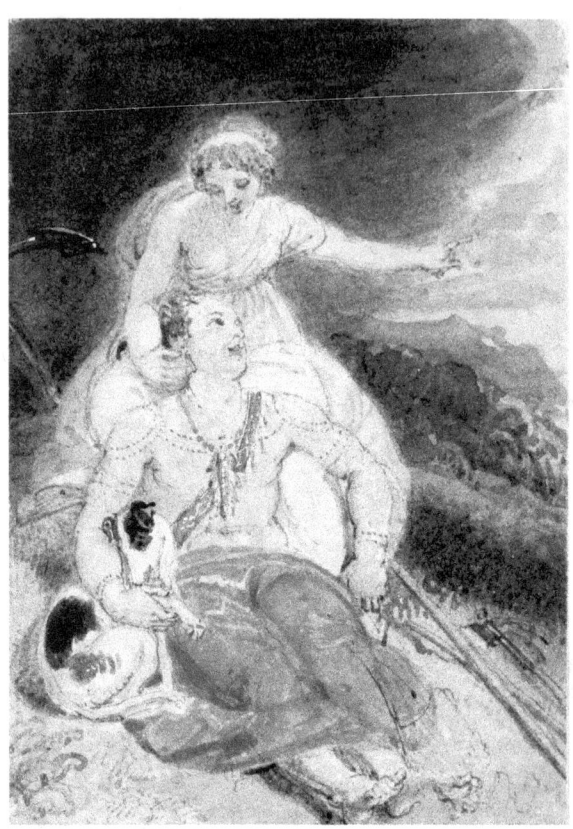

Plate 17. Thomas Stothard, *Lo! The Poor Indian*, watercolor and pen on paper, ca. 1790s, Prints and Drawings, The British Museum, London. Photo © Copyright The British Museum.

5   *Travel, Observation, and the Pathos of Decline*

ONE THEME THAT has emerged consistently in this book is the mediated nature of all the representations made of American Indians. From highly symbolic contexts, to history painting, to portraits of military and diplomatic figures, the artistic response can be shown to incorporate more than a simple visual response to the reality of American life. Indeed, to some extent these representations helped to construct that life in the minds of British viewers. In this final chapter, I examine representations of American Indians made in England over some forty years, the 1780s to the 1820s, concentrating especially on the theme of the "dying" Indian. In its construction of an image of cultural collapse, the dying Indian trope replaces any concern for the historical actuality of American Indian peoples with a more generalized and sentimental response to their existence and possible extinction.

It is tempting to link this emphasis with the loss of the American colonies following the Treaty of Paris in 1783. Certainly, with no direct involvement in the affairs of the United States, it is reasonable to suggest that interest in Indian peoples as active participants in Britain's affairs would decline. Yet as was shown in the preceding chapter, the administration of Canada included the welfare of the Indian communities living there, even if, as we shall see, many of them were deemed to have lost their nobility of spirit. For many witnesses, they were contaminated by too close a proximity to white settlement. Travel writers especially chose to comment on the degraded appearance of a once proud people.

These travel accounts can be linked, in their turn, with earlier voyages of "discovery." Notwithstanding our contemporary realization that travel literature was often corrupt, incorporating plagiarized or fictional material, it nevertheless offered its readers the promise of a direct engagement with cultures and environments far removed from their experience. Likewise, voyages of "discovery" were designed to accumulate data from remote or inaccessible regions for the benefit of education and edification back in England. Given the serious nature of these endeavors, the images produced by expeditionary artists seem to hold out the promise of a more direct engagement with American Indian culture. Disinterested and rational, here at least an unbiased witness might perhaps be found.

Initially, therefore, this chapter briefly examines some of the images derived from British expeditions to assess the effect such visual encounters had on general perceptions. Notwithstanding their origins in the desire for objective knowledge, even seemingly disinterested records are in fact contextualized by the circumstances of their production. This is not, of course, to deny the fact that these visual records have proved to be historically useful, routinely employed by today's scholars as evidence for understanding American Indian material culture, but it is to suggest that the expeditions were historically bound and responsive to contemporary circumstances. A proper consideration of voyage literature, expeditionary reports, and travel accounts of the Americas would require its own full-length account and is obviously beyond the scope of this book. What I hope to demonstrate, by making very abbreviated use of this material here, is how it contributes to the overall picture developed in the other chapters of this book. Placed alongside other manifestations of interest in American Indians, travel accounts helped to produce the idea of the Indian for readers at home. Their several accounts, ranging from sixteenth-century to nineteenth-century reports, chart the transition from fascination with the idea of the noble savage to the recording of a doomed race and observations of cultural contamination on the fringes of Anglo-American society.

Expeditions to America and the publications associated with them might best be understood as agents of the colonial situation. Accurate geographical surveys, analysis of flora and fauna, communication with the inhabitants, and a record of their way of life were certainly contributing to the general stock of human knowledge, but they also allowed an assessment of the new territory's peculiarities. The publication of an expedition's findings would not only represent a public exposure of what had been accomplished, it would also help disseminate the importance of the region and its potential for further investigation. The disinterested scientific account of the expedition, with its harvest of new information, was also the means by which other calculations of yield could be made.

This pattern can be detected early in the British exploration of America, in the example of the 1585 expedition to Virginia organized by Sir Walter Raleigh and led by Sir Richard Grenville, the commander of the flotilla of seven ships. On this important expedition to found a colony in America, visual representation was an important requirement, and the drawings in pen and watercolor by the voyage's artist, John White, still exist today as visual records of that encounter.[1] They, too, hold a special status as "ethnographic texts," being some of the earliest European images ever made of American Indians, but also because of their originality, extensiveness, and amount of detail (plate 14).[2] At the time of the Roanoke venture, Richard Hakluyt the elder was insisting that "a skilful painter" be taken on any North American expedition, probably in emulation of French and Spanish practices.[3] It seems apparent that the inclusion of John White on the early 1585 expedition was carefully planned. White's images were created without much written description on them, but, as the later published version of the voyage shows, he must have been working closely in collaboration with Thomas Hariot, the expedition's scientist and naturalist.[4] Hariot took detailed notes while on the spot, which were used when his account was published. Hariot's written account, minus White's images, appeared in print first in 1588 and then, more significantly, alongside engraved reproductions of White's images as volume one of Theodore de Bry's *Historia Americae* in 1590 (fig. 5.1).

A weroan or great Lorde of Virginia. III.

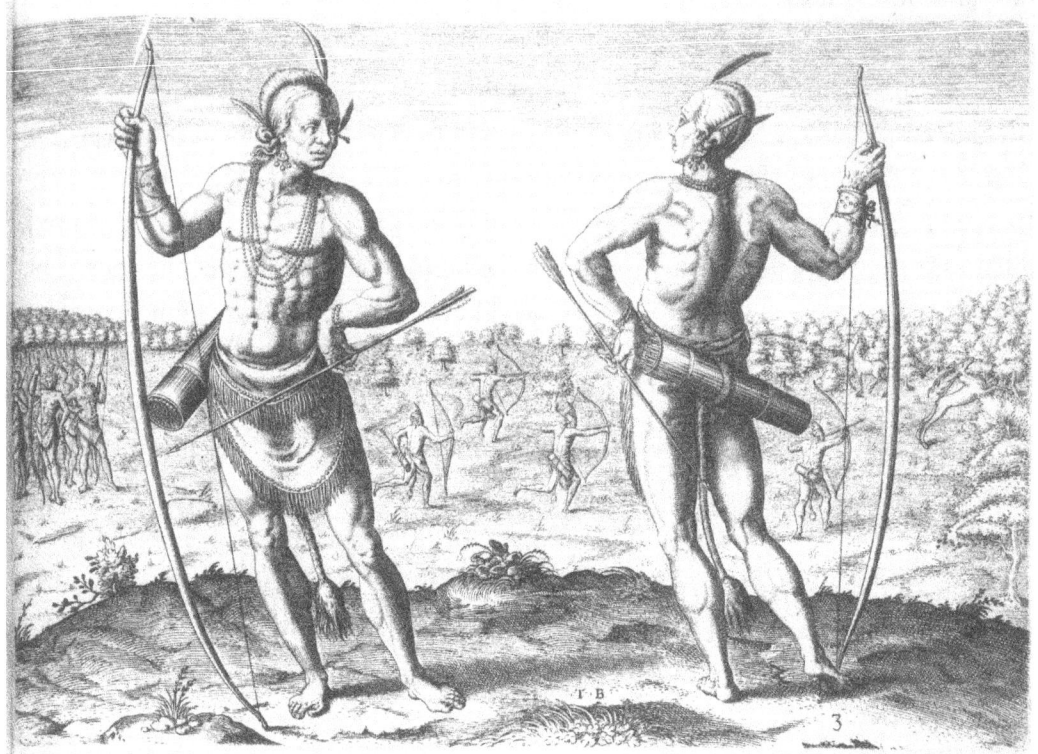

THe Princes of Virginia are attyred in fuche manner as is expreſſed in this figure. They weare the haire of their heades long and bynde opp the ende of the ſame in a knot vnder thier eares. Yet they cutt the topp of their heades from the forehead to the nape of the necke in manner of a cokſcombe, ſtirkinge a faier lóge pecher of ſome berd att the Begininge of the creſte vppun their foreheads, and another ſhort one on bothe ſeides about their eares. They hange at their eares ether thicke pearles, or ſomwhat els, as the clawe of ſome great birde, as cometh in to their fanſye. Moreouer They ether pownes, or paynt their forehead, cheeks, chynne, bodye, armes, and leggs, yet in another ſorte then the inhabitantz of Florida. They weare a chaine about their necks of pearles or beades of cop-per, wich they muche eſtee me, and ther of weat they alſo braſelets ohn their armes. Vnder their breſts about their bellyes appeir certayne ſpotts, whear they vſe to lett them ſelues bloode, when they are ſicke. They hange before thé the ſkinne of ſome beaſte verye ſeinelye dreſſet in ſuche ſorte, that the tayle hangéth downe behynde. They carye a quiuer made of ſmall ruſhes holding their bowe readie bent in on hand, and an arrowe in the other, radie to defend themſelues. In this manner they goe to warr, or tho their ſolemne feaſts and banquetts. They take muche pleaſure in huntinge of deer wher of theris great ſtore in the contrye, for yt is fruit full, pleaſant, and full of Goodly woods. Yt hathe alſo ſtore of riuers full of diuers ſorts of fiſhe. When they go to battel they paynt their bo-dyes in the moſt terible manner that thei can deuiſe.

Fig. 5.1. Theodor de Bry, after John White, *A Weroan Or Great Lorde of Virginia*, engraving, 1590, from *Historia Americae*, part I, shelfmark G.6837, the British Library, London. (Photo: By permission of the British Library)

Voyage literature, as a body of information, was ideally suited to express colonial aspirations for enhanced trading relationships with peoples and places distant from the European centers. The tenor and language and even the contents of such tracts started to become more officially and empirically constructed in order to counteract misinformation and hearsay. One product of this new attitude held by official bodies toward the recording of information collected abroad is the advice published by the Royal Society from the early seventeenth century onward concerning the ways travelers and seamen might systematize their written accounts. Taken from the *Transactions of the Royal Society*, these statements articulate concerns that must have been crucial to those protoscientific bodies representing the nation. Specifically,

> above the ignobler Productions of the Earth, there must be a careful account given of the Inhabitants themselves, both Natives and Strangers, that have been long settled there: And in Particular, their Stature, Shape, Colour, Features, Strength, Agility, Beauty (or want of it) Complexions, Hair, Dyet, Inclinations, and Customs that seem not due to Education. As to their Women (besides other things) may be observed their Fruitfulness or Barrenness; their hard or easy Labour, &tc. And both in Women and Men must be taken notice of what diseases they are subject to, and, in these whether there be any symptome, or any other Circumstance, that is unusual or remarkable.[5]

In addition, travelers were encouraged to bring back samples and other evidence of their findings in order that trained scientists could make closer study of them with proper instruments and methodical analysis.

The eighteenth century would see an unprecedented expansion of knowledge about the geography and biology of the earth garnered from colonial endeavors.[6] It was only after midcentury, however, that the employment of traveler-scientists and academically trained artists became more widely practiced in British expeditions to bring back new information about distant lands. The increasing attention given to training naval and military officers in draftsmanship indicates the extent to which it was understood that written descriptions, although helpful for accuracy

and attention to detail, were unlikely to be sufficient. A good example of one beneficiary of such training is provided by Thomas Davies, who had received instruction
in painting at the Woolwich Military Academy in 1755. Commissioned as a professional soldier in the artillery, he served in the Seven Years' War and the American
Revolutionary War and was posted to Canada in the 1780s. He exhibited as an
honorary exhibitor at the Royal Academy from 1771 until 1806.[7] His painting of
1788, *A View near Point Levy Opposite Quebec with an Indian Encampment* (plate
15), derives from his final period in Canada, shortly before his return to England
in 1790. It shows the Iroquois summer camp, the annual meeting place for the
reception of presents from the colonial government. Davies's image is typical of
his awkward and amateur style. Charming as his illustrations of early Canada are,
they are limited by the shortcomings of his technique. It is clear from this example
that such training as Davies received would not have equipped an officer to undertake ambitious visual records, and the eventual employment of professional artists,
especially on such important ventures as that of Captain James Cook's in the 1770s,
is a logical development of the aspirations enunciated by the Royal Society.[8]

Cook employed artists on all of his voyages, but only on his third and final
expedition (1776-80) did he visit America. His artist on that occasion was John
Webber, who recorded the people and places of the northern Pacific coast.[9] Webber's appointment as principal artist on Cook's third voyage took place through
the intervention of Dr. Carl Solander, who had accompanied Sir Joseph Banks on
Cook's first voyage in 1768. It had been established from the time of the second
voyage and the excellent work accomplished by William Hodges that the inclusion
of a competent artist was a high priority. In fact, the terms of Webber's appointment would be practically the same as those given to Hodges on the previous
voyage.[10] Webber had begun his training in Switzerland, primarily as a painter of
landscapes. Moving to England in 1775, he had undertaken further study at the
Royal Academy schools and had developed sufficient skill to be entrusted with
the appointment to Cook. As with Cook's other artists, Webber's studies of the
Nootka (Nuu-Chah-Nulth and Mowachaht) population at Yuquot and the watercolor paintings he made during the voyage represent a rare moment in the history

of organized scientific expeditions, for they follow a deliberate policy to gain direct likenesses of those peoples whom the British encountered.

Webber worked closely with his fellow artists and naturalists, combining his work with theirs to create a unified image of the voyage encounter for eventual presentation in a published account. Webber's pen-and-wash drawings, such as *A Woman of Nootka Sound* of April 1778 (fig. 5.2), may serve as an example of the kind of image the artist was required to make. In this finished study, the head, shoulders, and bust of the figure are shown in some detail down to just above the waist; but Webber's major concern lies with the hat she wears, which he depicts in great detail and whose designs can be compared closely with a number of similar examples of actual Nuu-Chah-Nulth or Mowachaht hats held in various ethnographic collections, including that of the British Museum.[11] The same type of decorated hat reappears in a number of other drawings made by Webber and those of other artists in this period, suggesting that its shape and decoration offered a particularly memorable instance of Mowachaht material culture. In this drawing, Webber has depicted a woman wearing a chieftain's hat, which suggests that he was unaware of its gendered significance.[12] No information is supplied for the woman, who seems to function merely as a visual prop or mannequin on which this beautifully crafted object might be displayed.

The record of this woman's appearance includes little that would place her specifically within the groups living in the Vancouver Island areas, apart from her anomalous chieftain's hat. Her style of dress, the way she arranges her hair, and indeed her overall facial expression reveal little of the individual woman being shown here. The lack of other visual information suggests that she is a "typical" "Nootka" woman, rather than an individual. Her iconic presentation closes down the proliferation of meanings another context would have provided and keeps her identity as two-dimensional as her image. Webber, like other artists employed on scientific missions, was impelled toward a taxonomic scrutiny of his subject, looking for the regular, the typical, and the most informative aspect, ignoring or overlooking the idiosyncrasies and irregularities of a specific situation.

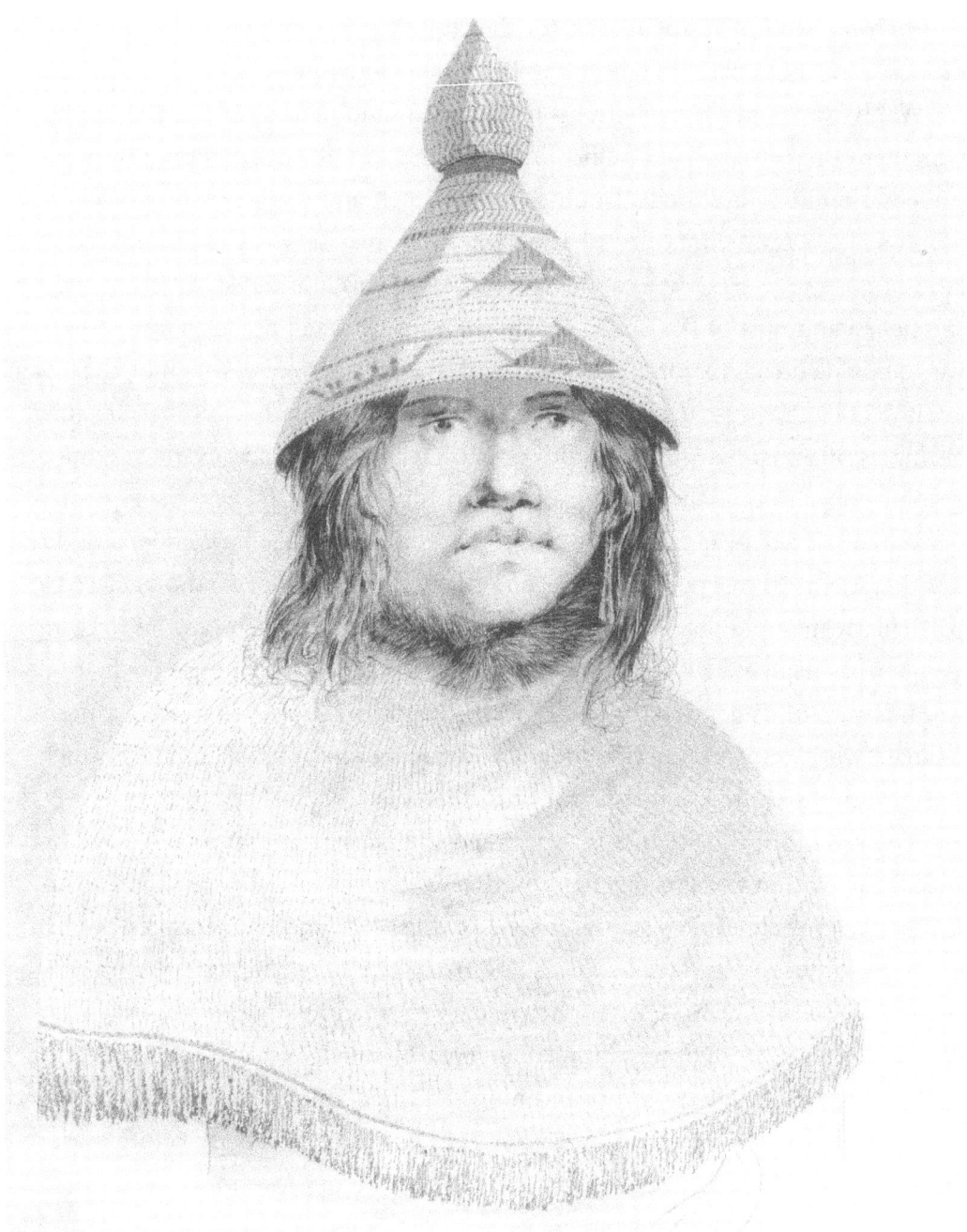

Fig. 5.2. John Webber, *A Woman of Nootka Sound*, pencil drawing, 1778, the Peabody Museum of Archaeology and Ethnography, Harvard University, Cambridge, Massachusetts. Photo © Copyright Presidents and Fellows of Harvard College. Courtesy of the Peabody Museum.

Yet for all the "objectivity" of Webber's approach, the nature of his presentation is anything but unmediated. The style and conventions associated with graphic illustration may have influenced the manner in which Webber delineated his American Indian subjects. Specifically, one must look at the general interest in foreign costume, dress, and habits provided by the costume books, which appeared from as early as the mid-seventeenth century and rose to prominence following the world voyages of the 1760s and 1770s. Like Webber's drawing, these works contained images rendered in a spare style, usually placed starkly against a plain white background in order to display information without any encumbrances. A good example of this kind of imagery is contained in Thomas Jefferys's *A Collection of the Dresses of Different Nations both Ancient and Modern* (1757 and 1772), which includes various representations of American Indian tribal groups, from the "Mohawk" to the "Native of Mexico" (fig. 5.3). Despite drawing on many sources, including travel accounts, for these images, once included in Jefferys's volumes, the arrangement of each figure is essentially the same, with a single individual displayed taxonomically against a bare background.

We can gain a perspective on Webber's images of the American Northwest if we compare them to a slightly later publication, Captain John Meares's *Voyages made in the Years 1788 and 1789, from China to the North West Coast of America*, published in 1790. The illustrations provided by Thomas Stothard include one *Callicum and Maquilla—Chiefs of Nootka Sound* (fig. 5.4).[13] In place of Webber's abstracted personages, whose depiction is subordinated to the need for empirical, even protoethnographical information, Stothard's image is of two historical figures of critical importance to their community and whose encounter with European explorers had exposed the economic motives supporting scientific curiosity.

Captain Meares had not visited the Nootka area in an official capacity, and some of his claims were hotly disputed by Captain George Dixon, who had explored the same region between 1785 and 1788.[14] Nevertheless, Meares had been successful in setting up trading relationships with the Indians, notably the two chiefs Callicum and Maquinna, seen in Stothard's print. Meares's account of the need to establish trading networks in the region and how the chieftains at Yuquot might

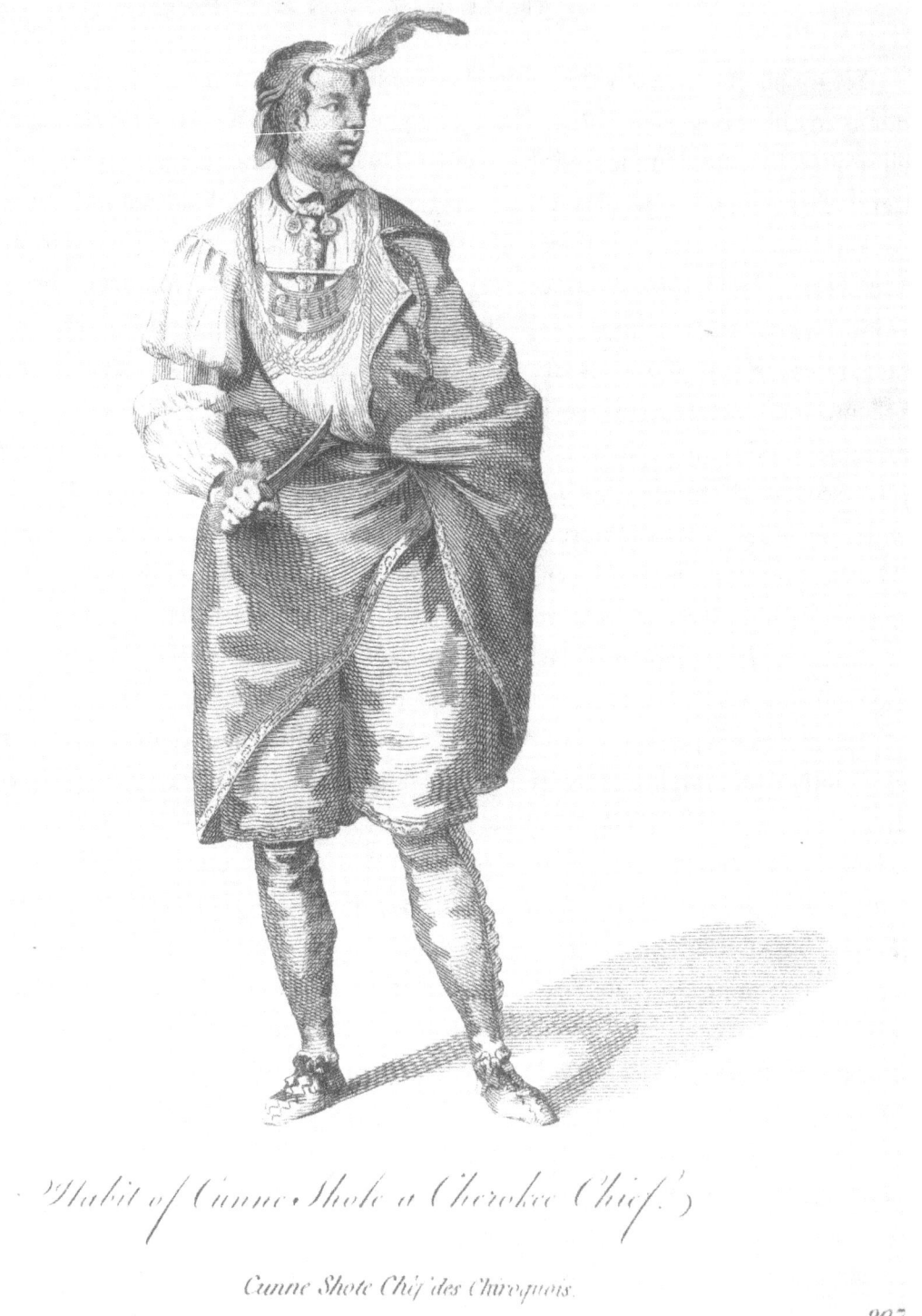

Habit of Cunne Shote a Cherokee Chief.

Cunne Shote Chef des Cherequois.

Fig. 5.3. Thomas Jefferys, *Habit of Cunneshote a Cherokee Chief*, engraving, 1771–72, from *A Collection of the Dresses of Different Nations both Ancient and Modern*, shelfmark C.11.g.2., the British Library, London. (Photo: By permission of the British Library)

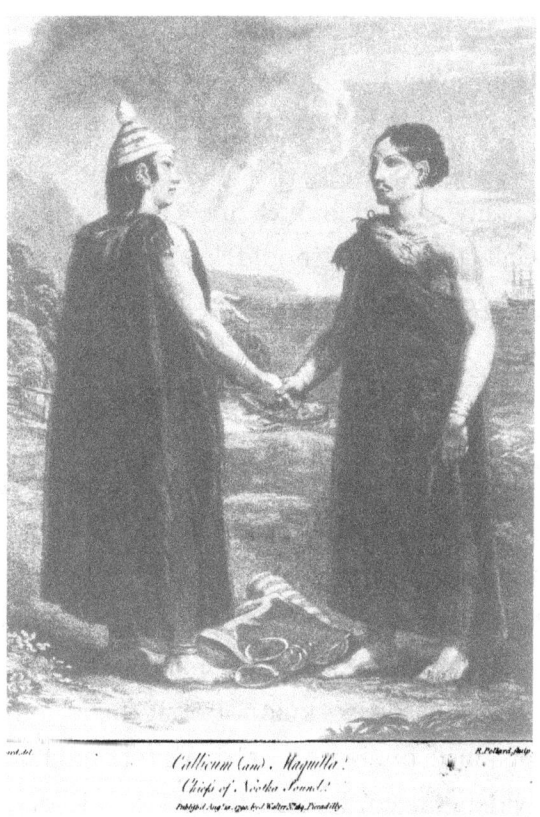

Fig. 5.4. R. Pollard, after Thomas Stothard, *Callicum and Maquilla—Chiefs of Nootka Sound*, engraving, 1790. Prints and Drawings, The British Museum, London. Photo © Copyright The British Museum.

play significant roles in the success of such ventures is alluded to in this image of an economic exchange, as though the two were meeting to cement a relationship with a handshake. Like Webber's image, there is much here that is materially accurate if we confine our attention to the chiefs' dress and ornamentation. But even though the specific cultural meaning of Nuu-Chah-Nulth trade and exchange is absent in Stothard's record of an economic exchange, he does at least locate Callicum and Maquinna as active participants in their culture, as opposed to the timeless and essentially passive behavior of the anonymous figures Webber had depicted.

Moreover, as Meares's text explained, by 1790 the Mowachaht leader Callicum was already dead, a victim of a misunderstanding with a Spanish exploratory expedition. For Meares, Callicum "possessed a delicacy of mind and conduct which would have done honour to the most improved state of our civilisation; a thousand instances of regard and affection towards us might be related of this amiable man, who is now no more."[15] This encomium on the dead chief is, of course, something of a trope in European dealings with American Indian leaders, but the text and the print work together to suggest British affinity with these people, whose generosity of spirit and readiness to trade justified their cultivation as an act of policy. Callicum's death should, in fact, give us pause when reviewing Webber's Nootka images, for Cook's voyage did not make landfall at an unknown and untouched area of the world. Instead, this area of the Pacific was contested by Britain, Russia, and Spain, all of which had advanced imperial claims for its possession. The 1780s saw an intensification of these arguments, which boiled up into the Nootka crisis of 1790, the same year in which Meares's *Voyages* were published. In these circumstances, to itemize the way of life of the inhabitants, depicting their dwellings, clothing, weapons, and means of subsistence, could not be a disinterested pursuit. The peoples and material culture in these images were already incorporated into a real or potential economic framework whose workings had historical consequences.[16]

From today's point of view, the idea that anthropology and ethnology are the products of discursive systems that militate against any possibility of objectivity is widely shared. In extending such considerations back to the eighteenth century, when studies of human cultures were in their infancy, we can see how the tension between the record itself and the motivation to make it was already apparent. Yet in the case of America particularly, our wish to accept the truthfulness of these representations is understandable. The tragic consequences of European expansion into America and the displacement or destruction of the peoples already living there have given a particular poignancy to any records that seem to offer reliable testimony of who and what were there.

As a result, the witness provided by artists as varied as John Webber, Thomas Davies, and George Catlin has been celebrated for its provision of a route back to a pristine world. The idea that these records offer the last glimpse of a vanishing culture is not, however, a purely modern response. As the U.S. government moved to open up the interior, artists were sometimes employed to record the tribes whose way of life was now under threat. Given this book's concentration on the British response to American Indians, however, I will touch briefly on the work of only one American artist, George Catlin, and then because Catlin's work was demonstrably successful in England.

Catlin had evidently assessed the plight of the western Indians as terminal, inevitably giving ground to white settlers until their way of life had disintegrated. He explored the Plains, Rocky Mountain, and Great Lakes areas between 1832 and 1834, traveling as far west as Fort Union and visiting many Indian settlements along the upper Missouri and Mississippi rivers. In the important account of his travels, *Letters and Notes on the Manners, Customs and Conditions of the North American Indians* (1841), Catlin sees himself as a final contributor to the study of American Indians before all their lands were absorbed into the larger confines of the American nation and their traditional life changed forever.

> I have, for many years past, contemplated the noble races of red men who are now spread over these trackless forests and boundless prairies, melting away at the approach of civilization. Their rights invaded, their morals corrupted, their lands wrested from them, their customs changed, and therefore lost to the world; and they at last sunk into the earth, and the plough-share turning the sod over their graves, and I have flown to their rescue—not of their lives or of their race (for they are "*doomed*" and must perish), but to the rescue of their looks and their modes, at which the acquisitive world may hurl their poison and every besom of destruction, and trample them down and crush them to death; yet, phoenix-like, they may rise from the "stain on a painter's palette," and live again upon canvass, and stand forth for centuries yet to come, the living monuments of a noble race.[17]

Catlin's enthusiastic wish to record these peoples relies essentially on his belief that their culture was worth commemorating. His sympathetic involvement in Indian life in the 1830s can be contrasted with the following wholly dismissive summary of their culture, published earlier in 1790.

> The North American natives are, in general, a wild and a faithless set of men. Their manners are a complication of ill-chosen customs, savage, ridiculous

and barbarous. Whatever some may say of their genius, it is certainly not equal to that of the inhabitants of our world; and America is, in this sense, justly styled the younger sister of Europe. The pains taken to instruct these savages in the laws and religion, have been mostly thrown away, and so bigoted are they to their own manner of living, that some of them have been regularly bred, clothed, and educated, have thrown away their clothes, run into the woods, forsaken society, and returned to their own barbarous manners, preferring what they foolishly termed liberty, among their savannahs and vast forests to all the benefits enjoyed in a well-ordered state.[18]

What separates these two perceptions is essentially a transition from one state of affairs, when Indian activities were central to any understanding of the American situation, to another, in which their way of life was no longer a central concern of statecraft.

Catlin assembled the numerous studies he made of Indian peoples into his Indian Gallery, a permanent exhibition he had always planned to create even before he had set out for the West.[19] When completed, his Indian Gallery met with some success at home, but his plan to sell the paintings to the U.S. government never materialized. Catlin made the decision to interest Europeans in his achievement, traveling to England in 1839. (His *Letters and Notes* was published in London in 1841.) He brought with him his collection of Indian artifacts, costumes, weapons, and other paraphernalia, displaying them at first on tailor's dummies, then on hired performers. In the early 1840s he recruited successively two American Indian groups already traveling in Europe, the Ojibwa and Iowa, to take part in animated displays of Indian life.[20]

Catlin's success in England makes sense against a background of European concern for the plight of American Indians in the United States. With the British government no longer facing them as adversaries or attempting to recruit them as allies, the Indian peoples of America had moved back from their prominence in current affairs to a more abstract entity. Removed in space and in military commitment, Britain had little reason to continue a detailed involvement with Indian affairs at the turn of the century. Direct contact with Indian nations, as a matter of state, was inconceivable with respect to those tribes in the United States, and foreign policy as regards the Indians in Upper and Lower Canada was less of an urgent preoccupation given Canada's formal recognition as a British colony by France and the United States. Many of the treaties mentioned in the preceding chapter, especially the Treaty of Ghent in 1814, established firmer national and international boundaries between the various nations involved in the conflicts, yet American Indian leaders and the resistance movements they led against assimilation and change were not at the negotiation table. Britain would only speak for itself and as a colonial power would turn its attention to other places in the world, leaving the competitive arena of North America to the emerging United States. The occasion for Indian diplomacy in London was effectively over.

Underlying this political agenda was a growing perception that American Indians and their culture were in decline and would soon disappear from any meaningful existence. European awareness of the collapse of classical and biblical civilizations suggested that historical processes could drive cultures into oblivion. As Indian communities gave ground to European and then American colonization and settlement, it seemed natural to characterize this as an inevitable process. The bishop of Quebec, Jacob Mountain, for example, taking tea with the artist Joseph Farington in April 1817, talked to him: "Of the American Indians, the Aborigines of the Country . . . are gradually reducing in number and by degrees will become extinct."[21] The bishop was not alone in believing this; as an idea, it had been explored with increasing frequency since the 1770s. Genocide, however, was not a concept that the visual arts could address, and in its place there developed a whole cluster of representations concerning the death of individual Indians. Standing metonymically for his or her entire community, the dying Indian figure was mobilized to represent the seemingly inevitable demise of Indian culture.

The origins of this trope derive from literary representations of American Indians, often taking the poetical form of an ode, song, or "death song" of the American Indian male or the widow's lament for him.[22] As a literary device, the dying Indian became popular in the late eighteenth century, especially after the success of the American poet Philip Freneau's poem "The Indian Burying Ground," first published in November 1787.[23] Although an American poem, this work spawned a literary response of some magnitude. American Indian songs, chants, and dirges appeared relatively frequently in works of English literature throughout the last quarter of the eighteenth century and into the nineteenth.[24] Sometimes, an Indian death song is expressed as a dying man's plea to his captors or tormentors to note the bravery with which he faces his own death. This subject revealed a wider interest in American Indian religious or spiritual practices as they related to a notion of ritual and how the dying and infirm were treated in American Indian society. All of these aspects of the dying Indian theme appealed to eighteenth-century notions of sensibility and stoicism under duress. Educated readers would have viewed such practices as somehow closer to a supposed primordial and rigorous form of human culture. Viewing American Indians in their so-called primitive or savage behavior was a means to uncover the past of all humanity in its remotest origins. But at the same time, in choosing death as a subject, a poet writing on this theme reinforced the association of Indian culture with extinction. Not only was such stoicism a throwback to earlier times, it was also untenable in the modern world. The death song trope inevitably positioned the Indian in the past, incapable of progress.

The most significant picture on the theme of the dying Indian, Joseph Wright of Derby's *The Indian Widow* (completed 1785; plate 16), was first exhibited with a companion piece, *The Lady in Milton's Comus*, at Mr. Robin's Rooms in London in 1785.[25] It is now believed that Wright's source was a quasi-historical text, James Adair's *The History of the American Indians*, published in London in 1775. The relevant passage reads:

Their law compels the widow, through the long term of her weeds, to refrain all public company and diversions, at the penalty of an adulteress; and likewise to go with flowing hair, without the privilege of oil to anoint it. The nearest kinsmen of the deceased husband, keep a very watchful eye over her conduct, in this respect. The place of interment is also calculated to wake the widow's grief, for he is entombed in the house under her bed. And if he is a war-leader, she is obliged for the first moon, to sit in the day-time under his mourning war-pole, which is decked with all his martial trophies, and must be heard to cry with bewailing notes.[26]

Elements that define the ethnicity of the figure are draped across the bare tree, blasted by the storm raging to the right of the figure. The widow is herself adorned only with the feathers she wears, attached to a decorated headband that stands out prominently against a luminous background, and a robe or shawl draped across her waist, hips, and one shoulder. It is known that Wright had difficulties knowing how to proceed on the dress of his figure and that he wrote to the poet William Hayley, explaining his difficulties.[27] One feels that Wright's solution to the problem, a figure turned away from the viewer, generalized and classically formulated such that the American Indian identifying marks are carefully minimized, stemmed as much from the requirements of painting and the use of the academic model as from any sense that he felt unequipped to paint Indian finery. Indeed, the pose of the figure is based on the classical prototype of the Weeping Dacia, an ancient figure expressing grief, and Wright's smooth modeling emulates the effect of relief sculpture.[28] The widow's stoic restraint is thus expressed through the agency of classical decorum. Her ethnic attributes, be they physical, ornamental, or behavioral, are played down in the interests of a classicizing aesthetic. A widow "crying with bewailing notes" and appropriately dressed in Indian garb could not, it seems, become the subject of a capital picture in 1785.

In this way, the figure in Wright's work has a connection with West's American Indian figure in *The Death of General Wolfe* (plate 4), for the treatment of both figures is classicizing and generalized in spite of West's attention to detail and Wright's recourse to Hayley. For all his adoption of Adair's text and his demonstration of American Indian nobility of emotion, Wright has shied away from detailed, particularizing representation and has presented the woman with a similar ambiguity to that found in West's *The Indian Family* (plate 6). That she is American Indian is not in doubt, but she is also the embodiment of a courageous and affecting temperament that any feeling European would wish to claim as his or her own sensibility. By employing a classicizing pose and avoiding too many specific details of skin color, accoutrement, and behavior, Wright's painting had a message not only for collectors of the antique but also for those who found "natural" emotion a topic of interest.

In Wright's painting, as in West's of the previous decade, an apotheosis was reached in the representation of American Indians, which in pictorial terms was never to be outdone. As it happened, very few painters chose to concentrate on similar subject matter after the appearance of Wright's work. Indeed, West's observation about the lack of public interest in American themes may apply to *The Indian Widow*, too, for despite Wright's painting it as a pendant to *The Lady in Milton's Comus*, which was bought by Josiah Wedgwood, *The Indian Widow* itself was not sold until after Wright's death.[29]

It should be kept in mind that similar themes concerning the American Indians' attitudes to death and dying not only entered poetry but also had appeared on stage, in novels, and in various tracts in the literature of travel.[30] It is a category that perhaps exceeds the boundaries of what one might call ethnographical interest or historical relevance because it touched on broader human themes such as filial commitment; loyalty to one's home, family, and country; and the rewards of virtuous behavior generally. These were important concerns for Europeans in a revolutionary climacteric. Likewise, the interest in American Indian methods of burial and mourning was stimulated by a Romantic concern with the idea of natural religion and related in a larger way to the question of the American Indians' beliefs in a single God or almighty creator and an afterlife. For instance, in Jonathan Carver's *Travels Through the Interior Parts of North America, in the Years 1766, 1767, and 1768*, the author tells of the practice in some tribes of the Northeast and Great Lakes areas of placing the dead on a bier or raised platform: "I observed that she [a widow] went almost every evening to the foot of the tree, on a branch of which the bodies of her husband and child were laid."[31] Wright's painting, like Adair's and Carver's testimony, can be understood as simply documenting Indian funerary practices, but all three representations are equally positioned within the world their readers knew. The idea of the virtuous wife, still faithful after death, necessarily provokes a comparison with the expectations surrounding marriage in a European context.

A few years later William Wordsworth wrote a poem concerning the treatment by the "northern" Indian tribes of those who were infirm and could not keep up with the tribes' wanderings. Entitled "The Complaint of a Forsaken Indian Woman"

(1798), the idea and subject matter were derived from Samuel Hearne's account of his travels, *Journey From Hudson's Bay to the Northern Ocean*, published in 1795. In this poem, the dying Indian woman seems to experience the heavens as a great force but does not directly address God:

> In sleep I heard the northern gleams;
> The stars, they were among my dreams;
> In rustling conflict through the skies,
> I heard, I saw the flashes drive[32]

Wordsworth, taking from the Hearne text the description of the "crackling" of the northern lights, has embellished the scientific aspect of the phenomenon and made it into a treatise about nature's divine forces, to which American Indians have direct connection. Again, Wordsworth's allusion to the woman's belief in higher forces is not only some compensation for the death that approaches but also something of a rebuke to his own increasingly materialist age.

To some extent, this idea of an American Indian belief system based on nature worship had been expressed as early as Alexander Pope's *Essay on Man*, written between 1730 and 1732 and published in 1733–34. Pope examines the cosmology of a natural religion:

> Lo! The poor Indian, whose untutor'd mind
> sees God in clouds, or hears him in the wind;
> his soul proud Science never taught to stray
> far as the solar walk, or milky way;
> yet simple Nature to his hope has giv'n,
> behind the cloud-topt hill, a humbler heav'n;[33]

A small watercolor drawing by Thomas Stothard from the 1790s engages with Pope's verse. Delicately drawn and of a size in keeping with book illustration, the drawing was reproduced as an engraving by James Parker in 1797 (plate 17). In the drawing, the figure of a male Indian warrior is shown reclining, his head supported from behind by the female figure of Hope, identified by her attribute of an anchor, who extends her arm to point to the distant setting sun and drifting clouds. Stothard's figure of the male warrior is mostly unclothed, with a small blanket draped across his legs. Underneath one arm sits his small dog, and to his left are the implements he must have carried in battle, his tomahawk and lance. Of interest is the detail given to his accoutrement and costume. His scalp appears bare except for a single topknot of hair, his shoulders have markings or tattoos, and he wears a strap across his chest and a knife case around his neck. The knife case and strap are a close approximation to the style of dress seen on the Choctaw Indian men in the *Townshend Monument* by Robert Adam of 1761 (see fig. 2.4, 2.4a). Significantly, however, Stothard's image suggests the imminence of death, with the figure of Hope offering the promise of some reward in the afterlife. Painted in the decade following Wright's *The Indian Widow*, this modest image further extends the increasingly prolific genre of dying Indians.

The representation of American Indian characters in literature to some extent substantiates the idea present in both Wright's and Stothard's images that this is a fragile culture on the edge of extinction. The emergence of a new literary type, the wise male tribal elder, can be adduced as a reinforcement of this perception. Whereas the earlier literary representation of American Indians had been preoccupied with young warriors and their adventures, this new character produces a more meditative effect. It is wisdom rather than action that he offers, be this a profound understanding of the forces of nature and a man's place in the world or, more tragically, a realization that his culture is declining and the world he knows is doomed to pass away. In 1787, for example, President Thomas Jefferson had popularized the "last" speech of Chief Logan, a leader of the Mingo group fighting in the conflict known as Lord Dunmore's War of 1774. Logan's family had been killed previous to the conflict, and Logan's hope of posterity was therefore extinguished. The killers, colonial soldiers, had left "not a drop of" Logan's blood running in the veins "of any person on earth," and so, "who will cry for Logan?"[34] In his aged state, with connotations of decrepitude and impotence, the Indian warrior lives on as a shadow of his former self. His physical decline and imminent death mirror the fate of his entire culture. Harmless and enfeebled, his philosophy rather than his feats of arms will be remembered. The Indian as quietist sage can meditate on the end of his or her community with a becoming sensibility.

The poetic nature of the speech of Ononthio in William Richardson's play *The Indians* of 1790, for example, departs from the Indian's earlier presentation as a rather classicized, senatorial speaker, as in John Dennis's *Liberty Asserted* of 1704. Now we find his speech is colored with metaphorical allusions to the stuff of nature—"the rushing of a mountain blast"—which mark him as a person who thinks in the language of a natural world. Ononthio's character may have sparked the imagination of the audience, for his eloquent patterns of speech and his insightful approach to his own culture reveal an intelligence and sensibility far removed from the fearsome tomahawk-wielding savages of popular report. The content and repetitive quality of Ononthio's words also draw on a growing recognition of the beauty and value of American Indian oratory as expressed in their songs and stories.[35] This, too, was part of a more general revival of earlier poetic forms and as such was linked with the primitivist tendencies that characterized the late eighteenth century.

In spite of this pleasing depiction of North American Indians, in creating the character of Ononthio Richardson began, if unwittingly, to initiate a chain of representation that resulted in the eventual mythification of the American Indian personage. Benjamin Bissell has pointed to the resemblance between Richardson's character and the figure of Chactas in François René de Chateaubriand's epic novel *Les Natchez* (1826); if one can say that the fate of Chactas was the inevitable result of exhibiting a delicate sensibility, then the consequences of that sensibility were annihilation and tragedy.[36] That is, at this point the American Indian character was entering into myth as his or her culture, beliefs, and style of existence were pushed back into a historical past, a fading memory that could not be recovered, as it had never been written down. In the presentation on stage of such characters, who speak with extreme eloquence and a profound understanding of humankind's foibles, the mythification of American Indians was made easier. The theater provided fictionalized characters, at best abstracted from historical events or exhibiting the noble qualities of rulers long deceased or those on the verge of extinction. With these personifications, dramatists could treat American Indians with a great amount of sympathy. But this sympathy relied upon the individual Indian being impotent to all intents and purposes, finding his or her role as an innocent, a disembodied commentator, or an isolated representative of a tribe. These plays accept the Indians' loss of autonomy in the face of British and American settlement and thus present Indians as posing no threat to the growth of a white America.

By the 1840s, the notion of the dying Indian was something of a literary commonplace. Probably the most significant instance of this tendency occurs in Thomas Campbell's poem "Gertrude of Wyoming." First published in 1809, it rapidly achieved popular success and went through a number of editions, at least two of them illustrated, up to 1840.[37] Campbell sought to provide a historical context for his poem by basing it on a notorious incident that had actually occurred in the American Revolutionary War, a battle in July 1778 known popularly as the Wyoming Valley Massacre.[38] The actual event was a Tory Rangers' raid on outlying settlements that were known to be sympathetic to the rebels. Few of the captive men survived, and much destruction of property took place. Joseph Brant was unfairly linked to the raid, when in fact it was John Butler, the British Indian agent, who led the squad responsible for the attack, a group that certainly included American Indian auxiliaries.[39] Rather unfortunately for the eventual treatment of all American Indians, the death of Jane MacCrea a year earlier, in 1777 (plate 8), became linked in the minds of eastern Americans and the British themselves with American Indian wartime cruelty and battlefield practices, such as scalping. It occasioned a certain level of hysteria on the frontier, causing many people to flee the outlying settlements, and brought forward the whole debate on whether American Indian fighters ought to be deployed at all in such battles. The Earl of Chatham's comments after the occurrence of such wartime atrocities as these speaks of a wider British consensus that American Indians were too readily connected with incidents of murder and mayhem out on the frontier.[40] (This despite the very real presence of American and European fighters who were adopting such tactics for their own purposes.)

In spite of his attested reliance on historical accounts, Campbell's poem emphasizes not the political and military reality of the Wyoming Valley incident but themes of love and loss concerning the intertwined lives of Henry Waldegrave; his protector,

Albert Waldegrave; Albert's daughter, Gertrude; and the Oneida chief Outalissi. Outalissi first discovers Henry, as a child, hiding in a tree and orphaned after a recent frontier battle. Outalissi takes Henry to Albert Waldegrave's house, where he grows to adulthood and falls in love with Gertrude. It is this same Outalissi, now an old man, who returns to warn the family of the impending destruction of their settlement in 1778.

To some extent, Campbell's poem is accurate. The Oneidas did attempt at first to remain neutral in the Revolutionary War, but their relations with the colonists would eventually influence their decision to take the side of the rebels. Outalissi's anger at the "accurs'd Brant" thus accurately mirrors the respective allegiances of the Oneida and the Mohawk peoples during the conflict. The Wyoming Valley itself is described by Campbell as some sort of paradise:

> Delightful Wyoming! Beneath the skies,
> The happy shepherd swains had nought to do
> But feed their flocks on green declivities
> Or skim perchance thy lake with light canoe.[41]

But we should recall that for all its beauty, its importance for the frontier region had produced many competing claims. The western Iroquois, the Senecas, considered it to be the portal to their hunting grounds; for the Delaware, or Lenape, Indians living in eastern Pennsylvania, it was their own homeland; for the settlers, it was theirs by right of land agreements and cessions. The Wyoming Valley's frontier significance also meant that it was vulnerable to attack, and the July 1778 massacre was widely regarded at one of the most savage of the entire war. As Campbell expresses it:

> And must I change my song? And must I show,
> Sweet Wyoming! The day when thou wert doom'd,
> Guiltless, to mourn thy loveliest bowers laid low!
> When where of yesterday a garden bloom'd,
> Death overspread his pall, and blackening ashes gloom'd![42]

Two of the many artistic responses to Campbell's poem will be considered here. The first derives from a meeting of the Sketching Society in 1810. The typical procedure of this group, established in the 1790s, was to meet at one another's houses to draw and to eat dinner. The host would select the theme for the evening, usually from a work of literature. The choice for the December 26 meeting was Campbell's "Gertrude of Wyoming," and four of the resulting sketches have come down to us.[43] Given the original name of the society, the "Society for the Study of Epic and Pastoral Design," Campbell's verses were obviously appropriate, especially his radiant descriptions of the Wyoming Valley at peace. The four extant wash drawings all depict the moment when Outalissi brings the young Henry to Albert Waldegrave. Alfred Chalon's version (fig. 5.5) is noteworthy for its very insecure placement of the protagonists in any credible setting. Albert Waldegrave wears a plantation-style hat and sits outside a wooden hut surrounded by palm groves; this tropical setting is matched by the distinctly South American appearance of Outalissi, whose feathered crown and skirt hark back to the earliest allegorical images of America. Chalon's interpretation of Campbell's poetry is understandable, given the lack of precision in the verse.

> And summer was the tide, and sweet the hour
> When sire and daughter, saw with fleet descent,
> An Indian from his bark approach their bower,
> Of buskin'd limb, and swarthy lineament;
> The red wild feathers of his brow were blent,
> And bracelets bound the arm that helped to light
> A boy, who seem'd, as he beside him went
> Of Christian vesture, and complexion bright,
> Led by his dusky guide, like morning brought by night.[44]

The position of the figures are explained in the next stanza:

> When, leaning on his forest-bow unstrung,
> Th' Oneyda warrior to the planter said,
> And laid his hand upon the stripling's head[45]

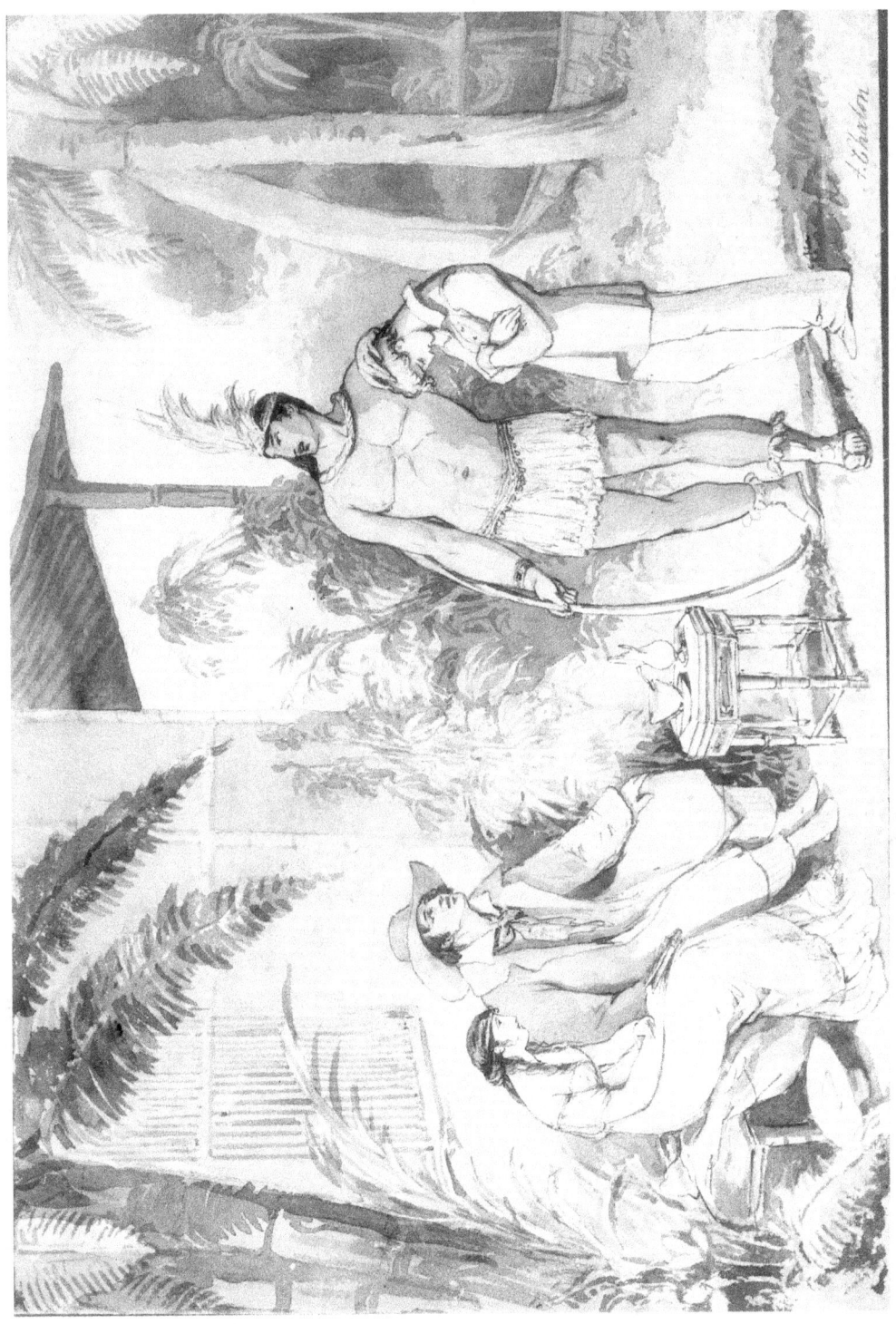

Fig. 5.5. Alfred Chalon, *Gertrude of Wyoming*, study, pen, ink and wash on paper, 1810, Laing Museum and Art Gallery, Newcastle upon Tyne. Courtesy of Tyne and Wear Museums.

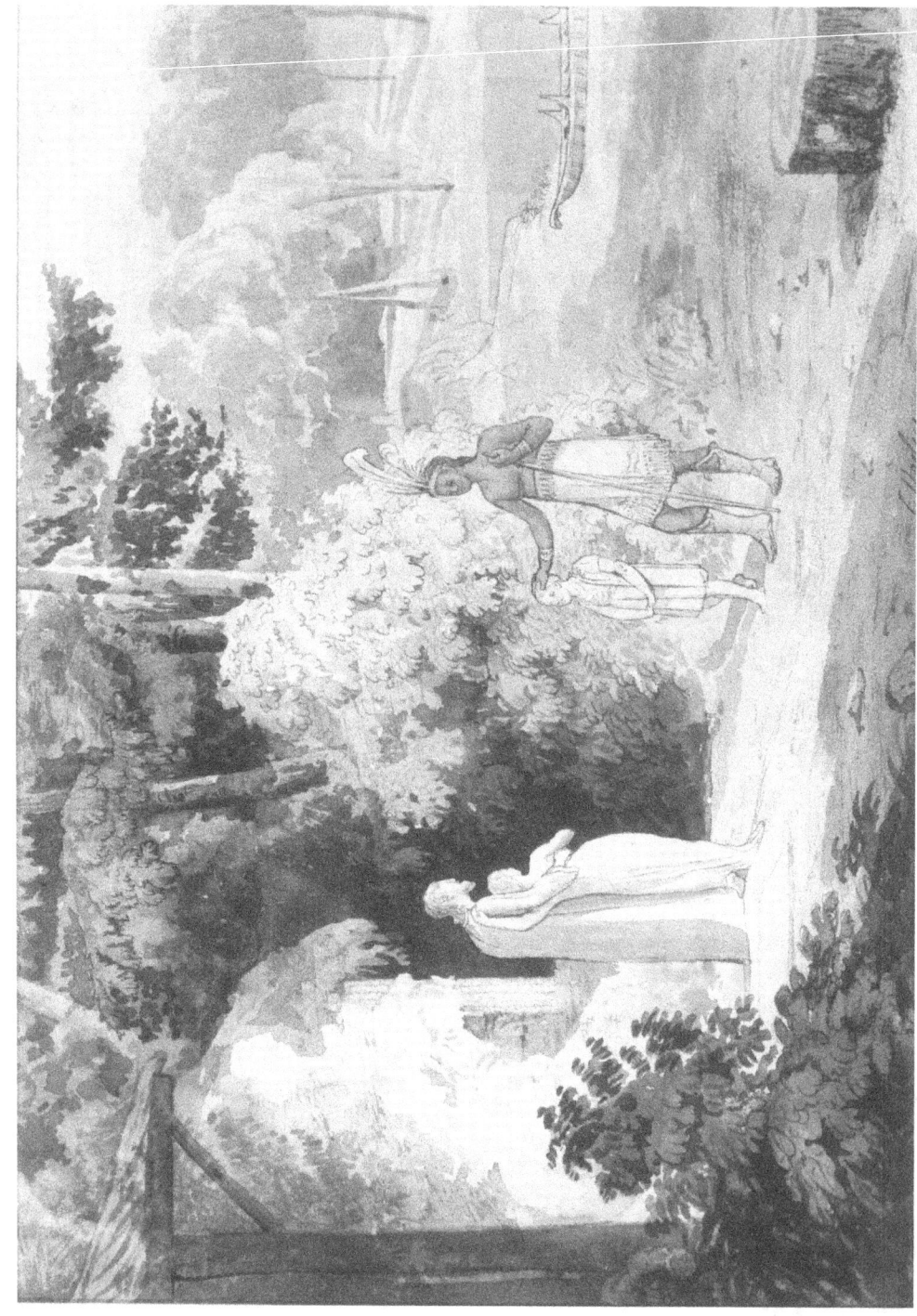

Fig. 5.6. Cornelius Varley, *Gertrude of Wyoming*, study, pen, ink and wash on paper, 1810, Laing Museum and Art Gallery, Newcastle upon Tyne. Courtesy of Tyne and Wear Museums.

It is surely noteworthy that an artist in 1810 could take these verses to mean something so vague as to allow a generalized exotic image. Given the significance of American Indian tribes for British concerns at midcentury, it is inconceivable that an artist of the 1760s or 1770s would have been at such a loss. By the early nineteenth century, however, specific understandings have given way to imprecise and exotic approximations. Of the four artists, only Cornelius Varley attempted anything remotely close to Oneida culture, kitting out his Outalissi with a buckskin apron and leggings (fig. 5.6). That the others could happily draw on South American imagery may be explained by the recent staging of Richard Sheridan's drama *Pizarro* (first performed in 1799), but the fact that no better stimulus for the work was in circulation in London in 1810 is a testament to the general decline in interest in American Indians during this period.

The second set of illustrations comes from an illustrated edition of "Gertrude" published in 1822. Richard Westall designed two plates to do with the figure of Outalissi for engraving, the first depicting the same meeting between the four protagonists chosen by the Sketching Society, the second showing Outalissi's return on the eve of the massacre (figs. 5.7, 5.8). In the second plate (fig. 5.7), the characters are arranged against a long, flat expanse of wall in a friezelike composition. The area around the figures is simplified, stripped of detail, while Outalissi's draped garments give him the appearance of a Roman figure dressed in a chiton rather than that of an aged chieftain of the "Oneyda" tribe. The incongruity of a curly-headed, bearded, and classicized figure has not troubled Westall in the creation of his American Indian figure. He may have been thinking more of an amalgamated type of "noble savage" in his design that would draw on a number of visual types as well as on more direct experiences with supposed "differing" peoples from diverse areas around the globe, including Oceanic peoples.[46]

The qualification of the American Indian figure is perhaps nowhere so insistent as in this small illustration, and it occurs for a number of reasons. First, this scene is itself part of the general theme that pervades the poem and which concerns the devotion of children to their parents or protectors; as a result, Outalissi is almost co-opted into European frontier society as a benevolent guardian or sage for the family. Westall's nonspecific treatment of the figure helps to blur the distinguishing

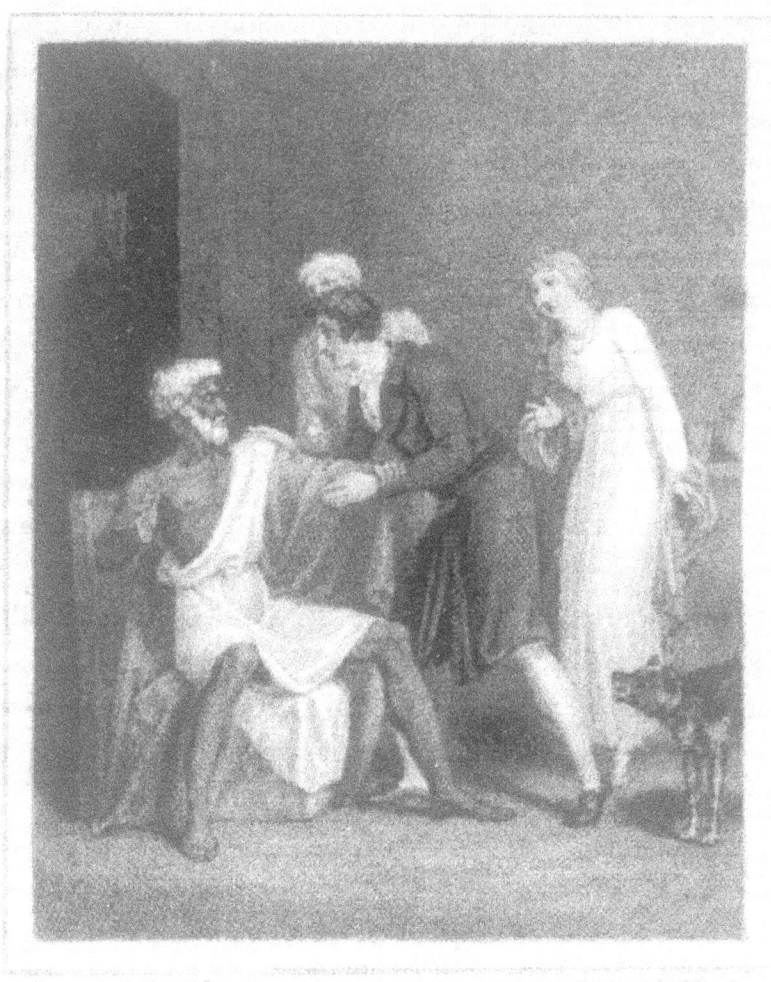

GERTRUDE OF WYOMING.

Fig. 5.7. Richard Westall, *The chief his old bewildered head withdrew, And grasp'd his arm, and look'd and look'd him through*, from Thomas Campbell, *Gertrude of Wyoming and Other Poems* (London: Longman et al., 1825), private collection. Photo by the author.

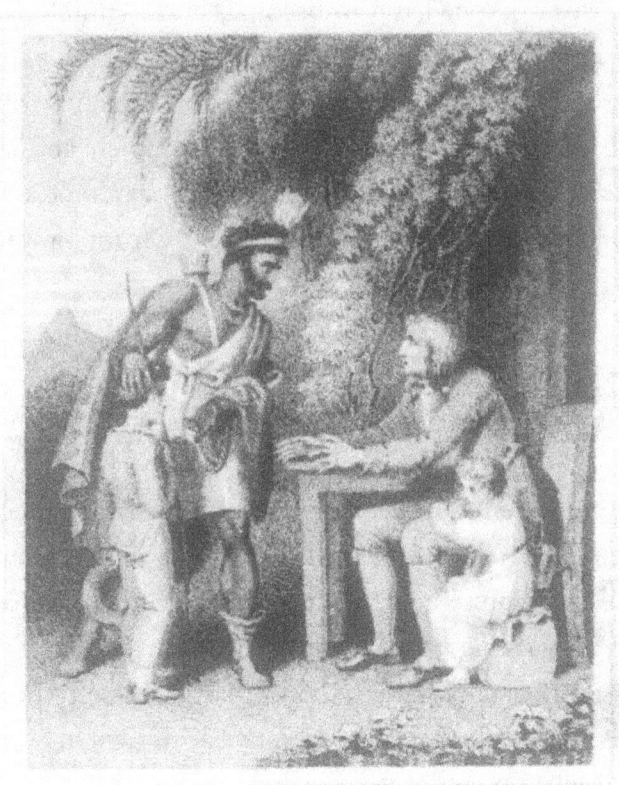

Fig. 5.8. Richard Westall, *And I, the eagle of my tribe have rush'd with this lorn dove,* from Thomas Campbell, *Gertrude of Wyoming and Other Poems* (London: Longman et al., 1825), private collection. Photo by the author.

American Indian traits that might have made this co-option problematic. Second, Outalissi's facial expression, in Westall's interpretation of the text, represents an intensity of feeling, which is not betrayed by the exterior features of the face. Stoicism like this had been identified as a classical virtue and championed by neoclassical theorists as an essential quality in noble behavior and the greatest art. Westall's image seems to owe allegiance to Grand Style history painting in its declamatory gestures, friezelike composition, and simplicity of presentation.

The implications of this procedure for the figure of Outalissi are complicated. In this work, he has now become almost entirely subsumed within a Europeanized vision, for he appears in Westall's illustration as a classicized, even senatorial figure, rather than as an Oneida leader with distinctive tribal adornment. He therefore is no longer viewed distinctively, as a complete and separate entity from the other characters. In the poem, Outalissi is shown to be a person without a home or family. His past has been completely cut away from him because of Brant's depredations.

All perish'd!—I alone am left on earth!
To whom no relative nor blood remains,
No!—not a kindred drop that runs in human veins![47]

Mimicking the speech of Chief Logan that had been popularized by Thomas Jefferson, the effect of this poem's storyline is to allow the character of Outalissi to divest himself of any traits that might make European assimilation problematic. He has been synthesized into an ancient healer of wrongs, a long-lost parent of the boy, and a friend to the European settlers whom he warns of the impending disaster. As the last of his race, he has thrown in his lot with the colonists to become a tutelary presence in their lives.

It is unlikely that Richard Westall ever had a chance to observe actual Northeastern Woodlands Indians, nor did he ever travel to the Americas where he might have seen Indians living on their own lands. It is fair, then, to conclude that the creation of his figure of Outalissi came almost entirely from his imagination. Campbell, too, would have found it difficult to observe actual American Indian peoples unless they came to Britain; however, as he gives frequent documentation of the historical bases of his poem, perhaps he hoped to make amends for this lack of visual experience by attesting to his knowledge of the literature of travel in North America. In fact, the name Outalissi may have some basis in the real-life personage of Outacity, who visited England in 1762 with other Cherokee men and whose image proliferated in a number of portrait engravings (see fig. 2.7). If so, there is a profound irony here, for whereas Outacity existed in history and was responded to as a significant player on the colonial stage, Outalissi is no more than a romantic fabrication, a fantasy of noble sentiment and exotic otherness quite removed from any colonial reality. In this context, it is surely significant that Campbell's illustrators seemed to have no need to draw on Indian culture. The Indian of concern to them was no longer an active agent of historical change but a denizen of another time and place, the genius loci of a continent whose relations with Europeans were already becoming something dreamlike.

Perhaps part of this change can be explained by the growth of travel literature concerning Canada and the United States whose reports were concerned less with the frontier than the settled eastern regions. Those Indians who were encountered often failed to elicit any favorable impressions. Dispossessed and corrupted by contact with Europeans, these groups offered merely a picture of marginal existence. As far as the bishop of Quebec was concerned, "the genuine American Indian [can be viewed] in a very favourable manner: as being inoffensive and faithful, but those who live upon the borders of the adjoining states, being a mixed breed of natives and Europeans, are a very profligate people in whom no confidence can be placed. They are barbarous, vicious and unfaithful."[48] Even when not betraying abject poverty, the Indians portrayed in the first decade of the nineteenth century were plainly subordinated to European culture. In his *Travels through the Canadas* (1807), George Heriot includes two illustrations of "Domiciliated Indians," showing them at one with nature in much the same way as British eighteenth-century artists, such as George Morland, had depicted gypsies, vagabonds, and migrant laborers (fig. 5.9). The comparison is not fortuitous. In his "Notices of the North American Indians" (1829), Dr. Edward Walsh wrote that "in Canada, many straggling parties are occasionally employed . . . others, of the Messuagues [*sic*] and Mukmaks [*sic*], wander about exactly like our gypsies . . . picking up a precarious existence."[49]

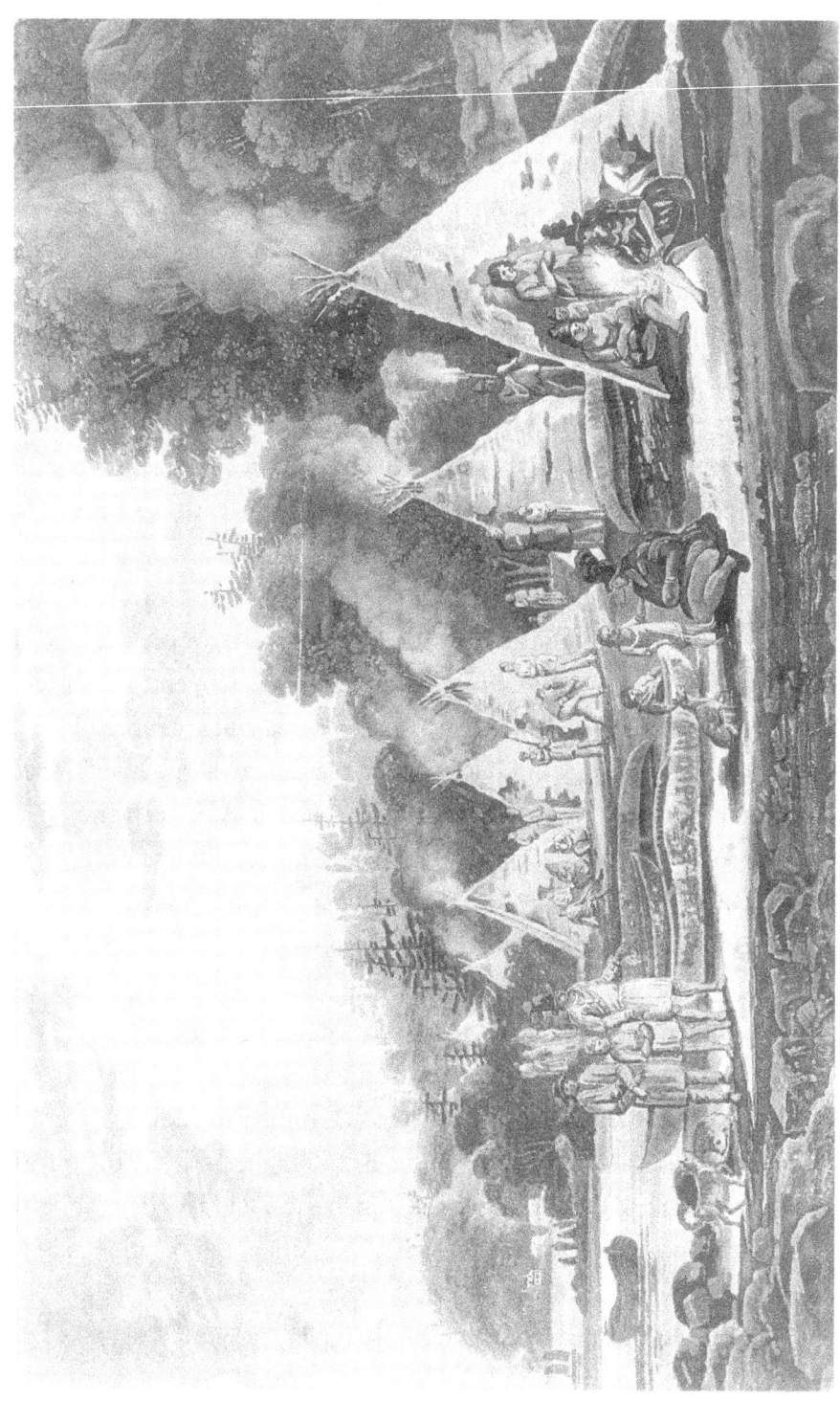

Fig. 5.9. George Heriot, *An encampment of Domiciliated Indians*, aquatint, from *Travels through the Canadas* (London, 1810), Edward E. Ayer Collection, the Newberry Library, Chicago. Courtesy of the Edward E. Ayer Collection, the Newberry Library.

Seen as a group, these Indians become the excuse for picturesque arrangement and enjoyable contemplation. They are reduced to an exotic ensemble; but no tribal affiliation, names of individuals, or explanations of culture or of history are offered. The Indians are there almost as part of the scenery, contributing to the characteristic experience of travel in Canada but decidedly not to its future development.

In further illustrations of the same period, these conclusions are more openly stated. Both Robert Sutcliff's *Travels in Some Parts of North America in the Years, 1804, 1805 & 1806* (1811) and John Lambert's *Travels through Lower Canada and the United States of North America in the Years 1806, 1807, and 1808* (1810) contain illustrations that show Indian family groups in rural landscape settings. In the sole plate depicting Indians in the Sutcliff volume (fig. 5.10), the itinerant aspect of the Indians' existence is elucidated, as the family is depicted in the process of moving their possessions and place of habitation, their backs loaded with bundles and their empty shelter left uninhabited in the background. Lambert's work is more openly derogatory. The title of his Indian plate is simply *An Indian and his Squaw,* where the two figures are depicted side by side and cast dark shadows on the shore behind them (fig. 5.11). The male figure wears a threadbare shirt of European make that has either stains or holes in it and a peaked hat on his head. The woman is entirely covered in a thick blanket and, in a strange juxtaposition of details, wears a crucifix at her throat. In contrast, the male's only possessions are his open bottle of spirits and a grotesque cow's skull in his right hand. Lambert makes the case evident in his description of the "domesticated Indians." Of the men, "Their external appearance is extremely forbidding, and often disgusting; a dark swarthy countenance, with high cheekbones, prominent nose and chins and long black, coarse hair, hanging in disorder over their face." Elsewhere he describes the men as "half-civilized, half-savage."[50] The attributes of the whiskey bottle and the dirty cow's skull are included to provide the viewer with pictures of those things that the text describes as being "favourites" of the Indians and used in great quantities.

Lambert's description offers a resolutely pessimistic vision of Indian existence in proximity to European settlement. In its picture of degradation, it promises nothing more than cultural collapse and even extinction. Yet in its iconic fashioning

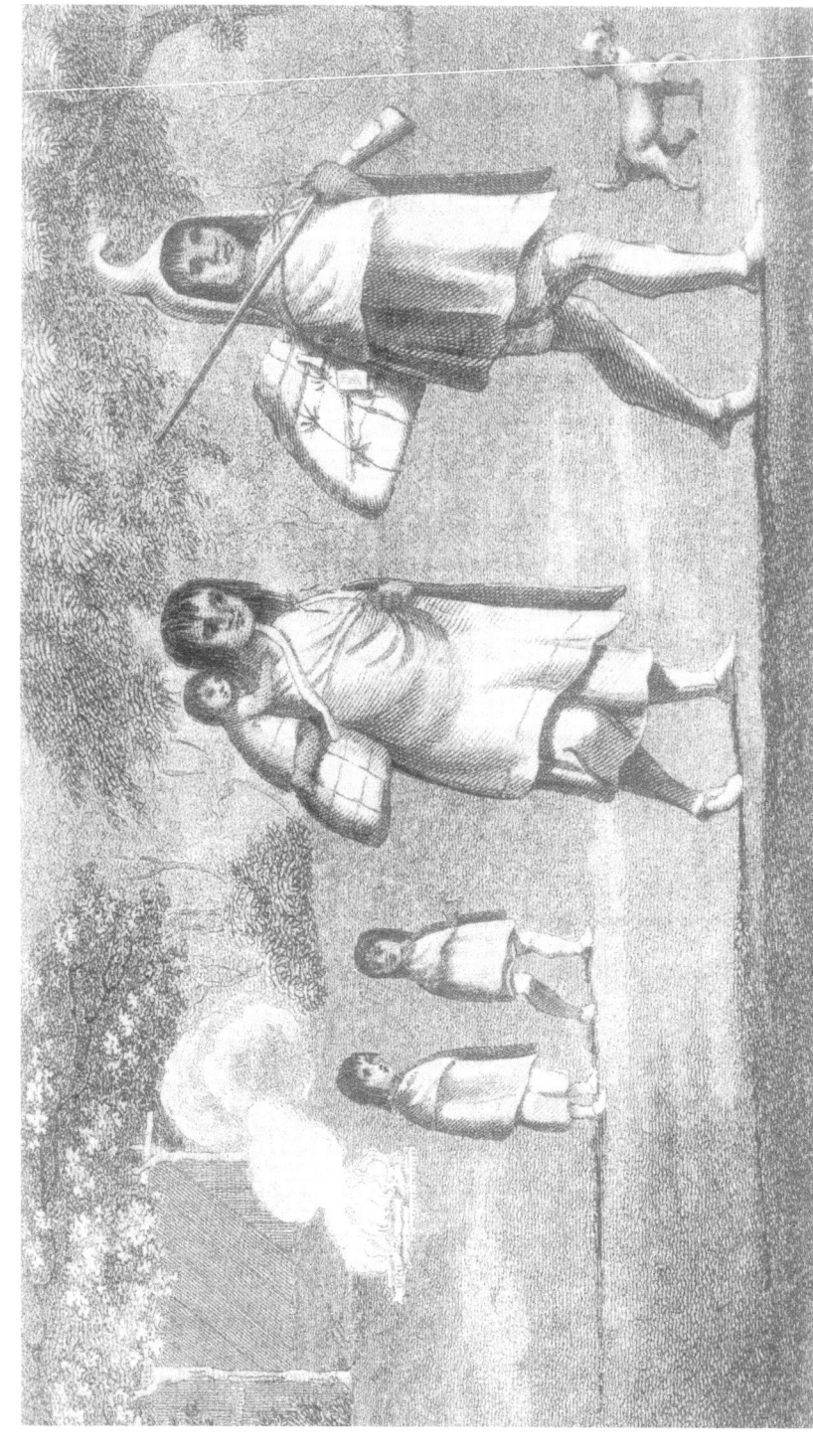

Fig. 5.10. Anon., *An Indian Family*, engraving, in Robert Sutcliff, *Travels in Some Parts of North America* (York, 1811), Edward E. Ayer Collection, the Newberry Library, Chicago. Courtesy of the Edward E. Ayer Collection, the Newberry Library.

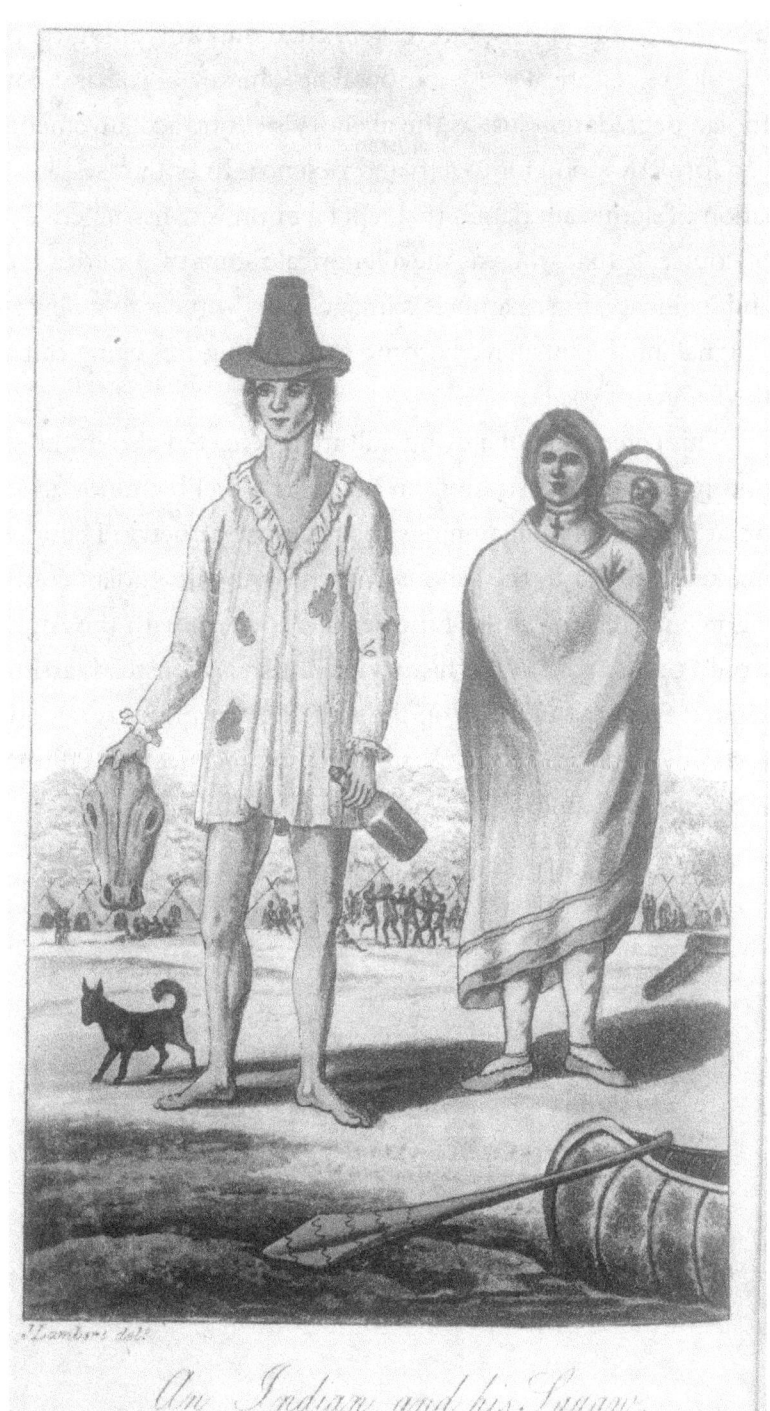

Fig. 5.11. John Lambert, *An Indian and his Squaw*, engraving, from *Travels through Lower Canada* (London, 1810), shelfmark 10408.c.32, the British Library, London. By permission of the British Library.

of an image of Indians, it reverts to that kind of typological presentation seen in the older allegorical presentation. The whiskey bottle and cow's skull stand for Indian degradation just as the allegory's exotic accoutrements and severed head had formerly stood for wealth and violence. In both cases, it is through the accumulation of significant details that a perception is constructed. The crucial distinction, of course, is that whereas the allegorical figure of America represented a continent and its inhabitants, Lambert's image bears witness to a new situation in which the original inhabitants have become marginal figures eking out a precarious living on the fringes of society.

This perception of a dying culture is reflected also in the status of those images: poorly executed illustrations in books of travel by minor artists with limited ability or, at best, fanciful imaginings to accompany poetry. These productions are in marked contrast to the serious engagement with Indian culture witnessed in the eighteenth century. In fact, no serious concern with the American Indian figure would occur again in the history of British art. Instead, artists working in the United States would take on the task of attempting to negotiate some sort of accommodation between Western artistic practice and cultural expectations and the complexity and resilience of American Indian life.

Conclusion

As THE FOREGOING chapters have demonstrated, the imagery associated with American Indians underwent a number of modifications in Britain during and immediately after the eighteenth century. The Renaissance-derived emblematic iconography of the American warrior, with its essentially atemporal representation of Indians, was joined by new visual possibilities capable of responding to the historical circumstances of the struggle for the continent. Delegations of Mohawks, Cherokees, and others were not only the product of contemporary policy but also contributions to a new language of empire, whose visual articulation spoke of Indian responses to British ascendancy on the Atlantic seaboard and increasingly in Canada. From the beginning of the century until the outbreak of the Revolutionary War, the importance of Indian peoples in diplomatic and military thinking was rarely in doubt. The visual depiction of Indians is marked by the same concerns, whether in portraits of delegations or in history painting. To generalize, the Indian figure is not a bloodless abstraction but a protagonist in a historical episode, responding to the exigencies of the time. Similarly, the old allegorical figure of America is itself radicalized in the political prints of midcentury to become an active agent rather than a passive emblem. With the loss of Britain's American colonies in the Revolutionary War, however, British interest in American Indians waned, and even in the circumstances of the second decade of the nineteenth century, no comparable imagery of Indians was produced. Instead, the trope of the "dying" Indian began to dominate artistic tradition, presenting a picture of extinction or cultural degradation.

The picture thus drawn delineates the rise and fall of an attitude to American Indian representation that responded to the historical circumstances of the eighteenth century but could not be sustained once those circumstances had altered. As we have seen, however, even when it most engaged with the particularities of the Indian presence, this engagement was never a transparent representation. In the texture of these images we can see the hesitation, doubts, and occlusions of vision that beset the whole enterprise. If the concept of the Indian underwent some modification in the eighteenth century, that change in understanding was never capable of overshadowing the framework of Eurocentric understandings that positioned the Indian within a context of expectations. The trope of the noble savage, and latterly its ignoble counterpart, came to infect much of the field of possibilities. However, the trope itself is reliant on earlier notions of European culture or its antipodes—civilization and barbarism, learning and ignorance, refinement and innocence, corruption and purity—producing the Indian as a conceptual alternative to European values. The repertoire the Indian was called upon to play may have been elaborated, especially in the middle decades of the eighteenth century, but his or her fundamental persona remained remarkably constant.

For all these reasons, the pressing task now is to work with these images and restore to them the complexity of their situation, that meeting point between history and fantasy in which the representation of American Indians was accomplished. What we cannot achieve satisfactorily at this remove is to restore the perspectives of American Indians to these representations. The scattered comments about portraiture, made by members of the 1762 Cherokee delegation, are insufficient to reclaim the opinions of those whose personality, way of life, or culture was represented thus.[1] What we can assume is that the labile culture of the "middle ground," which achieved a viable rapprochement between Indian and European conduct, would have articulated a sophisticated understanding of the differing modes of representation in Indian and European visual culture. Those engravings that circulated on the frontier might well have occasioned remark, but we have no means of knowing this; the records are silent.

It would be tempting, given this absence of eighteenth-century testimony, to turn to anthropology for insight and to judge these images by virtue of our presumed notions of accuracy. We would, in other words, examine them for their details, for their correct understanding of material culture, tribal behavior, and the like. Although there is much to learn from such investigations, the worry is that they close off the kind of inquiry I have undertaken with this book. Even if it were possible to prove that a particular artist had accurately depicted the hairstyle, facial decoration, body ornament, and clothing of a particular Eastern Woodlands tribe, such a conclusion is dangerous if it forestalls further inquiries into the circulation of the image. Visual accuracy of the sort a modern anthropologist might require was hardly a routine preoccupation of the eighteenth century. As Bernard Smith noted more than forty years ago, even on voyages of "discovery" artistic training and scientific procedures produced tensions in the field of vision. Moreover, a recourse to accuracy might suggest that "inaccurate" images are of less historical importance than seemingly more reliable ones. As I have hoped to show, however, every image has its tale to tell, all of them conspiring together to produce the eighteenth-century's concept of the Indian. It is not, therefore, so much a business of simply establishing how an image matches reality that concerns me. Rather, I am interested in the effects that images have, their ability to conjure up a compelling vision irrespective of any anthropological ignorance or artistic sleight of hand we might detect in them.

What, finally, can we make of this episode in visual culture? Is there anything in the British engagement with American Indians that leads to wider conclusions concerning the representation of race? One point that stands out prominently is the extent to which this imagery is not, at least initially, depicting subjugated peoples whose inferiority is marked by their subordinate position within the colonial experience. Instead, the representation of the various peoples who were of interest to Britain acknowledges their capacity for independent action, their military ability, and their strategic importance within the regions. Yet for all the avoidance of outright subjection within the imagery, in truth the Indians' entry into British recognition could not but be accomplished on anything other than prejudicial terms. Whether as useful allies or partners in trade, it is through the agency of British acceptance that these people gain whatever dignity and purpose their representations suggest. Filtered through the sensibilities of patrons, artists, and audiences, the image of American Indians is inescapably a confection that provides a pleasing surrogate to stand in for the alterity of an alien culture.

What follows from this, of course, is our realization that this imagery cannot be used to illustrate a historical account of colonial history in the eighteenth century, to assert that the Cherokees or the Iroquois are reliably present in the images that attempt to represent them. Frustrating as this is, we must accept that even the portraits of Indian delegates or tribal leaders are mediated images rather than truthful witnesses. The clash of cultures bound up in this imagery thus raises profound doubts about the ability of a culturally specific representational system to apprehend the complexity of lives lived so differently to European norms. This is not merely a question of artists lacking the direct knowledge of Indian customs and society that a colonial administrator, say, might possess. It points to the impossibility of fitting one people to another's precepts. The whole tradition of the fine arts in Europe grew up as a means to achieve some sort of cultural self-recognition, and the arts were tacitly accepted as one of the means by which the values of society might be projected. If there was a symbiotic relationship between the fine arts and society in Europe, it is understandable that the artists could only go so far when attempting to work with people whose cultural systems lay outside European experience. American Indians were translated into terms conformable to European values because the alternative, representing them in terms conformable to Indian values, was literally unthinkable.

What these images represent, therefore, is less a truthful record of their ostensible subjects and more a witness of the ways in which the concept of the American Indian was plastically produced. We should examine them as providing evidence of their own situation, attempting to make sense of American Indian culture at a particularly volatile moment in colonial history. Their partial truths and unreliable authority become, in this analysis, a route into the conceptual matrix that constructs the figure of the Indian. The "savage" surveyed in this book is thus neither a real individual in eighteenth-century America nor a complete figment of the European imagination but the product of a specific cultural encounter. The Indians presented in British eighteenth-century art were marked by the limits of European comprehension, certainly, but their depiction was occasioned by a pressing need to come to terms with them.

Notes

Introduction

1. Edward Said's *Orientalism: Western Concepts of the Orient* (New York: Pantheon Books, 1978) helped to open a field of study by giving formal analysis to a previously little understood European phenomenon. Ian Donaldson and Tamsin Donaldson, *Seeing the First Australians* (Sydney: George Allen and Unwin, 1985), and the four-volume publication underwritten by the Menil Foundation, Inc., *The Image of the Black in Western Art*, gen. ed. Ladislas Bugner (Cambridge, Mass.: Harvard University Press, 1989), with particular reference to vol. 4, part 1, written by Hugh Honour under the subtitle "Slaves and Liberators," are further examples.

2. There are at least two earlier studies of the imaging of American Indians with which one might compare more recent attempts to examine the idea of a racial type in art. The exhibition *The Noble Savage: The American Indian in Art* at the University Museum, Philadelphia, in 1958, and Elwood Parry, *The Image of the Indian and the Black Man in American Art* (New York: George Braziller, 1974), are both to a great extent concerned with American imagery of Indians and so are not strictly comparable to my own study. Hugh Honour's two major works on the question of the imaging of America come closest to my own area of concern. See Hugh Honour, *The New Golden Land: European Images*

of America from the Discoveries to the Present Time (New York: Pantheon Books, 1975) and Honour, *The European Vision of America* (The National Gallery, Washington, D.C.; the Cleveland Museum of Arts; and the Grand Palais, Paris, 1975–76, an exhibition catalog). In terms of comparative studies of blacks in art, I refer only to the Menil volume by Honour, which dealt extensively with eighteenth-century images of Africans in art.

3. Scholarly attention has often been directed toward the earliest visual imagery, as in the congress held at the University of California, Los Angeles in 1975. The congress published its papers under the title *First Images of America: The Impact of the New World on the Old*, edited by Fredi Chiapelli (Los Angeles: University of California Press, 1976). Exhibitions concerning the visual representation of American Indians were held in 1958 and 1975 (see note 2 above).

4. Exceptions to this stark division in the historiography are Hugh Honour's work and Mary Louise Krumrine and Susan Clare Scott, eds., *Art and the Native American: Perspectives, Reality and Influences*, Papers in Art History from Pennsylvania State University 10 (2001), which in its content straddles European-made and American-produced imagery of American Indians. Also of relevance are studies of the literature concerning American Indians, such as those found in the works of Richard Slotkin, Elemire Zolla, and Robert Berkhofer Jr.

5. See, for instance, Albert Boime, *The Art of Exclusion: Representing Blacks in the Nineteenth Century* (London: Thames and Hudson, 1990); Bernard Smith, *European Vision and the South Pacific* (New Haven, Conn.: Yale University Press, 1985); and Mary Ann Stevens, *The Orientalists: Delacroix to Matisse, European Painters in North Africa and the Near East* (London: The Royal Academy in association with Weidenfeld and Nicolson, 1984).

6. A related point concerns our understanding of the history of American art. If American-domiciled artists are to be considered the only legitimate contributors to such a history, then European images, often imaginary or literary confections, might appear somehow beside the point and largely irrelevant to such a history. Being neither illustrative of political history nor contributing to the history of American art, images made by Europeans of American Indian peoples might be precluded from examination.

7. See Colin G. Calloway, *Crown and Calumet: British and Indian Relations, 1783–1815* (Norman: University of Oklahoma Press, 1987); Richard White, *The Middle Ground: Indians, Empires, and Republics in the Great Lakes Region, 1650–1815* (Cambridge: Cambridge University Press, 1991); Anthony McFarlane, *The British in the Americas, 1480–1815* (London: Routledge, 1994).

8. See the seminal works of ethnohistorian James Axtell, such as *The Invasion Within: The Contest of Cultures in Colonial North America* (1985); Colin G. Calloway, *New Worlds for All: Indians, Europeans, and the Remaking of Early America* (Baltimore: Johns Hopkins University Press, 1997); and note 7 above.

9. The British Commonwealth Conference at University College London in 1997 held a session on British warfare and American Indian peoples; the British Association of American Studies (BAAS) Annual Conference at Glasgow University in March 1999 held one session having to do with eighteenth-century understandings of American Indians; and the Anglo-American Historians held a conference on race and ethnicity at the Institute of Historical Research June 30–July 2, 1999. Also, there is now a group of international scholars and academics who have founded an Early Americanist group to be part of the BAAS activities.

10. My doctoral dissertation, "The European Perception of the Native American, 1750–1850" (Council for National Academic Awards, 1990), provided the starting point for this book and operated with a wider focus, as its title suggests.

11. For instance, Olive P. Dickason, *The Myth of the Savage; And the Beginnings of French Colonialism in the Americas* (Edmonton: University of Alberta Press, 1984).

12. Roy Harvey Pearce, *Savagism and Civilization: A Study of the Indian and the American Mind* (Baltimore: Johns Hopkins University Press, 1953); Benjamin Bissell, *The American Indian in English Literature of the Eighteenth Century* (New Haven, Conn.: Yale University Press, 1925). See also Robert Berkhofer Jr., *The White Man's Indian* (New York: Alfred Knopf, 1978); Parry, *Image of the Indian*; and Honour, *New Golden Land*.

1. The Allegorical Representation of America

1. Joseph Warton, "Revenge of America," as quoted in *The Penguin Book of Eighteenth Century Verse*, edited by Dennis Davidson (Harmondsworth, U.K.: Penguin Books, 1973) 204. The poem reaches its conclusion when Warton reveals what the "revenge" of America will entail. The Spanish lust for gold will destroy them

I see all Europe's children cursed
With lucre's universal thirst:
The rage that sweeps my sons away,
My baneful gold shall well repay.

2. Accounts of the harsh treatment received by Indians at the hands of the Spanish first entered English literature in 1583, when Fra Bartolome de las Casas's *Brevissima relacion de la destruccion de las Indias* (1552–53) was published in translation. Las Casas's work was one of the first to express what would become a more commonplace representation of Peruvian or Mexican characters in English literature later in the seventeenth century, as the unfortunate victims of larger historical and colonizing forces. A number

of plays treated South and Central American subjects in this manner for the Restoration and post-Restoration stage, for instance, William Davenant's *The Cruelty of the Spaniards in Peru* (performed in 1658), based on a translation of Las Casas's entitled *Tears of the Indians* (1656); John Dryden and Sir Robert Howard's *The Indian Queen* (1664); Dryden's *The Indian Emperour* (1665); and, much later, Richard Brinsley Sheridan's *Pizarro, or the Spaniards in Peru* (first performed in 1799), an adaptation of Kotzebue's *Die Spanier in Peru, oder Rolla's Tod* (1795). In literature, for example, the poetry of Robert Southey and William Lisle Bowles offers further instances of this tendency in the very early nineteenth century. See, for example, Southey's "Mooma" in *Tale of Paraguay* (1814), an Indian woman who exhibits qualities of the allegory of America as an idealized symbol of place. Another is Bowles's *Missionary of the Andes* (1813), where the central figure of a young Indian woman strokes her pet alpaca and thus reiterates the allegory of America with appropriate attributes in the native flora and fauna surrounding her. For the dates and a discussion of these poems, see Hoxie Neale Fairchild, *The Noble Savage: A Study in Romantic Naturalism* (1928, repr., New York: Russell and Russell, 1961), 274.

3. Historically, the European "discovery" of the continent of America, with its previously unknown inhabitants, coincided with a development in art and culture that sought to understand and bring together both ancient and modern forms of knowledge. As a result of the Renaissance impetus to unify and make whole an increasingly fragmented view of the world and its contents, America's discovery came at a time that was auspicious for its being mapped into already existing structures of knowledge. A medieval view of the tripartite nature of the global landmasses shown on the *mappimundi* (such as the Hereford world map) was ameliorated and transformed with contemporary cartographic science to present a quadripartite division of the world according to its "four parts." This idea of a new, undiscovered continent was made more understandable by giving it an identity consonant with existing geographical understanding. America was thus given a classical status and a symbolic personage to represent its presence in the eternal scheme of things. The American Indian figure from the 1570s to the early nineteenth century became the standard way of elucidating America symbolically. For a discussion of early spectacles and fetes that included representations of America as allegory, see James Hazen Hyde, "The Four Parts of the World as Represented in Old-Time Pageants and Ballets," part I, *Apollo*, no. 4 (1926): 232–38; and Hyde, "Old-Time Pageants and Ballets," part II, *Apollo*, no. 5 (1927): 20–26. The "Allegory of America" as represented in art is chapter 4 of Honour's *New Golden Land*, 84–117. A discussion of the changes between medieval and Renaissance mapping of the world is found in J. R. Hale, *Renaissance Exploration* (London: British Broadcasting Corporation Publications, 1968).

4. The most influential of the allegorical handbooks was Cesare Ripa's *Iconologia*, first published in Rome in 1593 and illustrated in several of its subsequent editions.

5. In Cesare Ripa's *Iconologia*, the personification of America is a male figure, and the objects that ornament and surround him are intended to typify the essence of America.

6. Johann Georg Hertel, "Ripa's 'Iconologia,' illustrated with the help of the painter Gottfried Eichler the Younger" (1758–60), reprinted as Edward A. Maser, ed., *Baroque and Rococo Pictorial Imagery, the 1758–1760 Hertel Edition of Ripa's "Iconologia"* (New York: Dover Books, 1971).

7. Maser, *Baroque and Rococo*, entry no. 105, n.p.

8. Witness the mezzotint portraits by William Vincent and Bernard Lens of the actress Anne Bracegirdle in her role as "The Indian Queen."

9. For instance, Anne Bracegirdle playing the role of Semernia, or "The Indian Queen," as was acted onstage in Aphra Behn's *The Widow Ranter* (ca. 1700), exemplifies this tendency. A mezzotint of Bracegirdle in the role of "The Indian Queen" may represent the character Semernia and provides an apt visual equivalent to the combination of different genres found in Behn's writings. The subject of the print is either a representation of the actress in her role as Semernia or could refer to the main character in Dryden and Howard's play *The Indian Queen*, perhaps performed by Bracegirdle in its earliest stagings. See Emmett L. Avery, ed., *The London Stage, 1660–1800*, vols. 1–2 (Carbondale: Southern Illinois University Press, 1960), 7, 29, 92, 95, 122, where *The Indian Queen* is listed as an opera performance but the cast lists are unknown.

10. Aphra Behn, *Oroonoko, and Other Stories*, edited by Maureen Duffy (London: Methuen, 1986), 28.

11. Helen Carr, "Woman/Indian: 'The American' and His Others," in *Europe and Its Others: Proceedings of the Essex Conference on the Sociology of Literature* 2, (July 1984), University of Essex, Colchester, 1985, 49.

12. See Peter Hulme, "Polytropic Man: Tropes of Sexuality and Mobility in Early Colonial Discourse," in *Europe and Its Others*, 17–18.

13. Bacon was a historical figure involved in a small skirmish called Bacon's Rebellion that occurred in Virginia in the late seventeenth century.

14. Tongiori Tomasi argues that book frontispieces and title pages were a form of representing new knowledge and structuring that knowledge for the viewers of these texts. See Tomasi, "Image, Symbol and Word on the Title Pages and Frontispieces of Scientific Books from the Sixteenth and Seventeenth Centuries," *Word & Image* 4, no. 1 (January–March 1988): 372–79.

15. Christopher Hussey, *English Gardens and Landscapes, 1700–1750* (London: Country Life, 1967), 104.

16. See Francis Haskell and Nicholas Penny, *Taste and the Antique: The Lure of Classical Sculpture, 1500–1900* (New Haven, Conn.: Yale University Press, 1981), entry no. 8, 150.

17. Comparisons between ancient Greco-Roman myths and gods and American Indian beliefs and "deities" were not new in the eighteenth century. Such comparisons had several precedents in writings of the mid-seventeenth century and were initiated as early as the sixteenth century. See Sabine MacCormack, "Limits of Understanding: Perceptions of Greco-Roman and Amerindian Paganism in Early Modern Europe," in *America in European Consciousness, 1493–1750*, edited by Karen Ordahl Kupperman (Chapel Hill: University of North Carolina Press, 1995), 79–129.

18. As translated from the German by Henry Fuseli (London, 1765) and reprinted in Lorenz Eitner, ed., *Neo-Classicism and Romanticism*, vol. 1, 1750–1850 (London: Prentice-Hall, 1971), 6.

19. John Shebbeare, *Lydia; or Filial Piety* (1755 repr., London, 1786), 1:6.

20. The incident concerning West and his first viewing of the statue was initially committed to print in a footnote to the poem by Richard Payne Knight, *The Landscape: A Didactic Poem in Three Books* (1794). For mention of Payne Knight's poem and West's use of the pose of the Apollo Belvedere, see Matthew Craske, *Art in Europe 1700–1830: A History of the Visual Arts in an Era of Unprecedented Urban Economic Growth* (Oxford: Oxford University Press, 1997), 265. West's by then famous reaction to this statue was reiterated in 1816 in John Galt's biography of the artist and seems to play into his biographical image as the archetypal innocent artist, untrained and therefore unsullied by European values and customs. See John Galt, *The Life, Studies and Works of Benjamin West, Esq., President of the Royal Academy* (1816, Philadelphia; repr. London: T. Codell and W. Davies, 1820; repr., Gainsville, Fla.: Scholars' Facsimiles and Reprints, 1960), 103–6, 115.

21. Other examples of the use of the Apollo Belvedere pose can be found in costume book illustrations of this period. W. G. Hausleutner's *Gallerie der Nationen* (1793) includes a section on the Americas in which two images particularly borrow the pose: a Cherokee chief and an "Ottowa" Indian (Plates VII and IX). Hausleutner probably derived his figures from Thomas Jefferys's *A Collection of the Dresses of Different Nations both Ancient and Modern*, vol. 4 (London, 1772), which contains similarly posed figures (Plates CXCVII, CCV–CCVIII).

22. It has been suggested that a contemporary interpretation of the Apollo Belvedere as a hunter gained prominence in the second half of the eighteenth century, facilitating his identification with primitive hunters in real life. Benjamin West is reported to have remarked, on seeing the statue for the first time, "My God! . . . How like it is to a young Mohawk warrior." See Galt, *Life Studies and Works*, 103-6, 115 (as cited in Haskell and Penny, *Taste and the Antique*, 150). Evidence exists in contemporary fiction to show that West's comparison was not unique. In John Shebbeare's *Lydia* (1755), the narrator watches Cannassatego shoot an arrow, after which the American is animated by "the air,

attitude; and expression; of the beauteous statue of Apollo, which adorns the Belvidera [*sic*] Palace at Rome" (6). See also Stephanie Pratt, "From Cannassatego to Outalissi: Making Sense of the Native American in Eighteenth-Century Culture," in *An Economy of Colour: Visual Culture and the Atlantic World, 1660–1830*, edited by Geoff Quilley and Kay Dian Kriz (Manchester: Manchester University Press, 2003), 60–82.

23. A reference to the taking of scalps occurs in the background of the picture, where a similarly attired Indian is shown kneeling over a victim. In fact, the whole image seems to encompass a chronology, with the inclusion of tiny Indian figures on the right firing at European soldiers who point to the scalping vignette. The sequence culminates in and explains the dominant central figure, displaying his prize. The result is a brutality that is evident yet minimized, with incidental figures committing the atrocity, while its result is shown in a highly refined pose.

24. For the medieval association of difference with cannibalism, see John Block Friedman, *The Monstrous Races in Mediaeval Art and Thought* (Cambridge, Mass.: Harvard University Press, 1981), 34–35.

25. There could be confusion here between imagery associated with peoples of the West Indian colonies and those living in British North America. The figure is given a dark skin tone in the engraving (by the use of cross-hatching), which is unusual with respect to most images of American Indian peoples at this time. The curly hair is also unexpected for an Eastern Woodlands tribe. Some conflation of imagery culled from a variety of sources is most likely responsible for this figure. For a fuller analysis of this image, see Pratt, "From Cannassatego to Outalissi."

26. Robert N. Essick, *William Blake, Printmaker* (Princeton, N.J.: Princeton University Press, 1980), 52–53. A new critical reading of Blake's image is offered in Marcus Wood, "John Gabriel Stedman, William Blake, Francesco Bartolozzi and Empathetic Pornography in the *Narrative of a Five Years Expedition against the Revolted Negroes of Surinam*," in Quilley and Kriz, *An Economy of Colour*, 129–49.

2. Warfare, Diplomacy, and Visual Representation

1. Eric Hinderaker, "The 'Four Indian Kings' and the Imaginative Construction of the First British Empire," *William and Mary Quarterly*, 3rd series, 53, no. 3 (July 1996) 488.

2. Robert Utley and Wilcomb Washburn, *The History of the Indian Wars* (London: Mitchell Beazley, 1977), 71–73.

3. Ibid., 73–82. After 1722, the Tuscaroras would move from their homelands in North Carolina to become part of the Iroquois League, thus increasing the number to six nations instead of the original five (Mohawk, Oneida, Onondaga, Cayuga, and Seneca).

4. Cadwallader Colden, *The History of the Five Indian Nations, Depending on the Province of New York in America,* parts I and II (1727, 1747; repr., Ithaca, N.Y.: Cornell University Press, 1958), v.

5. Ibid., 77–78.

6. See Carl Waldman, *The Atlas of the North American Indian* (Oxford: Facts on File, 1985) 93.

7. According to historians, the "Covenant Chain" consisted of an "enduring partnership between the English and the Five Nations of Iroquois against the French and their Huron allies." It began in 1675-76 during King Philip's War in America, when the then governor of New York, Edmund Andros, formed an alliance with the Iroquois in order to quash New England Indian insurgency. See McFarlane, *The British in the Americas,* 120–21. See also the classic study of the Iroquois League by Francis Jennings, *The Ambiguous Iroquois Empire: The Covenant Chain Federation of Indian Tribes with the English Colonies from Its Beginnings to the Lancaster Treaty of 1744* (New York: Norton, 1984).

8. Fred Anderson, *Crucible of War: The Seven Years' War and the Fate of Empire in British North America, 1754–1766* (New York: Random House, 2000), 12–21.

9. See Daniel K. Richter, *The Ordeal of the Longhouse: The Peoples of the Iroquois League in the Era of European Colonization* (Chapel Hill: University of North Carolina Press, 1992), 236–54; Anderson, *Crucible of War,* 16–21; and Armstrong Starkey, *European and Native American Warfare, 1675–1815* (London: University College London Press, 1998), 33–34.

10. Herman J. Viola, *Diplomats in Buckskins: A History of Indian Delegations in Washington City* (Washington, D.C.: Smithsonian Institution Press, 1981), 13. This is also cited in Richmond P. Bond, *Queen Anne's American Kings* (Oxford: Clarendon Press, 1952), 33.

11. One of these men was identified as a Mahican, Schacook, or River Indian, the Mahicans being an Algonquian tribe living to the east of the Mohawks in the Hudson River valley, whom the latter seem to have considered under their suzerainty. Bond's *Queen Anne's American Kings* is the classic study of the visit of 1710. More recent discussion of the images that resulted from this visit is found in John G. Garratt, *The Four Indian Kings/Les Quatres Rois Indiens* (Ottawa: Public Archives of Canada, 1985); and Hinderaker, "Four Indian Kings." Bond suggests that another of the delegation may have been born a Mahican and then adopted by the Mohawks. This is Hendrick, known in the accounts of the 1710 visit as Tee Yee Neen Ho Ga Row, "Emperour of the Six Nations," or nominal leader of the group. His Iroquoian name is given as Theyanoguin or Teoniahigarawe in some accounts. See Bond, *Queen Anne's American Kings,* 39–40.

12. From the signed statement of Peter Schuyler et al. to Samuel Vetch, commander of the colonial invasion forces, in Bond, *Queen Anne's American Kings,* 32.

13. Foreman writes of the visit that "[they] received . . . much the same honours accorded Pocahontas, they were quite strange to the English, who followed them about the streets. The Archbishop of Canterbury gave each of the Mohawks a Bible, and an elaborate pamphlet was issued in London, giving a history of them and their tribe; pictures of them were sold on the streets." The Indians, conducted to court by Sir Charles Cotterell, had an audience with Queen Anne at St. James Palace on April 19, 1710. See Carolyn T. Foreman, *Indians Abroad, 1493–1938* (Norman: University of Oklahoma Press, 1943), 34–35.

14. At least three sets of mezzotints were published that contained the likenesses of each of the four Indian men, one of these apparently drawn from life; see Hinderaker, "Four Indian Kings," 507–23; Garratt, *Four Indian Kings;* and Bond, *Queen Anne's American Kings.*

15. Although somewhat confusing, the "six" here is a reference to the Mahican delegate, not the Tuscarora who would join the League only after 1722; see Hinderaker, "Four Indian Kings," 490. The wampum belt looks to have designs in the shape of small crosses picked out in contrasting white shell beads. This may have some connection with the fact that Hendrick, more certainly than the others, was Christianized and that the crosses allude to his conversion, as well as the desire on the part of the delegation to obtain missionaries to work among the Mohawks. See note 16 below.

16. This document was signed on the Mohawks' return to America to be sent in thanks to Queen Anne and her ministers for the favorable treatment given to the Indians on their visit. It was also written to reiterate their requests for missions to be established among the Mohawks, including the producing of translations of the Bible into the Mohawk language. See Bond, *Queen Anne's American Kings,* 8 and illustration facing page 8.

17. Hinderaker, "Four Indian Kings," 491. Bond gives an account of Samuel Vetch's preparations for the visit of the Mohawks, which include Vetch arranging for the Indians to be properly dressed and rested in order to meet with the queen. He "ordered his London agent, James Douglas, to provide funds for the sachems' transportation and correct clothing to wear before Her Majesty, as well as lodging and accommodation until they had waited upon his Lordship" (*Queen Anne's American Kings,* 43).

18. As quoted from William Smith Jr., *The History of the Province of New York* (1757), edited by Michael Kammen (Cambridge, Mass.: Harvard University Press, 1972), in Hinderaker, "Four Indian Kings," 491.

19. Hinderaker, "Four Indian Kings," 488, 487–526.

20. I have not attempted the almost impossible task of determining the actual status of these men in the 1710 delegation. A more fruitful mode of inquiry might be concerned with the impact, if any, these visits had on American Indian groups on the return of the

delegates. Some delegates went on to become leaders or influential members of their peoples on their return. One can note in particular from this era the figure of Attakulla-kulla, a member of Sir Alexander Cuming's 1730 delegation of Cherokees to London. Attakullakulla, who often spoke of his time in London, was a much-respected leader in Cherokee tribal politics of the midcentury and up until his death. Hendrick's later career in America and eventual death at the Battle of Lake George in 1755 speak of a continuing leadership role in Mohawk war making at least.

21. Foreman, *Indians Abroad*, 47; see also note 42 below.

22. As quoted from the *London Daily Journal* of June 18, 1730, in Foreman, *Indians Abroad*, 46.

23. Foreman quotes from the *Grub Street Journal* of July 30, 1730: "*The St. James's Evening Post* calls them 'Indian Kings; but this is not the first time that Kings have been confounded with their Ministers.'" For further contemporary reactions to this visit, see Foreman, *Indians Abroad*, 46. Bond cites a contemporary report by Daniel Defoe criticizing the presentation of the Indians in 1710 as "kings" (*Queen Anne's American Kings*, 74–77).

24. Jonathan Swift, in his *Journal to Stella*, claimed that it was he who "gave" Steele and Addison the idea of publishing the supposed "letters" of a visiting American Indian chieftain to London. He apparently had hoped to write a book about this himself, but all his ideas had been "used up" in Steele and Addison's article in the *Spectator* no. 50 (April 27, 1711). See Bond, *Queen Anne's American Kings*, 85–86.

25. Foreman, *Indians Abroad*, 39. Another commentator in the *Spectator* notes that this supposed letter from one of the Mohawks bears a striking relationship with "Notes from a Turkish Spy" and hence the whole tradition of the "Letters from a Foreigner Abroad in England." Bond, *Queen Anne's American Kings*, 86–87.

26. Fairchild, *Noble Savage*, 41.

27. Ibid.

28. Ibid.

29. Colden, *History*, 70–72.

30. Delawares and Shawnees had been driven out of eastern tribal lands earlier in the seventeenth and early eighteenth centuries. They were thought of as "younger relations" or "women' by the Iroquois leadership.

31. For an explanation of the role played by Canasatego, see Anderson, *Crucible of War*, 23–24.

32. John Fleming, "Robert Adam, Luc-François Breton and the *Townshend Monument* in Westminster Abbey," *Connoisseur* 150, no. 605 (July 1962): 171n10.

33. Ibid., 164. Townshend had brought home a French-speaking Indian boy "(design'd for Ld G:Sackville, but he did not chuse to take him) who goes about in his own dress, &

is brought into the room to divert his company." This suggests the boy was Choctaw. See Thomas Gray, *Correspondence of Thomas Gray*, edited by Paget Toynbee and Leonard Whibley, letter 308, January 23, 1760 (Oxford: Oxford University Press, 1935), 657.

34. See discussion of the monument in Honour, *New Golden Land*, 128–29. Adams's adaptation of the Wolfe Monument design for the Townshend Monument is discussed in Fleming, "Robert Adam," 163–71.

35. These two conflicts are described in Anderson, *Crucible of War*, 94–107, 185–201.

36. Anon., "American Affairs," *Gentlemen's Magazine* 27 (1757): 475.

37. Anderson, *Crucible of War*, 189.

38. Starkey, *European and Native American Warfare*, 19.

39. White, *Middle Ground*, 315.

40. For previous negotiations between Canasatego and the Pennsylvania colony, see Calloway, *New Worlds for All*, 131.

41. Anderson, *Crucible of War*, 457–71, 535–46. See also Gregory Evans Dowd, *A Spirited Resistance: The North American Indian Struggle for Unity, 1745–1815* (Baltimore: Johns Hopkins University Press, 1992), 25–27; and White, *Middle Ground*, 271–72.

42. Anderson, *Crucible of War*, 459–60.

43. See the discussion of Attakullakulla's role in bringing about a satisfactory arrangement for peace between the British and the Cherokees in 1761 in ibid., 467–68.

44. Foreman, *Indians Abroad*, 65.

45. Timberlake would later write of his experiences both in traveling to the Cherokee settlements and in conducting the delegation of Cherokees to London in his *Memoirs* (London, 1765).

46. As quoted in Foreman, *Indians Abroad*, 66.

47. Foreman, *Indians Abroad*, 65.

48. Ibid., 67.

49. Bond, *Queen Anne's American Kings*, 89. Presumably, the letter quoted here refers to the visit of the Cherokees in 1730, including Attakullakulla, and to the interpreter in that situation, Sir Alexander Cuming.

50. Ibid., 89–90.

51. Foreman, *Indians Abroad*, 67.

52. For a discussion of Parsons's portrait and the mezzotint engraving of it by James MacArdell, see ibid., 70–71n9. For a fuller discussion of the Cherokee delegates and questions over their identities, see Stephanie Pratt, "Reynolds' 'King of the Cherokees' and Other Mistaken Identities in the Portraiture of Native American Delegations, 1710–1762," *Oxford Art Journal* 21, no. 2 (1998): 133–50.

53. Foreman, *Indians Abroad*, 70.

54. Ibid., 74–76.

55. Henry Howard, "A New Humorous Song, on the Cherokee Chiefs. Inscribed to the Ladies of Great Britain," broadsheet, London, 1762. British Library, accession no. 1850.c.10.(79).

56. J. C. H. King, *Smoking Pipes of the North American Indian* (London: British Museum Press, 1977), 24–27.

57. Foreman, *Indians Abroad*, 70–71.

58. See Pratt, "Reynolds' 'King of the Cherokees,'" 150.

59. Foreman mentions a "portrait group of Indian Chiefs who visited England in 1763. Engraved by McArdell" (*Indians Abroad*, 70). Perhaps this is the engraving of the "Three Cherokee Chiefs and Their Interpreter who Was Poisoned" (1762) (British Museum, London), long thought to be after a portrait group by Reynolds. See William P. Cumming et al., *The Exploration of North America 1630–1776* (London: Paul Elek, 1977). Another print (anon.) depicts the "Chief Warrior, Outacity" (1762) (British Museum, London) and is thought to be based on a portrait by Reynolds. However, this latter print bears little resemblance to the only existing portrait by Reynolds of this man (*Scyacust Ukah* [oil on canvas] [1762], Thomas Gilcrease Institute, Tulsa, Ok.).

60. One example produced in the year of the Cherokee visit seems to point to the ways that American Indians had been manipulated and exhibited by unscrupulous entrepreneurs. The satiric print by Hogarth called *The Times* (1762) includes a reference to the then-visiting group of Cherokee Indians in 1762. In the print, a naked Indian male is shown on a pub sign above the notice "Alive from America" and wearing a belt hung with bagged coins around his middle, some of which he holds forward in his hands.

61. To find the American Indian figure represented in the design of such items as a ship's figurehead or as a support figure in the arrangement of a coat-of-arms such as that of the Company of Distillers is to perceive that this personage is merely a token not of ethnographic content but of exotic or economic qualities. Similar to this are the commemorative coins and trading tokens that sometimes contained an image of an "Indian," witnessed in the examples of a coin minted for the Distillers in about 1770 and depicting an Indian in a feather skirt with a feather "crown" on his head and in the trading token used by an Exeter merchant in the seventeenth century. The image of an American Indian contained in an item of tableware or as part of the design of a tobacco label cannot aspire to the same kind of tone as it might in instances of high art, such as painting and sculpture. Secondary sources pertaining to decorative items include R. J. Charleston, ed., *World Ceramics—An Illustrated History* (London: Paul Hamlyn, 1968), 253, where there is a discussion of Plymouth porcelain; medals are discussed and illustrated in Christopher Eimer, *British Commemorative Medals* (London: B. A. Seaby, 1987), 100; trading tokens are listed in R. H. Thompson, *The Sylloge of Coins of the British Isles (31) Norweb Collection,*

Tokens of the British Isles, 1575–1750, Part I, *Bedfordshire to Devon* (London: Spink and Son, 1984), see Plate XXVIII, no. 663.

62. M. Dorothy George, *English Political Caricature to 1792: A Study in Opinion and Propaganda* (Oxford: Clarendon Press, 1959), 135.

63. The shop windows were a place where items could be displayed without charging the usual entrance fee. Inside, "the usual price was 6d. for plain and 1s. for coloured prints" (F. D. Klingender, ed., *Hogarth and English Caricature* [1944; repr. London: Transatlantic Arts, 1945], iii). See also Peter D. G. Thomas, *The American Revolution: The English Satirical Print 1600–1832* (Cambridge: Cambridge University Press, 1986).

64. See Elizabeth McClung-Fleming, "The American Image as Indian Princess, 1765–1783," *Winterthur Portfolio* 2 (1965): 65–81; and McClung-Fleming, "From Indian Princess to Greek Goddess—The American Image, 1783–1815," *Winterthur Portfolio* 3 (1967): 37–66.

65. Conventionally, the central figure of Hercules must make a choice between a life of virtue or a life of vice, as represented by the figures of goddesses of their respective worlds. The appropriateness of this subject for serious history painting is discussed in Lord Shaftesbury, *Treatise VII, Characteristicks, III* (London, 1714).

66. In the section of William Smith's *Historical Account of the Expedition Against the Ohio Indians* (Philadelphia, 1765), which was composed by Thomas Hutchins, it states that "the love of liberty is innate in the savage; and seems the ruling passion in the state of nature." Quoted in Richard Slotkin, *Regeneration through Violence: The Mythology of the American Frontier, 1600–1860* (Middletown, Conn.: Wesleyan University Press, 1973), 233.

67. One puzzling aspect of America's adornment at this time seen in many of the political prints is the criss-cross pattern placed on the skirt tied about the figure of America. This pattern (a plaid?) may be a contemporary allusion to the "Scotch" government of George III, which it was thought had been too easily influenced by Scottish ministers like Lord Bute. In the language of the political satirists, America has come under Scottish control. See George, *English Political Caricature*, 123-25.

68. The Chelsea factory figurines are discussed in Honour, *European Vision of America*, n.p., catalog no. 147.

69. See Charleston, *World Ceramics*, 253, where there is a discussion of Plymouth porcelain.

70. See discussion of this group in the British Museum, *British Museum Department of Medieval and Later Antiquities-Porcelain Catalogue* (London: British Museum, 1958), 2:48.

71. McClung-Fleming, "From Indian Princess," 37-66.

72. Ibid., 38-39. Two prints published during the hostilities, *Bunker's Hill, or the Blessed Effects of Family Quarrels* of 1775 and *The Parricide* of 1776, show the situation in the American colonies as a physical feud between two females. Both are illustrated in Thomas, *American Revolution.*

73. For example, the speech of American Indians is often portrayed as simple, unadorned, and childlike, either due to their lack of understanding the English language or to the idea that their culture was itself simple, pure, and primitive. See various extracts of contemporary accounts of American Indian culture in Wilcomb E. Washburn, ed., *The Indian and the White Man* (New York: Doubleday, 1964); see also Cumming, *Exploration of North America.*

3. History Painting and American Indians

1. Alan Staley and Helmut von Erffa, *The Paintings of Benjamin West* (New Haven, Conn.: Yale University Press, 1986), 213.

2. These comments by West were originally published in his biography by Galt, *Life, Studies and Works*, 2:48. West's attitudes to his picture were also discussed in Staley and Von Erffa, *Paintings of Benjamin West*, 212.

3. Charles Mitchell, "Benjamin West's 'Death of General Wolfe' and the Popular History Piece," *Journal of the Warburg and Courtauld Institutes* 7 (1944): 20–33.

4. Edgar Wind, "The Revolution of History Painting," *Journal of the Warburg and Courtauld Institutes* 2 (October 1938): 116–27.

5. The image of a snake seems significant here, as Benjamin Franklin in 1754 adopted this precise symbol in a print he designed. There the divided pieces of a snake make reference to the colonies, inciting them with the phrase "Join, or Die." See illustration 4.23 in David Bjelajac, *American Art: A Cultural History* (London: Laurence King, 2000), 133.

6. Bromley's analysis is cited in Barbara A. C. Saunders, "A European Image of the Noble Savage: Joseph Wright's 'Indian Widow'" (master's thesis, University of Leiden, 1977), 4n77.

7. William Pressley, *The Life and Art of James Barry* (New Haven, Conn.: Yale University Press, 1981), 60.

8. For an analysis of the picture and its visual effects, as well as Barry's surviving notes on it, see ibid., 61.

9. One exception to this might be the connection between Benjamin West's picture of Wolfe's death and John Trumbull's of the Revolutionary War general Montgomery. *The Death of General Wolfe* was possibly the inspiration for the painting by Trumbull, who was working abroad in England during the last quarter of the eighteenth century

and was associated with West's studio. Trumbull's *The Death of General Montgomery* (1786), like West's picture of Wolfe's demise, includes an American Indian figure placed in a central position within the work's formal and narrative structures.

10. Galt, *Life, Studies and Works*, 18.

11. *Storia degli stabilimenti europei in America* (Venice, 1763). Burke's account had first been published in London in 1757. See Hugh Honour, "Benjamin West's *Indian Family*," *Burlington Magazine* 125 (1983): 726–33.

12. The text is reproduced in Honour, "Benjamin West's *Indian Family*," appendix, 732–33.

13. See discussion of the classical pose of the Roman togate magistrate, as it was adapted to suit portraiture of noted leaders in England and Scotland in the 1740s and 1750s, particularly Ramsay's *Macleod of MacCleod* (1748) and Sir Joshua Reynolds's *Commodore Augustus Keppel* (1753), in Alastair Smart, *Allan Ramsay 1713–1784* (Edinburgh: Scottish National Portrait Gallery, 1992), 112–13; and David Solkin, "Great Pictures or Great Men? Reynolds, Male Portraiture, and the Power of Art," *Oxford Art Journal* 9, no. 2 (1986): 42–49. The pose of General Robert Monckton in West's portrait of him (ca. 1764) is very similar to that adopted by the sitters in the portraits by Ramsay and Reynolds mentioned above.

14. This incident was relayed to the general reading public via Diderot's *Memoirs*, relating a 1760 meeting with Von Dieskau. It is thought that the Mohawks who attacked the French commander were acting in retaliation for the death in battle of Hendrick, the Mohawk leader and longtime ally of the English since his visit with other young Mohawk leaders in 1710. As Von Dieskau spent some years in England, West may have actually met him. See Staley and Von Erffa, *Paintings of Benjamin West*, entry no. 92, 211.

15. Chatham's speech and the debates in Parliament are referred to in Robert Lawson-Peebles, *Landscape and Written Expression in Revolutionary America: The World Turned Upside Down* (Cambridge: Cambridge University Press, 1988), 26.

16. Samuel Y. Edgerton Jr., "The Murder of Jane MacCrea: The Tragedy of an American 'Tableau d'histoire,'" *Art Bulletin* 47, no. 4 (1965): 482–92.

17. Eventually, the task would be given to another artist, Robert Smirke; see ibid., 482.

18. The historical accounts are not in agreement over what actually occurred to result in the death and scalping of Jane MacCrea.

19. Her case is discussed in Starkey, *European and Native American Warfare*, 111–12.

20. Although Vanderlyn's composition is striking and seemingly original, it is possible that other extant illustrations of Jane MacCrea's death may have influenced his thinking. An aquatint of 1778 entitled *The Closet* contains several compartments depicting important episodes from the Revolutionary War. In the top left compartment is an image of the MacCrea murder scene showing the young woman kneeling with her hands clasped

together in a supplicant position. An American Indian man is shown rushing in from the right in a manner very similar to that seen on the right-hand side in Vanderlyn's painting. To the left of this central figure group in the print, a subsequent event is shown, the restraining of the victim by both American Indian men so that her scalp can be taken. As *The Closet* was a political print, and therefore meant to arouse criticism of wartime practices, its brutality is strategic, as it was intended to shock or horrify. When Vanderlyn revisited this scene in his painting of 1804, not only were the events securely passed, but the function of the image had altered as well. A history painting, designed to arouse general reflections on human behavior, transfers actual historical events to the realm of the epic. The 1778 print, on the other hand, in its almost casual depiction of what it presents as a genuine atrocity, gives MacCrea's murder all the horror of a documentary report.

21. For instance, see Kathleen Moss Pritchard, "John Vanderlyn and the Massacre of Jane MacCrea," *Art Quarterly* 12 (1949): 361–65.

22. The story was recounted for a popular audience in Parson M. L. Weems, *The Life of William Penn, the Settler of Pennsylvania* (1822; repr., Philadelphia, 1845), 146–56. It would eventually become engrained in the American historical consciousness down even to the present day. For a discussion of the painting and its connection to the Pennsylvanian colonial situation at the time, see Ann Uhry Abrams, "Benjamin West's Documentation of Colonial History: *William Penn's Treaty with the Indians*," *Art Bulletin* 47, no. 4 (1982): 59–75; see 59n1 for details of early sources of the Penn legend.

23. The Paxton Boys were Scots-Irish immigrants living on the eastern Pennsylvania frontier who were angry over the lack of armed defense provided for those families exposed to violence perpetrated by American Indian irregulars during the Seven Years' War. They rose up as a force in 1763–64 and attacked and killed a group of pacifist Conestoga Indians before turning to the Moravian Indians. Current online encyclopedic sources discuss the moves by Governor John Penn to bring the Paxton Boys to justice. See "Early History of Pennsylvania," found at *www.u-s-history.com/pages/h1188.html* (2002). See also "Paxton Boys Uprising," Encyclopedia Britannica, 2004, Encyclopedia Britannica Premium Service, February 11, 2004, *www.britannica.com/eb/article?eu=60305*.

24. Abrams, "Benjamin West's Documentation," 72–73.

25. Galt, *Life, Studies and Works*, 15.

26. Abrams, "Benjamin West's Documentation," 69.

27. Ibid., 61.

28. The Lenni Lenape came under the designation of "Delaware" Indians due to their Algonquin-language grouping. The Delaware Indians migrated westward to the Ohio Valley regions from eastern Pennsylvania during the period known as the Beaver Wars. See Helen Hornbeck Tanner, ed., *Atlas of Great Lakes Indian History* (Norman: Oklahoma University Press, 1987), 2.

29. This is an extract of a letter written in February 1805 to William Darton, cited in Staley and Von Erffa, *Paintings of Benjamin West*, entry no. 85, 207-8.

30. Staley and Von Erffa, *Paintings of Benjamin West*, 210-11.

31. *Gentleman's Magazine* 25 (1755): 486-87.

32. Galt, *Life, Studies and Works*, 67.

33. Joseph Farington, *The Diary of Joseph Farington*, edited by Kathryn Cave, vol. 4, entry for March 15, 1801 (New Haven, Conn.: Yale University Press, 1984), 1521–22.

34. These are discussed in Abrams, "Benjamin West's Documentation," 66–68, and mentioned in Honour, *New Golden Land*, 129.

35. J. C. H. King, "Woodlands Artifacts from the Studio of Benjamin West, 1738–1820," *American Indian Art Magazine* 27 (Winter 1992): 34–47.

36. See, for instance, the identifications proposed in ibid., 34–47; see also Arthur Einhorn and Thomas S. Abler, "Bonnets, Plumes and Headbands in West's Painting of Penn's Treaty," *American Indian Art Magazine* 21 (Summer 1996): 44–53. These contrast with Honour, "Benjamin West's *Indian Family*."

37. Galt, *Life, Studies and Works*, 105–6.

38. Honour, "Benjamin West's *Indian Family*."

39. See the discussion of the painting's ambiguities in Courtney Noble, "Rescuing Difference: Ambiguous Heroism in Benjamin West's *General Johnson Saving a Wounded French Officer from the Tomahawk of a North American Indian,*" *Immediations—The Research Journal of the Courtauld Institute of Art* 1, no. 1 (Spring 2004): 60–75.

40. Ann Uhry Abrams, *The Valiant Hero: Benjamin West and Grand-Style History Painting* (Washington, D.C.: Smithsonian Institution Press, 1985), 177.

41. Gregory H. Nobles, *American Frontiers: Cultural Encounters and Continental Conquest* (Harmondsworth, U.K.: Penguin Books, 1997).

42. It is possible, however, that the Indian figure in *The Death of General Wolfe* may betray other sympathies. In 1765 in the *Gentleman's Magazine*, the following lines were written by an anonymous poet who imagined the "speech" of an Indian who looked upon the battlefield at Quebec.

> Those who most boast of their humanity,
> content themselves, forsooth, to seize each chace
> and fishery, to drive us from each spot
> where plenty or fertility can make
> a settlement agreeable, and boast
> of strictest justice, only making war
> when we intrude on lands that are our own . . .
> When the dire pride of these usurping tyrants

shall happily be crushed, and we revenge
the cruelties long practiced on our race
for see! these forms of rapine have now drawn
their swords upon each other, and referred
their idle and imaginary claime
to the decision of a war; let us
look on with pleasure, still remembering
that when an European falls, there falls
a tyrant and a robber;

West could conceivably have seen this text, published in the middle of the decade in which most of his own Indian subjects were painted. If he did follow the poem's thesis, then West's Indian figure can no longer be viewed in the restive position, which his seated pose seems to suggest. Instead, what we find here, if his mute figure could speak, would be something altogether more resentful and aggressive. It is, in his eyes, still the land of his ancestors, but is being fought over by European usurpers. See *Gentleman's Magazine* 35 (1765): 526. This poem also appeared in *The Idler* for 1765.

4. Secret Diplomacy and Uneasy Alliances

1. See, for example, the discussion of the Battle of Fallen Timbers and General Anthony Wayne's preparation for it in Starkey, *European and Native American Warfare*, 153–54.

2. Helen A. Cooper, *John Trumbull: The Hand and Spirit of a Painter* (New Haven, Conn.: Yale University Art Gallery, 1982), 54n9.

3. For American Indian movements for unity within this period, see Dowd, *Spirited Resistance*.

4. Ibid., xxii, 184–85.

5. Starkey, *European and Native American Warfare*, 149–51.

6. For discussion of official geographical surveys in the nineteenth century in America, see Andro Linklater, *Measuring America: How the United States Was Shaped by the Greatest Land Sale in History* (London: Harper Collins, 2002).

7. See the introductory comments regarding the term "cultural broker" and its usage in historical interpretation in Larry L. Nelson, *A Man of Distinction among Them: Alexander McKee and British-Indian Affairs along the Ohio Country Frontier, 1754–1799* (Kent, Ohio: Kent State University Press, 1999), xiii.

8. Hendrick's important role is discussed at some length in Timothy J. Shannon, "Dressing for Success on the Mohawk Frontier: Hendrick, William Johnson, and the Indian Fashion," *William and Mary Quarterly*, 3rd series, 53, no. 1 (January 1996): 13–42.

9. Calloway, *New Worlds for All*, 131.

10. Isabel Thompson Kelsay, *Joseph Brant, 1743–1807, Man of Two Worlds* (Syracuse, N.Y.: Syracuse University Press, 1984), 190.

11. Thomas Campbell, *Gertrude of Wyoming and Other Poems*, 9th ed. (London: Longman, Hurst, Rees, Orme, Brown and Green, 1825), 37, stanza 16. Campbell added a note at the bottom of the page on this edition stating that "Brandt [*sic*] was the leader of those Mohawks, and other savages, who laid waste this part of Pennsylvania." The poet also misspelled Brant's name in the poem as "Brandt" (37). In later editions of his poems, Campbell told of his meeting with Brant's son (John Brant) in London after publication of the poem. Campbell later had a retraction of his denigration of Brant placed in the *New Monthly Magazine* of 1822. See note to page 167, line 10, in Thomas Campbell, *The Poetical Works of Thomas Campbell* (London: Edward Moxon, 1840), 339. A recent history of American Indian warfare in the eighteenth century places Brant squarely at the scene of battle in the Cherry Valley in Pennsylvania in 1778. However, evidence suggests that Brant promoted restraint against attacks on noncombatants. See Starkey, *European and Native American Warfare*, 119.

12. Sa Ga Yeath Qua Pieth Tow signed his name as "Brantt." However, "Sa Ga Yean Qua Rah Tow" was used as this man's name on the set of portraits of this delegation by Bernard Lens. It is the latter name that is placed next to "Brantt" in the signed document but must refer back to the sitter "Sa Ga Yeath Qua Pieth Tow, King of the Maquas," as portrayed by John Verelst. Joseph was related to him through the partnership of his mother with a noted Mohawk leader named Brant. See Kelsay, *Joseph Brant*, 13–14. Bond mentions the link between Joseph Brant and his earlier relation. See Bond, *Queen Anne's American Kings*, 44. The signature of Sa Ga Yeath Qua Pieth Tow is illustrated in ibid., facing page 8.

13. J. R. Fawcett Thompson, "Thayendanegea the Mohawk and His Several Portraits," *Connoisseur*, no. 170 (1969): 49–53. His biographer, Kelsay, states that Brant was probably of undistinguished ancestry, as this sort of hierarchical distinction was passed through the mother's lineage and not the father's. Kelsay, *Joseph Brant*, 1.

14. Kelsay, *Joseph Brant*, 171; Arthur J. Pound, *Johnson of the Mohawks: A Biography of Sir William Johnson* (1930; repr., Freeport, N.Y.: Books for Libraries Press, 1971) (the portrait of Brant owned by Boswell is facing page 382).

15. Kelsay, *Joseph Brant*, 14, 171.

16. Ibid., 51.

17. Shannon, "Dressing for Success."

18. The artist who painted Caldwell's portrait in 1782 is not yet identified. Another example of this tendency is Benjamin West's portrait of Sir Joseph Banks in a Maori cloak exhibited at the Royal Academy in 1773 with the title *A Whole Length of a Gentleman with a New Zealand Mantle around Him*.

19. Kelsay, *Joseph Brant*, 182.

20. Ibid., 165–66, 172–73.

21. Utley and Washburn, *History*, 120.

22. There is evidence that in the period from Pontiac's Rebellion to the end of the American Revolution, the British had been moving toward a more accommodating style of negotiation based on precedents set by the French during the late seventeenth and early eighteenth centuries, known as the "middle ground" by scholars. See Starkey, *European and Native American Warfare*; and White, *Middle Ground*.

23. Kelsay, *Joseph Brant*, 179.

24. Utley and Washburn, *History*, 121.

25. Ontario Heritage Foundation, *John Graves Simcoe, 1752–1806* (Toronto: Ontario Heritage Foundation, 1984), 5.

26. Starkey, *European and Native American Warfare*, 138.

27. On Simcoe's introduction to Brant, see Carl F. Klinck and James J. Talman, eds., *The Journal of Major John Norton* (1816; repr., Toronto: Champlain Society, 1970), lxxxiii. Simcoe's assessment of Brant comes from Calloway, *Crown and Calumet*, 239. Elizabeth Simcoe's diary also provides a telling observation about her response to Joseph Brant in that she saw his countenance as "expressive of art or cunning." See Kelsay, *Joseph Brant*, 558.

28. See contemporary comments about Brant in D. B. Read, *The Life and Times of General John Graves Simcoe, Commander of the Queen's Rangers during the Revolutionary War and first Governor of Upper Canada. Together with some account of Major André and Captain Brant* (Toronto: George Virtue, 1890), 143, 161, 265.

29. J. T. Smith, *Nollekens and His Times* (London, 1828), 2:308.

30. Dowd, *Spirited Resistance*, 96–98.

31. See the discussion of the "Nootka crisis" and Alexander MacGillivray's reactions in William C. Sturtevant, "The Cherokee Frontiers, the French Revolution, and William Augustus Bowles," in *The Cherokee Indian Nation: A Troubled History*, edited by Duane H. King (Knoxville: University of Tennessee Press, 1979), 63–66.

32. Anthony A Pearson, "John Hunter and Two Cherokee Indians," *Annals of the Royal College of Surgeons of England* 58 (September 1976): 374–81.

33. From the *Kentish Gazette*, quoted in Foreman, *Indians Abroad*, 103.

34. Foreman, *Indians Abroad*, 101.

35. Ibid., 101–2.

36. This conclave at Glaize has been compared with another coming together of many tribal groups seen at the pantribal Indian congress at Lower Sandusky in 1783. See John Sugden, *Tecumseh: A Life of America's Greatest Indian Leader* (1997; repr., London: Pimlico, 1999), 61–62.

37. The names of the American Indian men accompanying Bowles are listed in Foreman, *Indians Abroad*, 103. Geoff Quilley has mentioned his recent doubts over the security of the attribution to Hodges, for which I am in his debt.

38. *Miko* is a Muskogean term signifying "chief." It was first seen in British representations of American Indians on a 1734 engraved portrait, *Tomochaqu, Miko of the Yamacraw* [*sic*], by William Verelst.

39. "In London they met John Hunter at a party given by the famous naturalist Sir Joseph Banks, who, with Hodges, had accompanied Captain Cook in the Endeavour to Australia" (Pearson, "John Hunter," 374).

40. This attitude to physiognomy may link up with earlier instances, such as the illustration for George Alexander Stevens's "Celebrated Lecture on Heads," which circulated popularly as an engraving in 1766. In Stevens's frontispiece, the second "head" is that of a Cherokee chieftain. This illustration can be found in a recent reprint of Stevens' lecture. See *A Lecture on Heads*, (English and German translation) by Michael Hellenthal, Athena-Verlag, 1999.

41. For a recent proposed identification of some of the sitters in Verelst's painting, see Donald Panther-Yates, "A Portrait of Cherokee Chief Attakullakulla from the 1730s? A Discussion of William Verelst's 'Trustees of Georgia' Painting," *Journal of Cherokee Studies* 23 (2001): 4–20.

42. William Bartram, *Travels Through North and South Carolina, Georgia* . . . (1791; repr., New York: Penguin Books, 1988), 388.

5. Travel, Observation, and the Pathos of Decline

1. Paul G. Hulton, keeper of the prints and drawings collection at the British Museum for many years, has described the vicissitudes of the drawings' history and their publication in Hulton, *America 1585: The Complete Drawings of John White* (Chapel Hill and London: University of North Carolina Press and British Museum Publications, 1984), 22–23.

2. Hulton discusses White's achievement as an artist in ibid., 27, 35–38.

3. See Paul Hulton and David Beers Quinn's *The American Drawings of John White, 1577–1580, with Drawings of European and Oriental Subjects* (London and Chapel Hill: Trustees of the British Museum, British Museum, and University of North Carolina Press, 1964), 34–35n1, where they cite E. G. R. Taylor, ed., *The Writings and Correspondence of the Two Richard Hakluyts* (London: Hakluyt Society, 1935), 338.

4. Hulton and Quinn suggest that Hariot and White moved around together on site making sketches (White) and taking notes (Hariot) as a "method of working." See Hulton and Quinn, *American Drawings of John White*, 15.

5. Quoted in R. W. Frantz, *The English Traveller and the Movement of Ideas, 1660–1732* (*University of Nebraska Studies* 32–33 [1934]; repr., Lincoln: University of Nebraska Press, 1967), 23.

6. P. J. Marshall and Glyndwr Williams, *The Great Map of Mankind: British Perceptions of the World in the age of the Enlightenment* (London: J. M. Dent and Sons, 1982).

7. R. H. Hubbard, ed., *Thomas Davies in Early Canada* (Ottawa: Oberon Press, 1972), 17, 44–47.

8. Kim Sloan, *Alexander and John Robert Cozens—The Poetry of Landscape* (New Haven, Conn.: Yale University Press, 1986), 21-22.

9. Rüdiger Joppien and Bernard Smith's seminal study concerning the artists taken on Captain James Cook's voyages of circumnavigation in the years 1768–80 developed a considered and nuanced approach to the expeditionary artists. Joppien and Smith's work began to create distinctions in the ways that art historians and ethnologists might regard such imagery, and they successfully demonstrated the way such imagery was manipulated as it entered the public realm. Nevertheless, their account is predicated on the idea of a truthful record as a standard with which to judge visual representation. Rüdiger Joppien and Bernard Smith, *The Art of Captain Cook's Voyages*, vol. 3, *The Voyage of the "Resolution" and "Discovery" 1776–1780* (New Haven, Conn.: Yale University Press, 1988).

10. Ibid., 1. His detailed charge given by the Admiralty (via orders given to Cook) was as follows:

> Whereas we have engaged Mr. John Webber, Draughtsman and Landskip [*sic*] painter . . . in order to make Drawings and Paintings Of such places in the Countries you may touch at in the Course of the said Voyage as may be proper to give a more Perfect idea thereof than can be formed by written descriptions Only . . .taking care that he does diligently employ himself in Making Drawings and Paintings of such places . . . as may be Worthy of notice . . . also of such other objects and things as May fall within the compass of His abilities.

Taken from John Frazier Henry, *Early Maritime Artists on the Pacific North West Coast, 1741–1841* (Vancouver: Douglas and MacIntyre, 1984), 75.

11. In the current displays at the British Museum, shown in the Americas Gallery under the title The Mowachaht of Vancouver Island, are several woven basketry hats, one of which offers a good comparison with one depicted by Webber; see information on the wall text "Basketry," hat cited as Ethno: NWC7 (JB). This information was gathered on January 27, 2004.

12. Joppien and Smith, *Art of Captain Cook's Voyages*, entry no. 3, 223, 460. Other examples of drawings depicting the male chieftain's hat at the Mowachaht village are

illustrated in Thomas Vaughan, E. A. P. Vaughan, and Mercedes Palau Iglesias, *Voyages of Enlightenment: Malaspina on the Northwest Coast, 1791/1792* (Portland: Oregon Historical Society, 1977).

13. Meares consistently refers to Maquilla, the chief at Nootka, but his name was Maquinna or, in some of the Spanish accounts, Macuina.

14. The controversy is discussed in Henry, *Early Maritime Artists*, 92–93. A full account is given in Frederic W. Howay, ed., *The Dixon-Meares Controversy* (Toronto: Ryerson Press, 1929).

15. John Meares, *Voyages made in the Years 1788 and 1789, from China to the North West Coast of America* (London: Logographic Press, 1790), 117.

16. See the discussion of the significance of Meares's voyages in Barry M. Gough, "Meares and a Scheme of Empire," in *The Northwest Coast: British Navigation, Trade and Discoveries to 1812* (Vancouver: University of British Columbia Press, 1992), 96–99.

17. George Catlin, *Letters and Notes on the Manners, Customs, and Conditions of the North American Indians*, vol. 1, a facsimile of the first edition with an introduction by Marjorie Halpin (London, 1844; repr., New York: Dover, 1973), 16.

18. J. H. Wynne, *General History of the British Empire in America* (London, 1770), 1:241, quoted in Thomas Peardon, *The Transition in English Historical Writing, 1760–1830* (New York: AMS Press, 1966), 121.

19. Brian W. Dippie, *Catlin and His Contemporaries: The Politics of Patronage* (Lincoln: University of Nebraska Press, 1990), 10–11.

20. Ibid., 98–105.

21. Farington, *Diary* 14:5009, entry for April 23, 1817.

22. Frank Edgar Farley's study is seminal for this discussion. See Farley, "The Dying Indian," in *Anniversary Papers: By Colleagues and Pupils of George Lyman Kittredge . . .* (Boston: Ginn, 1913), 251–60.

23. For poetry of the period that supposedly emulated American Indian songs or chants, see Fairchild, *Noble Savage*, 441–97. See also Farley, "Dying Indian."

24. Bissell, *American Indian in English Literature*.

25. Theodore Crombie, "Wright of Derby's Indian Widow," *Apollo* (October 1959): 107.

26. Honour, *European Vision of America*, n.p., catalog no. 184.

27. Benedict Nicolson, *Joseph Wright of Derby, Painter of Light* (London: Routledge and Kegan Paul, 1968), 1:148.

28. Haskell and Penny, *Taste and the Antique*, 193–94.

29. Crombie, "Wright of Derby's Indian Widow," 107.

30. For example, the theme appears in William Richardson's play *The Indians* of 1790.

31. Jonathan Carver, *Travels Through the Interior Parts of North America, in the Years 1766, 1767, and 1768* (London: 1778), as quoted in Fairchild, *Noble Savage*, 467.

32. H. M. Margoliouth, ed., *Wordsworth: Selected Poems* (London: Collins, 1959), 196–98.

33. John Butt, ed., *The Poems of Alexander Pope* (London: Methuen, 1965), 508, lines 99-104.

34. Logan's speech was first recounted in Thomas Jefferson, *Notes on the State of Virginia* (London, 1787), and is reprinted in Wilcomb E. Washburn, ed., *The Indian and the White Man* (New York: Anchor Books, 1964), 426–28.

35. Witness the early accounts of Cadwallader Colden regarding the oratory of Mohawk and Iroquois leaders (see chapter 1). Onnontio was the name given to the colonial representative in Canada by the local Algonquins living in that region. Richardson's play of 1790 is discussed in Bissell, *American Indian in English Literature*, 142–46.

36. Bissell, *American Indian in English Literature*, 143.

37. Thomas Campbell's "Gertrude of Wyoming" first appeared in print in 1809 and was reprinted every year after that up until the 1820s. The two illustrated editions of Thomas Campbell's *Poems* are the 1825 and 1840 editions.

38. In the preface to the 1825 edition of his poems, Campbell inserted an advertisement stating how he had taken his information from Isaac Weld's *Travels in America* (1796).

39. Kelsay, *Joseph Brant*, 218–22.

40. See discussion in chapter 3 and its note 15. See also Lawson-Peebles, *Landscape and Literary Expression*, 26.

41. Thomas Campbell, "Gertrude of Wyoming," in *The Poetical Works, illustrated with thirty seven woodcuts by designs by Harvey* (London: Edward Moxon, 1860), part 1, stanza 2, 134.

42. Ibid., part 3, stanza 5, 162.

43. Now in the prints and drawings collection at the Laing Art Gallery, Newcastle Upon Tyne, a part of Tyne and Wear Museums' collections.

44. Campbell, "Gertrude of Wyoming," part 1, stanza 13, 138.

45. Ibid., stanza 14, 139–40.

46. See discussion in Pratt, "From Cannassatego to Outalissi," 74–75.

47. Campbell, "Gertrude of Wyoming," part 3, stanza 17, 167.

48. Farington, *Diary*, 5009.

49. Walsh's quotation is taken from his "Notices of the North American Indians," first published in 1829 and reprinted in S. C. Hall, ed., *The Amulet—A Christian and Literary Remembrancer* (London, 1833). I am indebted to Michael Pidgley for bringing this book to my attention.

50. John Lambert, *Travels through Lower Canada and the United States of North America in the Years 1806, 1807, and 1808,* 2 vols. (London, 1810), 367–68.

Conclusion

1. Pratt, "Reynolds' 'King of the Cherokees.'"

Bibliography

Abrams, Ann Uhry. "Benjamin West's Documentation of Colonial History: William
    Penn's Treaty with the Indians." *Art Bulletin* 47, no. 4 (1982): 59–75.

———. The *Valiant Hero: Benjamin West and Grand-Style History Painting*. Washington,
    D.C.: Smithsonian Institution Press, 1985.

Anderson, Fred. *Crucible of War: The Seven Years' War and the Fate of Empire in British
    North America, 1754–1766.* New York: Random House, 2000.

Anon. "American Affairs." *Gentleman's Magazine* 27 (1757).

———. *Gentleman's Magazine* 25 (1755): 486–87.

———. *Gentleman's Magazine* 35 (1765): 526.

Avery, Emmett L., ed. *The London Stage, 1660–1800*, vols. 1–2. Carbondale: Southern
    Illinois University Press, 1960.

Axtell, James. *The Invasion Within: The Contest of Cultures in Colonial North America.*
    New York: Oxford University Press, 1985.

Bartram, William. *Travels Through North and South Carolina, Georgia, East and West
    Florida, the Cherokee Country, the Extensive Territories of the Muscogulges, or Creek
    Confederacy, and the Country of the Chactows.* 1791. Reprint, New York: Penguin
    Books, 1988.

Behn, Aphra. *Oroonoko, and Other Stories.* Edited by Maureen Duffy. London: Methuen, 1986.

———. *The Widow Ranter.* 1690.

Berkhofer, Robert F., Jr. *The White Man's Indian.* New York: Alfred Knopf, 1978.

Bissell, Benjamin. *The American Indian in English Literature of the Eighteenth Century.* New Haven, Conn.: Yale University Press, 1925.

Bjelajac, David. *American Art: A Cultural History.* London: Laurence King, 2000.

Boime, Albert. *The Art of Exclusion: Representing Blacks in the Nineteenth Century.* London: Thames and Hudson, 1990.

Bond, Richmond P. *Queen Anne's American Kings.* Oxford: Clarendon Press, 1952.

Butt, John, ed. *The Poems of Alexander Pope.* London: Methuen, 1965.

Calloway, Colin G. *Crown and Calumet: British and Indian Relations, 1783–1815.* Norman: University of Oklahoma Press, 1987.

———. *New Worlds for All: Indians, Europeans, and the Remaking of Early America.* Baltimore: Johns Hopkins University Press, 1997.

Campbell, Thomas. *Gertrude of Wyoming and Other Poems*, 9th ed. London: Longman, Hurst, Rees, Orme, Brown and Green, 1825.

———. *The Poetical Works of Thomas Campbell.* London: Edward Moxon, 1840.

Carr, Helen. "Woman/Indian: 'The American' and His Others." In *Europe and Its Others: Proceedings of the Essex Conference on the Sociology of Literature* 2 (July 1984), University of Essex, Colchester, 1985.

Carver, Jonathan. *Travels Through the Interior Parts of North America, in the Years 1766, 1767, and 1768.* London, 1778.

Catlin, George. *Letters and Notes on the Manners, Customs, and Conditions of North American Indians*, vol. 1. A facsimile of the first edition with an introduction by Marjorie Halpin. London, 1844. Reprint, New York: Dover, 1973.

Charleston R. J., ed. *World Ceramics—An Illustrated History.* London: Paul Hamlyn, 1968.

Chiapelli, Fredi, ed. *First Images of America: The Impact of the New World on the Old.* Los Angeles: University of California Press, 1976.

Colden, Cadwallader. *The History of the Five Indian Nations, Depending on the Province of New York in America.* Parts I and II. 1727, 1747. Reprint, Ithaca, N.Y.: Cornell University Press, 1958.

Cooper, Helen A. *John Trumbull: The Hand and Spirit of a Painter.* New Haven, Conn.: Yale University Art Gallery, 1982.

Craske, Matthew. *Art in Europe 1700–1830: A History of the Visual Arts in an Era of Unprecedented Urban Economic Growth.* Oxford: Oxford University Press, 1997.

Crombie, Theodore. "Wright of Derby's Indian Widow." *Apollo* (October 1959): 107.

Cumming, William P., Susan Hillier, David Beers Quinn, and Glyndwr Williams. *The Exploration of North America 1630–1776*. London: Paul Elek, 1977.

Dickason, Olive P. *The Myth of the Savage; And the Beginnings of French Colonialism in the Americas*. Edmonton: University of Alberta Press, 1984.

Dippie, Brian W. *Catlin and His Contemporaries: The Politics of Patronage*. Lincoln: University of Nebraska Press, 1990.

Donaldson, Ian, and Tamsin Donaldson. *Seeing the First Australians*. Sydney: George Allen and Unwin, 1985.

Dowd, Gregory Evans. *A Spirited Resistance: The North American Indian Struggle for Unity, 1745–1815*. Baltimore: Johns Hopkins University Press, 1992.

Edgerton, Samuel Y., Jr. "The Murder of Jane MacCrea: The Tragedy of an American 'Tableau d'histoire.'" *Art Bulletin* 47, no. 4 (1965): 482–92.

Eimer, Christopher. *British Commemorative Medals*. London: B. A. Seaby, 1987.

Einhorn, Arthur, and Thomas S. Abler. "Bonnets, Plumes and Headbands in West's Painting of Penn's Treaty." *American Indian Art Magazine* 21 (Summer 1996): 44–53.

Eitner, Lorenz, ed. *Neo-Classicism and Romanticism*. Vol. 1, *1750–1850*. London: Prentice-Hall, 1971.

Essick, Robert N. *William Blake, Printmaker*. Princeton, N.J.: Princeton University Press, 1980.

Fairchild, Hoxie Neale. *The Noble Savage: A Study in Romantic Naturalism*. 1928. Reprint, New York: Russell and Russell, 1961.

Farington, Joseph. *The Diary of Joseph Farington*, vol. 4. Edited by Kathryn Cave. New Haven, Conn.: Yale University Press, 1984.

Farley, Frank Edgar. "The Dying Indian." In *Anniversary Papers: By Colleagues and Pupils of George Lyman Kittredge: Presented in Completion of His Twenty-fifth Year of Teaching in Harvard University, June MCMXIII* Boston: Ginn, 1913.

Fleming, John. "Robert Adam, Luc-François Breton and the Townshend Monument in Westminster Abbey." *Connoisseur* 150, no. 605 (July 1962): 164–71.

Foreman, Carolyn T. *Indians Abroad, 1493–1938*. Norman: University of Oklahoma Press, 1943.

Frantz, R. W. *The English Traveller and the Movement of Ideas, 1660–1732*. Reprint, Lincoln: University of Nebraska Press, 1967.

Friedman, John Block. *The Monstrous Races in Mediaeval Art and Thought*. Cambridge, Mass.: Harvard University Press, 1981.

Galt, John. *The Life, Studies and Works of Benjamin West, Esq., President of the Royal Academy*. 1816, Philadelphia. Reprint, London: T. Codell and W. Davies, 1820. Reprint: Gainsville, Fla.: Scholars' Facsimiles and Reprints, 1960.

Garratt, John G. *The Four Indian Kings/Les Quatres Rois Indiens.* Ottawa: Public Archives of Canada, 1985.

George, M. Dorothy. *English Political Caricature to 1792: A Study in Opinion and Propaganda.* Oxford: Clarendon Press, 1959.

Gough, Barry M. "Meares and a Scheme of Empire." In *The Northwest Coast: British Navigation, Trade and Discoveries to 1812.* Vancouver: University of British Columbia Press, 1992.

Gray, Thomas. *Correspondence of Thomas Gray.* Edited by Paget Toynbee and Leonard Whibley. Oxford: Oxford University Press, 1935.

Hale, J. R. *Renaissance Exploration.* London: British Broadcasting Company Publications, 1968.

Hall, S. C., ed. *The Amulet—A Christian and Literary Remembrancer.* London, 1833.

Haskell, Francis, and Nicholas Penny. *Taste and the Antique: The Lure of Classical Sculpture, 1500–1900.* New Haven, Conn.: Yale University Press, 1981.

Henry, John Frazier. *Early Maritime Artists on the Pacific North West Coast, 1741–1841.* Vancouver: Douglas and MacIntyre, 1984.

Heriot, George. *Travels through the Canadas.* London, 1807.

Hertel, Johann Georg. "Ripa's 'Iconologia', illustrated with the help of the painter Gottfried Eichler the Younger." 1758–60. Reprinted as Edward Maser, ed., *Baroque and Rococo Pictorial Imagery: The 1758–1760 Hertel Edition of Ripa's "Iconologia."* New York: Dover Books, 1971.

Hinderaker, Eric. "The 'Four Indian Kings' and the Imaginative Construction of the First British Empire." *William and Mary Quarterly*, 3rd Series, 53, no. 3 (July 1996): 487–526.

Hobson, R. L. *Catalogue of the Collection of English Porcelain in the Department of British and Mediaeval Antiquities and Ethnography of the British Museum.* London: Longmans, 1905.

Honour, Hugh. "Benjamin West's Indian Family." *Burlington Magazine* 125 (1983): 726–33.

———. *The European Vision of America.* The National Gallery, Washington, D.C.; the Cleveland Museum of Arts; and the Grand Palais, Paris, 1975.

———. *The New Golden Land: European Images of America from the Discoveries to the Present Time.* New York: Pantheon Books, 1975.

———. "Slaves and Liberators." In Ladislas Bugner gen. ed., *The Image of the Black in Western Art*, vol. 4. Menil Foundation. Cambridge, Mass.: Harvard University Press, 1989.

Howard, Henry. "A New Humorous Song, on the Cherokee Chiefs. Inscribed to the Ladies of Great Britain." *Broadsheet,* London, 1762. British Library, accession no. 1850.c.10.(79).

Howay, Frederic W., ed. *The Dixon-Meares Controversy.* Toronto: Ryerson Press, 1929.

Hubbard, R. H., ed. *Thomas Davies in Early Canada.* Ottawa: Oberon Press, 1972.

Hulme, Peter. "Polytropic Man: Tropes of Sexuality and Mobility in Early Colonial Discourse." In *Europe and Its Others.* Colchester, U.K.: University of Essex, 1985.

Hulton, Paul. *America 1585: The Complete Drawings of John White.* Chapel Hill and London: University of North Carolina Press and British Museum Publications, 1984.

Hulton, Paul, and David Beers Quinn. *The American Drawings of John White, 1577–1580, with Drawings of European and Oriental Subjects.* London and Chapel Hill: Trustees of the British Museum, British Museum, and University of North Carolina Press, 1964.

Hussey, Christopher. *English Gardens and Landscapes, 1700–1750.* London: Country Life, 1967.

Hyde, James Hazen. "The Four Parts of the World as Represented in Old-Time Pageants and Ballets," part I. *Apollo,* no. 4 (1926): 232–38.

———. "Old-Time Pageants and Ballets," part II. *Apollo,* no. 5 (1927): 20–26.

Jefferson, Thomas. *Notes on the State of Virginia.* London, 1787.

Jefferys, Thomas. *A Collection of the Dresses of Different Nations both Ancient and Modern,* vol. 4. London, 1772.

Jennings, Francis. *The Ambiguous Iroquois Empire: The Covenant Chain Federation of Indian Tribes with the English Colonies from Its Beginnings to the Lancaster Treaty of 1744.* New York: Norton, 1984.

Joppien, Rüdiger, and Bernard Smith. *The Art of Captain Cook's Voyages.* Vol. 3, *The Voyage of the "Resolution" and "Discovery" 1776–1780.* New Haven, Conn.: Yale University Press, 1988.

Kelsay, Isabel Thompson. *Joseph Brant, 1743–1807, Man of Two Worlds.* Syracuse, N.Y.: Syracuse University Press, 1984.

King, J. C. H. *First Peoples, First Contacts: Native Peoples of North America.* London: British Museum Press, 1999.

———. *Smoking Pipes of the North American Indian.* London: British Museum Press, 1977.

———. "Woodlands Artifacts from the Studio of Benjamin West, 1738–1820." *American Indian Art Magazine* 27 (Winter 1992): 34–47.

Klinck, Carl F., and James J. Talman, eds. *The Journal of Major John Norton.* 1816. Reprint, Toronto: Champlain Society, 1970.

Klingender, Francis D., ed. *Hogarth and English Caricature.* 1944. Reprint, London: Transatlantic Arts, 1945.

Krumrine, Mary Louise, and Susan Clare Scott, eds. *Art and the Native American: Perspectives, Reality and Influences.* Papers in Art History from Pennsylvania State University 10 (2001).

Kupperman, Karen Ordahl, ed. *America in European Consciousness, 1493–1750.* Chapel Hill: University of North Carolina Press, 1995.

Lambert, John. *Travels through Lower Canada and the United States of North America in the Years 1806, 1807, and 1808,* 2 vols. London, 1810.

Las Casas, Fra Bartolome de. *Brevissima relacion de la destruccion de las Indias.* Seville, 1552–53. Translated into English as *Tears of the Indians,* 1656.

Lawson-Peebles, Robert. *Landscape and Written Expression in Revolutionary America: The World Turned Upside Down.* Cambridge: Cambridge University Press, 1988.

Linklater, Andro. *Measuring America: How the United States Was Shaped by the Greatest Land Sale in History.* London: Harper Collins, 2002.

Lord Shaftesbury. *Treatise VII, Characteristicks, III.* London, 1714.

Margoliouth, H. M., ed. *Wordsworth: Selected Poems.* London: Collins, 1959.

Marshall, P. J., and Glyndwr Williams. *The Great Map of Mankind: British Perceptions of the World in the Age of the Enlightenment.* London: J. M. Dent and Sons, 1982.

McClung-Fleming, Elizabeth. "The American Image as Indian Princess, 1765–1783." *Winterthur Portfolio* 2 (1965): 65–81.

———. "From Indian Princess to Greek Goddess—The American Image, 1783–1815." *Winterthur Portfolio* 3 (1967): 37–66.

McFarlane, Anthony. *The British in the Americas, 1480–1815.* London: Routledge, 1994.

Meares, John. *Voyages made in the Years 1788 and 1789, from China to the North West Coast of America.* London: Logographic Press, 1790.

Mitchell, Charles. "Benjamin West's 'Death of General Wolfe' and the Popular History Piece." *Journal of the Warburg and Courtauld Institutes* 7 (1944): 20–33.

Nelson, Larry L. *A Man of Distinction among Them: Alexander McKee and British—Indian Affairs along the Ohio Country Frontier, 1754–1799.* Kent, Ohio: Kent State University Press, 1999.

Nicolson, Benedict. *Joseph Wright of Derby, Painter of Light.* 2 vols. London: Routledge and Kegan Paul, 1968.

Noble, Courtney. "Rescuing Difference: Ambiguous Heroism in Benjamin West's *General Johnson Saving a Wounded French Officer from the Tomahawk of a North American Indian.*" *Immediations—The Research Journal of the Courtauld Institute of Art* 1, no. 1 (Spring 2004): 60–75

Nobles, Gregory H. *American Frontiers: Cultural Encounters and Continental Conquest.* Harmondsworth, U.K.: Penguin Books, 1997.

Ontario Heritage Foundation. *John Graves Simcoe, 1752–1806.* Toronto: Ontario Heritage Foundation, 1984.

Panther-Yates, Donald. "A Portrait of Cherokee Chief Attakullakulla from the 1730s? A Discussion of William Verelst's 'Trustees of Georgia' Painting." *Journal of Cherokee Studies* 23 (2001): 4—20.

Parry, Ellwood. *The Image of the Indian and the Black Man in American Art.* New York: George Braziller, 1974.

Payne Knight, Richard. *The Landscape: A Didactic Poem in Three Books.* N.p., 1794.

Pearce, Roy Harvey. *Savagism and Civilization: A Study of the Indian and the American Mind.* Baltimore: Johns Hopkins University Press, 1953.

Peardon, Thomas. *The Transition in English Historical Writing, 1760–1830.* New York: AMS Press, 1966.

Pearson, Anthony A. "John Hunter and Two Cherokee Indians." *Annals of the Royal College of Surgeons of England* 58 (September 1976): 374–81.

Pound, Arthur. *Johnson of the Mohawks: A Biography of Sir William Johnson.* 1930. Reprint, Freeport, N.Y.: Books for Libraries Press, 1971.

Pratt, Stephanie. "From Cannassatego to Outalissi: Making Sense of the Native American in Eighteenth-Century Culture." In *An Economy of Colour: Visual Culture and the Atlantic World, 1660–1830,* edited by Geoff Quilley and Kay Dian Kriz. Manchester, U.K.: Manchester University Press, 2003.

———. "Reynolds' 'King of the Cherokees' and Other Mistaken Identities in the Portraiture of Native American Delegations, 1710–1762." *Oxford Art Journal* 21, no. 2 (1998): 133–50.

Pressley, William. *The Life and Art of James Barry.* New Haven, Conn.: Yale University Press, 1981.

Pritchard, Kathleen Moss. "John Vanderlyn and the Massacre of Jane MacCrea." *Art Quarterly* 12 (1949): 361–65.

Read, D. B. *The Life and Times of General John Graves Simcoe, Commander of the Queen's Rangers during the Revolutionary War and first Governor of Upper Canada. Together with some account of Major André and Captain Brant.* Toronto: George Virtue, 1890.

Richardson, William. *The Indians.* Edinburgh, 1790.

Richter, Daniel K. *The Ordeal of the Longhouse: The Peoples of the Iroquois League in the Era of European Colonization.* Chapel Hill: University of North Carolina Press, 1992.

Said, Edward. *Orientalism: Western Concepts of the Orient.* New York: Pantheon Books, 1978.

Saunders, Barbara A. C. "A European Image of the Noble Savage. Joseph Wright's 'Indian Widow.'" Master's thesis, University of Leiden, 1977.

Shannon, Timothy J. "Dressing for Success on the Mohawk Frontier: Hendrick, William Johnson, and the Indian Fashion." *William and Mary Quarterly*, 3rd series, 53, no. 1 (January 1996): 13–42.

Shebbeare, John. *Lydia; or Filial Piety*, 2 vols. 1755. Reprint, London, 1786.

Sloan, Kim. *Alexander and John Robert Cozens—The Poetry of Landscape*. New Haven, Conn.: Yale University Press, 1986.

Slotkin, Richard. *Regeneration through Violence: The Mythology of the American Frontier*. Middletown, Conn.: Wesleyan University Press, 1973.

Smart, Alastair. *Allan Ramsay 1713–1784*. Edinburgh: Scottish National Portrait Gallery, 1992.

Smith, Bernard. *European Vision and the South Pacific*. New Haven, Conn.: Yale University Press, 1985.

Smith, J. T. *Nollekens and His Times*. Vol. 2. London, 1828.

Smith, R. C. *The Noble Savage: The American Indian in Art*. Philadelphia: University Museum, 1958.

Smith, William. *Historical Account of the Expedition Against the Ohio Indians*. Philadelphia, 1765.

Smith, William, Jr. *The History of the Province of New York*. Edited by Michael Kammen. 1757. Reprint, Cambridge, Mass.: Harvard University Press, 1972.

Solkin, David. "Great Pictures or Great Men? Reynolds, Male Portraiture, and the Power of Art." *Oxford Art Journal* 9, no. 2 (1986): 42–49.

Staley, Alan, and Helmut von Erffa. *The Paintings of Benjamin West*. New Haven, Conn.: Yale University Press, 1986.

Starkey, Armstrong. *European and Native American Warfare, 1675–1815*, London: University College London Press, 1998.

Steele, Richard, and Joseph Addison. "The Indian Kings in London." *Spectator*, no. 50, April 27, 1711. In *Selections from "The Tatler" and "The Spectator" of Steele and Addison*, edited by Angus Ross. Harmondsworth, U.K.: Penguin Books, 1982.

Stevens, Mary Ann. *The Orientalists: Delacroix to Matisse, European Painters in North Africa and the Near East*. London: The Royal Academy in association with Weidenfeld and Nicolson, 1984.

Sturtevant, William C. "The Cherokee Frontiers, the French Revolution, and William Augustus Bowles." In *The Cherokee Indian Nation: A Troubled History*, edited by Duane H. King. Knoxville: University of Tennessee Press, 1979.

Sugden, John. *Tecumseh: A Life of America's Greatest Indian Leader*. London: Pimlico, 1999.

Sutcliff, Robert. *Travels in Some Parts of North America in the Years 1804, 1805, & 1806*. York: W. Alexander Darton, Harvey and Darton, and W. Phillips, 1811.

Tanner, Helen Hornbeck, ed. *Atlas of Great Lakes Indian History.* Norman: University of Oklahoma Press, 1987.

Taylor, E. G. R., ed. *The Writings and Correspondence of the Two Richard Hakluyts.* London: Hakluyt Society, 1935.

Thomas, Peter D. G. *The American Revolution: The English Satirical Print 1600–1832.* Cambridge: Cambridge University Press, 1986.

Thompson, J. R. Fawcett. "Thayendanegea the Mohawk and His Several Portraits." *Connoisseur,* no. 170 (1969): 49-53.

Thompson, R. H. *The Sylloge of Coins of the British Isles (31) Norweb Collection, Tokens of the British Isles, 1575–1750.* Part I, *Bedfordshire to Devon.* London: Spink and Son, 1984.

Timberlake, Henry. *Memoirs.* London, 1765.

Tomasi, Tongiori. "Image, Symbol and Word on the Title Pages and Frontispieces of Scientific Books from the Sixteenth and Seventeenth Centuries." *Word & Image* 4, no. 1 (January–March 1988): 372–79.

Utley, Robert, and Wilcomb Washburn. *The History of the Indian Wars.* London: Mitchell Beazley, 1977.

Vaughan, Thomas, E. A. P. Vaughan, and Mercedes Palau Iglesias. *Voyages of Enlightenment: Malaspina on the Northwest Coast, 1791/1792.* Portland: Oregon Historical Society, 1977.

Viola, Herman J., Jr. *Diplomats in Buckskins: A History of Indian Delegations in Washington City.* Washington, D.C.: Smithsonian Institution Press, 1981.

Waldman, Carl. *The Atlas of the North American Indian.* Oxford: Facts on File, 1985.

Warton, Joseph. "Revenge of America." In *The Penguin Book of Eighteenth Century Verse,* edited by Dennis Davidson. Harmondsworth, U.K.: Penguin Books, 1973

Washburn, Wilcomb E., ed. *The Indian and the White Man.* New York: Doubleday, 1964.

Weems, Parson M. L. *The Life of William Penn, the Settler of Pennsylvania.* 1822. Reprint, Philadelphia, 1845.

White, Richard. *The Middle Ground: Indians, Empires, and Republics in the Great Lakes Region, 1650–1815.* Cambridge: Cambridge University Press, 1991.

Wind, Edgar. "The Revolution of History Painting." *Journal of the Warburg and Courtauld Institutes* 2 (October 1938): 116–27.

Wynne, J. H. *General History of the British Empire in America.* 2 vols. London, 1770.

Zolla, Elemire. *The Writer and the Shaman: A Morphology of the American Indian.* Translated by Raymond Rosenthal. New York: Harcourt, Brace Jovanovich, 1973.

Index

www.ingramcontent.com/pod-product-compliance
Lightning Source LLC
Chambersburg PA
CBHW080908170526
45158CB00008B/2040